GW00786772

JANNER'S
EMPLOYMENT FORMS

GREVILLE JANNER

JANNER'S EMPLOYMENT FORMS

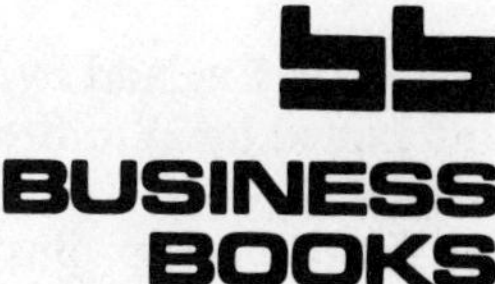

First published 1979

ISBN 0 220 67027 7

Printed in England by The Anchor Press Ltd.
and bound by Wm Brendon & Son Ltd.,
both of Tiptree, Essex,
for the publishers, Business Books Ltd.,
24, Highbury Crescent, London N.5.

For
Cllr Mrs Janet Setchfield
with love, admiration – and thanks for so many years of happy comradeship and service

OTHER BOOKS BY GREVILLE JANNER, QC, MP (EWAN MITCHELL) INCLUDE:

Janner's Compendium of Employment Law
Janner's Product Liability
The Employer's and Personnel Manager's Handbook of Draft Letters of Employment Law
The Employer's Guide to the Law on Health, Safety and Welfare at Work
The Director's and Company Secretary's Handbook of Draft Legal Letters
The Director's and Company Secretary's Handbook of Draft Contract Letters
The Caterer's Lawyer and Restaurateur's Legal Guide
The Retailer's Lawyer
The Sales Executive's Lawyer and Businessman's Guide to the Laws of Buying and Selling
The Business and Professional Man's Lawyer
The Businessman's Guide to Letter-writing and to the Law on Letters
The Businessman's Guide to Speech-making and to the Laws and Conduct of Meetings
The Director's Lawyer and Company Secretary's Legal Guide
The Lawyer and His World
Farming and the Law
You and the Law
Your Property and the Law and Investor's Legal Guide
Coping with Crime — the businessman's guide to dealing with stealing, spying, fraud, false trade descriptions and other common commercial crimes
The Businessman's Legal Lexicon
The Employer's Lawyer
The Businessman's Guide to Travel
The Businessman's Guide to Commercial Conduct and the Law
The Transport Manager's Lawyer and Transport Operator's Legal Guide
RAC Motorist's Lawyer

Contents

Book Three OFFICIAL FORMS

Introduction

Documentation is the key to the avoidance of expense, anxiety and potential disaster from the vast array of employment and industrial relations law. The employer may, of course, evolve his own documents, as he goes along. But he may prefer to take a leaf out of the lawyer's book and to rely on precedents. This book is a collection of these precedents — to be used or adapted, copied, duplicated, amended, added to — as you see fit.

The forms cover all those topics now vital to the employer — from the birth of the employment (contracts . . . written terms . . . requirements of law and of common sense . . .) — to the employment's end (warnings . . . dismissal forms . . . written reasons . . .).

Health and Safety at Work means protection for employees and self-preservation for employers. So here are more forms — ranging from sample safety policies (including 'organisation' and 'arrangements') to systems for employees to follow . . . forms for safety representatives and safety officers, for everyday routine and for (hopefully rare) disasters.

Please use these forms with care and with discretion. As 'references' should state: 'No legal responsibility can be accepted' — in this case, by the author or publishers.

Of course, the object of using forms is to keep you as far away from courts and tribunals, the law and lawyers, as is reasonably possible in the world of employment protection. Systems, routines and forms may be regarded as bureaucracy and red tape — until the day when you recognise that they save time, anxiety and money — and, on occasion, life and limb.

If you have trouble in deciding which form to use or on how to adapt it, consult your solicitor. You may even find this book on his shelf — quite likely, disguised in a plain cover.

* * *

In most cases, the identity of the signatory of a form or notice will either be obvious or not of great importance. A signature, though, there should normally be — if only to personalise the document. The personnel director or manager, the industrial relations or safety officer, or even the managing director may sign, as appropriate. But as the forms (except where indicated) are guides, drafts and precedents, rather than in a form prescribed by statute or regulation, the presence or absence of a signature is immaterial. Where it is believed that a particular person should sign, however, the form so states.

* * *

I am extremely grateful to my friends in industry who have provided me with copies of their own documentation, some of which is so excellent that I have reproduced it almost verbatim and some of which has provided ideas or bases for other precedents.

My especial thanks to: Mr Lewis Goodman, Miss Diana Rookledge and Miss Jenny Hurd (Marks and Spencer Ltd); Mr Errol Bateman and Mr Peter Daniel (Amoco [UK] Ltd); Mr Don Chappell and Miss Joan Townsend (The Johnson Matthey Group); Mr J.C.J. Catt (Unigate Foods Ltd); and to Professor Peter Wallington, of Lancaster University, whose advice, help and contributions have been absolutely invaluable. To my assistants, Mr William Sandover and Mr Paul Secher, and to my wife — my appreciation, as always, for their efforts and assistance.

June 1979 GREVILLE JANNER

STOP PRESS — Unfair dismissal and redundancy

As we go to press, Draft Orders under *The Employment Protection Act, 1975*, have been laid before Parliament and are expected to come into operation on 1 October 1979. The effect of these Orders will be as follows:

1 *Unfair dismissal* The qualifying period of service for the right not to be *unfairly* dismissed will be increased from 26 to 52 weeks.

2 *Redundancy consultation* The required period for consultations with trade unions and notification to the Secretary of State concerning redundancies of 10-99 employees at one establishment will be reduced from 60 to 30 days. The maximum protective award will be reduced from 60 to 30 days too. The remaining periods are unchanged.

The Introductions to the sections on 'Dismissal' and 'Redundancy' and the forms that follow them should now be read in conjunction with these two new Draft Orders.

Book One

DRAFT FORMS

Part One

Appointments

Introduction

Every employee has a contract of employment, oral or written — or partly oral and partly in writing. There is no law which requires an employment contract to be written, for it to be binding. However, *The Contracts of Employment Act, 1972*, as amended by *The Employment Protection Act, 1975*, and now incorporated in *The Employment Protection (Consolidation) Act, 1978*, requires employers to provide all employees with particulars of the main terms of their contracts *(a)* within 13 weeks of the commencement of the employment and *(b)* within 4 weeks of any variation.

While 13 weeks' delay is permitted, it is generally best to provide employees with written particulars before their employment begins. Neither on these particulars nor on almost any other document is a signature necessary to ensure validity. Anyone who signs a document is unlikely thereafter to be heard to say that he did not know or understand its contents. If an employee refuses to sign to indicate his agreement with the terms of service you offer to him, then — subject (as always) to industrial relations considerations — you may refuse to employ him. Alternatively, as in the case of all other documents including disciplinary and dismissal warning notices, you should make and keep a record that the document was handed to and received by the employee but that he refused to sign for it.

The main particulars which must be recorded in writing are the following:

1 The name and address of the employer. This is especially important where a company is part of a group — but less important than it used to be, thanks to the new protection given to employees when their employers became insolvent.
2 The employee's name.
3 The title of the job which the employee is required to do.
4 The place of work. (If flexibility is required, say so — otherwise the employee need not move.)
5 Hours of work. (*Again:* If these may have to be changed, say so. *Likewise:* For voluntary and required overtime.)
6 Remuneration: How much and how often? (*Again:* Make careful distinction between entitlement and voluntary additions. Also detail fringe benefits, e.g. a company car and use of canteen facilities.)
7 Pension rights. (Have you contracted in or out? Have you additional schemes — and if so, then on what basis?)
8 Sick pay entitlement (if any). Remember that if you dismiss an employee

after his sick pay rights have expired, they will revive during his period of notice.

9 Notice which the employee is entitled to receive and which he is bound to give. (Do not say: 'You are entitled to statutory notice' — the law provides only for a statutory *minimum*. Also, the employee's duty to give notice is more theoretical than real because you cannot successfully sue if he fails to comply, as you cannot prove your damage.)

10 Holiday entitlement. (Remember especially a statement of the employee's entitlement when the employment ends, i.e. on a pro-rata basis?)

11 Disciplinary procedures or state where these may be found (in a place that is readily accessible). Also state who will exercise these disciplinary measures and to whom the employee can appeal.

12 Grievance procedures. (State to whom the employee should turn if he has a grievance.)

In addition to the required particulars, there are many others which should be considered. Composite Form 10 should serve as a complete checklist. Remember especially, where appropriate: right to search; requirement that a woman employee should give written notice of intention to return to her job after pregnancy or childbirth, where practicable at least 3 weeks before she departs; especially serious disciplinary offences which will give rise to dismissal with notice/instant dismissal; agreement to undergo medical examinations; and any special requirements applicable to the particular employee or his job.

Form 1 Requisition for replacement staff

XYZ Co. Ltd
Requisition for Staff

Part 1 *(to be filled in by head of section, etc., making requisition).*

Location:

Department/Section:

Name of departing employee:

Grade and salary/wage:

Hours of work/overtime:

Date of leaving:

Reason for leaving: Resigned/retired/transferred/promoted/dismissed/deceased/temporary leave

Title of post:

Summary of duties (if not standard for post):

Reasons for requiring to replace departing employee:

(Approval will not be given automatically. The head of section is to indicate whether all or any of the duties of the post could be reallocated, and whether there is any likelihood of a reduction in requirements for this type of work.)

Proposed grade for replacement employee *(Give reasons for any proposed change, and if a change is proposed give details of other employees doing similar work who might be affected.)*

Changes in job specification, hours of work, overtime or other requirements:

Proposed starting date:

Likely duration of job (temporary replacement only):

Names of existing employees who should be considered for this vacancy:

Signed: *Date:*

(Continued)

(Continued)

Part 2 Authorisation — to be filled in by personnel manager

Authority to fill granted/refused.

Method of recruitment:
- External advertising
- Internal advertising
- Invitation to . . .

Details of advertising (if any):

Changes in job specification (if any):

Grade and starting pay range:

(NOTE: Authority not to fill, and changes from previous job specification or grade, may not be given without consultation with any relevant Trade Union. If grade is to be changed, the position of all personnel performing similar work is to be reviewed.)

Signed: *Date:*

Part 3 Record of recruitment *(offer details to be filled in AFTER acceptance is signified)*

Advertisements placed (date):

Shortlist and interviewing completed:

Offer made to:

Conditions satisfied: medical
references
qualifications
trade union membership
other

Offer accepted:

Date started:

Starting grade and pay:

Form 2 Requisition for additional staff

XYZ Co. Ltd.
Requisition for Additional Staff

Part 1 *(to be filled in by head of section, etc., making requisition)*

Location:

Department/Section:

Number of staff required: Full time/Part time:

Job title and summary of proposed duties *(A separate form is to be filled in for each type of job):*

Starting date:

Proposed hours of work:

Overtime requirements:

Proposed grade and pay level:

Is requirement temporary or permanent?

If temporary, for how long?

Are any existing employees engaged in similar jobs? Yes/No

If yes, job details for new staff should normally be the same. Give reasons for any changes proposed:

State the reasons for requiring additional staff:

What financial benefits will accrue to the Company from the additional staff proposed? Give details as indicated:

Value of additional production
Reduction in overtime
Removal of bottlenecks
Improved staff co-operation
Other

Will any additional facilities be required to accommodate staff, e.g. cloakrooms, office furniture, work benches?

Give details and approximate cost:

Give names of any existing employees who should be considered for this/these post(s):

(Continued)

(Continued)

Part 2 Authorisation *(to be filled in by Personnel Manager and approved by Financial Controller)*

Estimated cost:
Recruitment
Capital equipment
Annual pay and overheads

Estimated benefits:
Value added (annual)
Overtime saved (annual)
Allowance for value of other benefits

Recruitment: Approved — Number . . ./Refused.

Method of recruitment:
External advertising
Internal advertising
Invitation(s) to:

Details of advertising (if any):

Job title and specification:

Hours of work/overtime:

Grading and starting pay:

Authority for provision of extra facilities as required:

NOTE: if existing personnel are engaged in similar jobs to that proposed, a different grade must not be approved without consultation with any relevant trade union, and a review of the position of all existing personnel performing similar jobs undertaken.

Signed:	*(Personnel Manager)*	*Date:*
Signed:	*(Financial Controller)*	*Date:*

Part 3 Record of recruitment *(Additional copies of this part to be filled in for second and each subsequent post and clipped to this form. Offer details to be filled in* after *acceptance signified)*

Advertisements placed (date):

Shortlisting and interviewing completed:

Offer made to:

Conditions satisfied:
Medical
References
Qualification
Trade union membership
Other

Offer accepted:

Date started:

Starting grade and pay

Form 3 Application form for manual workers

XYZ Co. Ltd

Position applied for:

A Personal details

Name in full *(underline surname)*:

Address:

Telephone No.

Date of birth: Sex: Male/Female

Marital status: Single/Married/Widowed/Divorced

Place of birth: Nationality:

B Qualifications

List schools and colleges attended since age 11, and examinations passed, and other qualifications obtained e.g. apprenticeships, with dates.

School/College/Employer	Examination/Qualification	Date

Do you have any other qualifications or skills which might be useful for this job?

(Continued)

C Employment

Please give name and address of present employer, the nature of your job and salary/wages, and the date started. (If you are at present unemployed give details for your most recent employer and include the date and reason you left work.)

Name and address of employer	Post	Pay details	Date of starting/leaving

Reason for leaving:

If we offer you employment we shall wish to approach the employer you have named above for a reference. No contact will be made with the employer unless an offer is made, but any offer will be conditional on our getting a satisfactory reference from this employer.

Previous employment: please give details of previous employment within the last two years, other than your present/most recent employer.

Name and address of employer	Post	Pay details	Dates of starting/leaving

School leavers If you have not previously been in employment a reference will be requested from the school or college which you attended most recently.

D Personal reference

Please give the name of one person who is not related to you whom we can contact for a confidential assessment of your suitability for this job.

Name:

Address:

Telephone No:

E Availability

How much notice would you require to give to leave your present employment?

Give dates of any holidays already arranged which you would like us to honour:

What rate of pay are you seeking?

Are you willing to work:
- Nights? Yes/No
- Shift work? Yes/No
- Overtime? Yes/No

Why do you wish to change your job?

Are you in good health? Yes/No

If no please give details?

Are you registered as disabled? *(Please note that offers of employment may be conditional on your passing a medical examination.)* Yes/No

Have you ever worked for XYZ Co. Ltd before? Yes/No

If yes give dates, position held and reason for leaving:

Do any close relatives of yours work for XYZ Co. Ltd? Yes/No

If yes, give names:

Have you any previous convictions for a criminal offence (other than motoring offences)? Yes/No

If yes, give full details and dates:

How did you come to know of this job? *(Please tick)*
- Advertisement/state name of newspaper ....)
- Informed by friend/relative.
- Direct inquiry.
- Other (please state ....)

Please read and sign the following declaration:

I apply for employment with XYZ Co. Ltd. To the best of my knowledge and belief all the particulars I have given above are true. I understand that any false statement may disqualify me from employment or render me liable to instant dismissal.

Signed: *Date:*

Form 4 Application form for monthly paid staff

(This is intended as a more comprehensive form where a more detailed scrutiny of applicants may be required. Not all the questions will be appropriate to every company or post, and the form may be used as a checklist for deciding what should be included.)

XYZ Co. Ltd

Position applied for:

A Personal details

Full name *(underline surname)*:

Private address:

Telephone No:

Business Address:

Telephone No:

(Place a cross in the box if you do not wish to be contacted at work ☐).

Date of birth: Sex: Male/Female

Marital status: Single/Married/Widowed/Divorced

Place of birth: Nationality:

B Education and qualifications

Schooling Please give the names and dates of schools attended since age 11, and the details of all public examinations attempted, with results (including any examinations failed).

Schools attended	Dates	Subject and grade of examinations	Dates	Results

(Continued)

(Continued)

Further and higher education Please give details of any University or College attended with dates, subject studied, and details of qualifications (including class of degree, and failures if any). Include details of any public examinations attempted after leaving school through private study correspondence, etc.

College or university attended	Dates	Subjects and level of qualification	Date of examination	Result

Please state any other qualifications, distinctions or skills which you consider might be particularly useful to the XYZ Co. Ltd.

Foreign languages spoken Please list any foreign languages spoken or understood together with the degree of proficiency in reading and speaking.

Membership of professional body Please state whether you are a member of any professional body or institution, and if so, which.

Do you have a current driving licence? Yes/No

C Employment

Please list in reverse order the names and addresses of all your employers during the last five years, together with dates of starting and leaving, the reason for leaving, posts held and initial and leaving salary in each case.

Name and address of employer	Dates of starting/ leaving	Post held	Starting/ leaving salary	Reasons for leaving

(Continued)

Please confirm that we may approach your present/most recent employer for a confidential assessment of your suitability for employment. Yes/No.

Unless you tick here we shall not approach your employer before making you an offer of employment.☐

Please give details of any special responsibilities or achievement in your most recent employment which might be relevant.

Why do you wish to leave your present employment?

D Personal reference

Please give the names and addresses of two people personally known to you but not related to you whom we can contact for a confidential assessment of your suitability for this job.

Name:

Address:

Telephone No:

Name:

Address:

Telephone No:

E Health

Are you in good health? Yes/No

Are you registered as disabled? Yes/No

Have you suffered from any serious illness or undergone any major operation? Yes/No

Please give details in each case if relevant.

It will be a condition of any offer of employment XYZ Co. Ltd may make to you that you either provide satisfactory evidence of your state of health or undergo a medical examination.

(Continued)

(Continued)

F Availability

How much notice would you require to give to leave your present employment?

Please give dates of any holidays already arranged which you would like us to honour:

What rate of pay are you seeking?
Are you willing to work on shift supervision involving night work? Yes/No

Are you willing to work overtime and weekends as required: Yes/No

It is company policy to give preference to applicants willing to work anywhere within the United Kingdom. Are you willing to do so? Yes/No

If no, please state areas you are willing to work in:

G Supplementary information

Have you ever worked for XYZ Co. Ltd before? Yes/No

If yes, give details including dates and reason for leaving:

Have you ever been convicted of a criminal offence? Yes/No

If yes, please give full details. You need not include motoring convictions unless your driving licence has a current endorsement as a result.

Any other information which may assist the company in deciding whether to appoint you:

Leisure interests and activities (including details of any positions of responsibility and voluntary work):

H Declaration

I apply for employment with XYZ Co. Ltd. To the best of my knowledge and belief all the particulars I have given are true. I understand that any false statement may disqualify me from employment or render me liable to instant dismissal.

Signed *Date*

Form 5 Request for employer's reference

(To be duplicated on headed company notepaper.)

To: Date:

Dear

Application for Employment: J. Smith

The above has applied to this company for employment in the post of . . . and the company is considering the possibility of appointing him/her. He/she has informed us that you are his/her current/most recent employer, and has given details of his/her employment with you. I should be very grateful if you would confirm the correctness of these particulars as set out below and overleaf and give me your assessment of the applicant's suitability in relation to the questions overleaf. Your reply will of course be treated as strictly confidential. If you would prefer to reply by letter I should be perfectly happy. A reply paid envelope is enclosed.

May I take the opportunity of thanking you in advance for your assistance.

Yours faithfully,

Personnel Manager

Details of employment given by applicant

Location:

Starting date: Leaving date:

Salary/wage:

Post and responsibilities:

Are these particulars accurate? Yes/No

If no, please give details:

If the applicant has left your employment please give the reason (if known):

(Continued)

(Continued)

Please give a brief assessment of the applicant's qualities under each of the following headings:

Timekeeping:

Realiability:

Honesty:

Attitude to work:

Quality of work:

Responsibilities assumed:

Ability to work with others:

Health:

Absenteeism:

Breaches of discipline:

Would you re-employ the applicant? Yes/No

If not please give reasons:

Any other comments:

Signed: *Date:*

Position:

Form 6 Invitation to interview

(To be duplicated on company headed paper. Also, employers may prefer to fill in as much as possible of the reply slip before sending the invitation out.)

To: Date:

Dear

Your Application for Employment

With reference to your recent application for the post of . . . , I am pleased to inform you that we should like to interview you for possible appointment. The interview will be at the above address at . . . am/pm . . . on the . . . 19. . . Please report to the *reception desk/security gate about 15 minutes before the time of your interview, and bring this letter with you.

I enclose a map showing the location of our offices/works. If you are coming by car you may park in the visitors car park. *The company will pay your expenses (2nd class rail fare or . . .p per mile for car travel) *but I regret that this can only be done if you have agreed that if we offer you the post you will accept the offer. If you require overnight accommodation this can be arranged.

I must formally advise you that it is company policy not to make any appointment except by way of a formal written contract. If therefore we decide after your interview to make you an offer of a post, this will be subject to the formal terms of appointment which will be communicated to you in writing.

Please let me know if you will attend the interview by completing and returning the tear-off slip. A reply paid envelope is enclosed.

I look forward to meeting you at the interview.

Yours faithfully,

Personnel Manager

Enc.

**Delete as required*

- -

To: The Personnel Manager,
XYZ Co. Ltd

Interview for post of:

Name:

I *shall/shall not attend the interview arranged for me at . . . am/pm on . . . the . . . 19. . .

I *shall/shall not require overnight accommodation for the night(s) . . .

*I agree to accept appointment to this post if it is offered to me.

Signed: *Date:*

**Delete as appropriate.*

Form 7 Assessment and interview record

(This form serves both as an aid to selection and a record of the selection process. It should be kept for six months *after the final decision whether to appoint, as a record in case a claim is made by an unsuccessful candidate.)*

Part 1 Initial assessment for shortlisting *(to be completed for all applicants being considered for shortlisting).*

Name:

Address:

Age:

Marital status: Nationality:

Present employment:

Post applied for:

Location of post:

Grading and salary of post:

Formal qualifications/experience required for post (*underline essential requirements*):

Does applicant possess all relevant qualifications/experience? Yes/No

Comment if no:

Other relevant qualifications/experience of applicant:

Any other comments:

Recommendation as to shortlisting: Yes/Possible/No

Any relevant points for interviewers to raise with applicant:

Decision as to shortlisting: Yes/No

Reasons:

Invited to interview — date:

Accepted/declined/no reply:

(Continued)

(Continued)

Part 2 Interview record *(to be completed for all candidates invited to interview).*

Date of interview: Duration:

Number of applicants interviewed:

Number of posts:

Names of interviewer(s):

Decision: Accept/Reject:

Conditions of acceptance (delete as relevant):
- References
- Medical examination
- Membership
- Work permit
- Examinations (give details)
- Other (give details)

Proposed starting salary/grade:

Proposed starting date:

Interviewers' report and reasons for decision:

Part 3 Appointment record *(to be completed for applicants offered employment).*

Conditional offer letter sent — date:

Applicant's acceptance/refusal/no reply:

Requests for references sent — date:

Employer reference: Wholly favourable/satisfactory/suspect/unsuitable/refused.

Personal reference: Wholly favourable/satisfactory/suspect/unsuitable/refused.

Referred to doctor/medical reports provided — date:

Medical assessment: Wholly favourable/satisfactory/suspect/unsuitable.

(Note any special points about applicant's health that should be retained on his/her personal record):

Other conditions satisfied — date:

Formal offer sent — date:
(Special conditions to be added to formal offer):

Acceptance received — date:

Date employment commenced:

Form 8 Rejection of application

(To be duplicated on headed company notepaper. It is suggested that separate forms be prepared for each of the asterisked alternative middle paragraphs.)

To: Date:

Dear

Your Application for Employment

I refer to your recent application for employment as . . .

*I regret to inform you that at present we have no vacancies for this kind of post. I will write to you again should any vacancies arise in the near future for which we may wish to consider you.

*I regret to inform you that we have no vacancies of this kind.

*There is at present a waiting list for this work, and I have added your name to the waiting list. We shall give your application further consideration when you reach the top of the list, but I cannot promise you a job then as it will depend on the circumstances at that time.

*There was a very large number of applications for this post, and I regret that we have not been able to make you an offer of employment on this occasion.

In conclusion may I thank you for your interest in the Company.

Yours faithfully,

Personnel Manager

Form 9 Conditional offer of employment

(To be duplicated on headed company notepaper. Asterisked conditions can be deleted as required or additional ones inserted.)

To: Date:

Dear

Offer of Employment

Further to your recent application for employment I am pleased to inform you that the Company has decided, subject to the conditions set out in this letter, to make you an offer of employment as . . . .

This offer is conditional on

*a) receipt of satisfactory reference from your previous employer and the personal referee named in your application form;

*b) your passing a medical examination or providing satisfactory evidence of medical fitness;

*c) your assurance that you are or will become a member of the . . . Trade Union;

*d) the Department of Employment approving the transfer of your work permit;

*e) your passing the following examinations;

*f) *(insert other conditions here).*

If you are able to satisfy these conditions and you accept our offer, you will be given a formal written statement of the terms and conditions of your employment. I must stress that this letter is not a formal offer, and it is subject to the Company's terms and conditions of employment. However I can confirm that you will be offered a starting *salary/wages of . . . *per week/per year, and that your normal hours will be: . . . .

You will be working at: . . . .

Please report there at . . . a.m. on . . . 19. ., which is the date your employment is to commence, and ask for . . . .

Please let me know whether you intend to accept this offer by filling in the tear-off slip and returning it to me. A reply paid envelope is enclosed.

Yours faithfully,

Personnel Manager

- -

To the Personnel Manager
XYZ Co. Ltd

Offer of employment: Post:

Starting date:

Name:

I accept your offer of employment as stated above and subject to the conditions in your letter and the company's terms and conditions of employment.

I authorise you to approach my present/previous employer for a reference. *(Please give the name and address to which the company should write)*:

I enclose a recent medical report/I agree to be examined by a doctor selected by the company. *(Delete as appropriate).*

Signed: *Date:*

Contract of employment between
XYZ COMPANY LIMITED ('the Company')
and
. . . . ('the employee')

A Preamble

1 This document sets out the terms on which the Company has offered to employ the employee, and which the employee has accepted in writing by his signature at the end hereof.

2 The employee agrees and affirms that he has not been induced to accept this offer of employment by any representation, assurance or warranty made to him by any servant or agent of the Company as to any matter not expressed in this agreement.

3 This agreement constitutes a written contract of employment for the purposes of Section 5 of *The Employment Protection (Consolidation) Act, 1978.*

4 The terms of this contract will not be varied except as provided in Clause 6 otherwise than by notice in writing from the Company to the employee.

5 This contract is governed by English Law. The employee will be based in the UK/in. . .

6 This contract is subject to the terms of the agreements between the Company and the . . . Trade Union relating to monthly paid staff in force at the date hereof, and shall continue to be so subject notwithstanding that the said agreements or any of them shall cease to have effect through expiry, termination, non-renewal or otherwise.

7 In the event of a conflict between a term of this contract and the terms of an agreement incorporated by Clause 6, this contract shall prevail over any such term as is in force at the date hereof.

8 This contract is subject to the terms of any agreement which may in the future be made between the Company and the Trade Union relating to monthly paid staff, and any such terms shall prevail over the terms of this contract in the event of a conflict between them.

9 For the purposes of Section 18(4) of *The Trade Union and Labour Relations Act, 1974*, it is hereby declared that the terms of the agreement between the . . . Trade Union and the Company dated . . ., whereby the Trade Union agreed that its members would not take part in a strike or other industrial action until all agreed procedures had been followed, is incorporated into this contract.

B Period of employment

10 The employee will be employed by the Company from . . . until such time as this contract is determined as provided for below, or comes to an end by operation of law, but will otherwise terminate on the date of the employee's . . .th birthday.

11 For the purpose of *The Employment Protection (Consolidation) Act, 1978*, the employee's previous employment from . . . to . . . with the Company/. . . does/does not count as continuous with this employment and the date from which continuous employment is to be computed is . . .

12 Either party may terminate this contract on the last day of any calendar month by giving notice in writing to that effect. The employee shall give at least one calendar month's notice, or if at the time such a notice would expire the employee would have completed three years' continuous employment as defined in Clause 11 at least three calendar months' notice.

C Title and duties of employment

13 The employee's job title is . . . . The duties of the employee are as set out in the job description annexed to this contract and which forms part of the contract. The employee may also be required as a

(Continued)

condition of employment to undertake duties not specified in the job description reasonably required of him by the Company.

14 Instructions which may be given to the employee by the Company may be given by any person authorised to do so by the Company, and in particular by the person designated as the employee's supervisor. The employee's supervisor shall be . . . .

D Place of employment

15 The employee's place of work will be the Company's district office for . . . district/head office *(and the employee will be required to travel to the premises of customers within that district).

16 The employee may be required on one month's notice in writing from the Company to work at any other of the Company's offices, in the United Kingdom. If in the opinion of the Company it is reasonable for the employee to move house in order to fulfil such a requirement (or if it is necessary for the employee to do so in order to comply with Clause . . .) he will be entitled to the financial assistance and paid removal leave set out in the relevant agreement for the time being in force between the Company and the Trade Union.

E Hours of employment

17 The hours of employment are . . . each week, normally from . . . to . . . with a one-hour lunch break to be taken at a time to be agreed between the employee and his supervisor.

18 The employee will work reasonable overtime when required. While every effort will be made to give reasonable notice of overtime, no minimum period of notice is guaranteed by the Company.

19 The employee is not entitled to additional remuneration for overtime as this is regarded as an integral feature of the post. However the Company will at its discretion allow the employee time off in lieu, or an *ex gratia* payment, where substantial overtime is worked. Time off in such cases will be one day for each five hours of overtime, and *ex gratia* payments will be at the rate of 3/80 of a week's salary per hour.

F Remuneration

20 The employee will be paid on the company's scale . . . which is £ . . . p.a. increasing by . . . annual increments of £ . . . to £ . . . p.a. The employee's initial salary will be £ . . . p.a. The incremental date is . . . and the employee will be entitled to an increment of salary on . . . and annually thereafter.

21* In addition the employee is entitled to commission of 2 per cent of the gross value of sales by the Company to customers for whom he is responsible. Sales shall be deemed to take place at the time at which payment becomes due. The employee shall not be entitled to commission on sales which take place before the date of commencement of the employment or after it has terminated.

22 The Company pays all employees an annual bonus of one week's salary *(and 1/52 of a year's commission); this is payable at the end of November each year.

23 Salary is payable monthly in arrears into a bank account nominated by the employee. The employee will be notified each month in writing of the amount of net and gross salary and the nature and amount of all deductions. (Commission is payable together with the salary for the month following that in which the commission is earned.) Overtime payments are payable together with salary for the month following that in which the overtime is worked.

24 The employee will be reimbursed by the Company for expenses incurred in the course of Company business at the rates prescribed for the time being by the Company, on condition that claims are duly submitted on the forms provided. Expenses will be paid at the end of the month after that in which the claim is submitted. Cash advances in respect of expenses will be given at the Company's discretion.

(Continued)

25 It is hereby declared that the employee's salary accrues due from day to day.

G Fringe benefits

26 The employee is entitled to the use of a Company-provided car of not more than . . . cc engine size, to be chosen from a list of approved models published by the Company from time to time. The Company reserves the right to decide at its discretion at what intervals the car will be changed.

27 The Company will tax the vehicle and insure it in the joint names of itself and the employee and pay for the cost of maintenance and repairs so far as occasioned by fair wear and tear or defects in the vehicle. The employee is responsible for oil and petrol and the first £ . . . of any accidental damage due to his negligence (or such larger sum as may from time to time be required by way of Excess by the Company's insurers) and for any repairs occasioned by misuse of the vehicle. The Company will reimburse the employee for the cost of oil and petrol for travel on Company business, including travel between the employee's home and place of work.

28 The vehicle will at all times remain the property of the Company and any attempt to sell hire assign or pledge it will be regarded as a serious offence. No modification may be made to the vehicle without the Company's consent. The employee shall surrender the vehicle to the custody of the Company forthwith on leaving the Company's employ.

29 The employee is permitted to use the vehicle for private as well as business travel, but this is a concession which the Company reserves the right to withdraw at any time without notice.

30* Where as a result of the vehicle not being useable, the employee is prevented from working, the Company shall at its expense provide alternative transport or at its discretion pay to the employee a reasonable sum in recompense for any commission which the employee was thereby prevented from earning.

31 The employee is entitled to free membership of the Company Sports and Social Club and the use of its facilities in accordance with the rules, a copy of which is displayed on the notice board at each branch of the Club. If the employee is married then his spouse is also entitled to membership.

32 The Company provides a scheme for health and accident insurance. The employee is entitled to the benefits of the scheme in accordance with its terms. The principal benefits are outlined in the Company rules for monthly paid staff.

33 The employee is entitled in March each year to purchase up to 200 of the Company's £1 Ordinary shares at a discount of 20 per cent. Payment may be made by six equal deductions from the employee's salary over the six months following the purchase. This right does not apply to a probationary employee.

H Indemnity

33 The Company undertakes to indemnify the employee in respect of any liability he may incur in defending or as a result of civil proceedings brought against him for any act or omission in the course of his employment, including debts reasonably incurred, unless in the Company's opinion the act or omission constituted wilful disobedience of rules or instructions. This undertaking is conditional on the employee agreeing to be represented by lawyers chosen by and acting under the instructions of the Company as to the conduct of proceedings or the approval of any settlement.

34 The Company cannot and does not indemnify employees in respect of criminal liability but it may in its discretion provide the employee with assistance in conducting his defence in any criminal proceedings where the Company's interest is or may be affected.

I Holiday

35 The employee is entitled to paid holidays as follows: 4 weeks (20 days) in any calendar year

(Continued)

commencing before the employee has completed 5 years' continuous employment; thereafter 5 weeks (25 days) in any calendar year. In addition the employee is entitled to the following Bank or Statutory holidays without loss of pay: New Year's Day, Good Friday, Easter Monday, May Day, Spring Bank Holiday, Summer Bank Holiday, Christmas Day, Boxing Day. If the employee is required to work in Scotland, or Northern Ireland, he will be entitled to the equivalent Bank or Statutory holidays for that country. The employee will also be entitled to a holiday without loss of pay on any other day which may proclaimed by the Queen as a public holiday. Where a Statutory or Bank holiday occurs on a Saturday or Sunday the Company will nominate an alternative day which will be deemed to be the Bank Holiday for the purposes of the employee's holiday entitlement.

36* 'Paid' or 'without loss of pay' means that the employee shall be entitled to receive his salary in full but shall not receive any additional sum by way of commission other than commission actually earned, nor any compensation for loss of opportunity to earn commission.

37 The Company reserves the right to require the employee to work on a Bank or Statutory or other public holiday when circumstances require. In that event the employee will be entitled to either two days' additional paid holiday or an additional payment of 2/5 of a week's salary, at the Company's discretion.

38 The employee is required to take part of his holiday entitlement on such dates as the Company may direct that the establishment at which he is for the time being employed shall be closed (normally the period between Christmas and New Year) and the remainder at times agreed with his supervisor.

39 The employee is required to take the whole of his holiday entitlement during the calendar year in which it accrues. Holiday entitlement cannot be carried over to the next year.

40 If the employee leaves the Company's employment other than at the end of a calendar year, the holiday entitlement will be calculated on a proportionate basis for each whole month's service, reduced to the next whole number of days' holiday. If on this basis the employee has not used up the whole of his holiday entitlement he will be paid at the rate of a day's salary for each unused day. If he has exceeded the entitlement there will be a deduction from salary due accordingly.

J Sickness and medical examinations

41 The employee is entitled to paid sick leave for up to . . . weeks in each calendar year at full pay and up to a further . . . weeks at half pay. During the first year of continuous employment as defined in Clause 11 the employee shall be entitled only to one half of these periods of paid leave.

42 The employee is entitled to unpaid sick leave for periods of absence occasioned by illness for which he is not entitled to paid sick leave.

43 The granting of sick leave is subject to the condition that the employee furnishes a certificate signed by a duly qualified medical practitioner stating that the employee was unable to work because of illness on each day for which sick leave is sought. As a concession the Company has agreed to waive the requirement for a medical certificate for absences not exceeding three consecutive working days, but this concession may be withdrawn by the Company for any employee at any time in its absolute discretion.

44 The granting of sick leave is subject to the further condition that the Company may at any time require the employee to submit to a medical examination, in which case sick leave will not be granted until such time as the employee has complied with the requirement.

45 Where the employee is unable to work by reason of illness on a date on which he would otherwise have been on holiday, and furnishes a certificate from a qualified medical practitioner to that effect, he is entitled to an additional day's holiday in lieu to be taken in accordance with the conditions as to holidays (but if it would otherwise not be possible to take it, this holiday may be carried over to the next calendar year).

46 'Full pay' in this part of the contract means the appropriate proportion of the employee's gross salary, less the amount which he could on a claim duly made receive in state sickness or industrial

(Continued)

injuries benefit including any earnings-related benefit); and 'half pay' means half of the appropriate proportion of the employee's gross salary, less half of the benefits claimable as stated above. State benefits are deducted whether they are paid or not, and the employee is required as a condition of payment of sick pay to claim state benefits where applicable and to give the employer details of the amounts to which he is entitled.

47 The Company reserves the right to withhold sick pay in any case where the employee is incapable of work because of addiction to drugs, accidents sustained in participation in any dangerous sport, or deliberate self-injury.

48 Where incapacity to work is a result of an accident occurring during the course of the employee's employment, the Company may in its discretion extend the period of time for which sick leave (both at full pay and at half pay) is available.

49 Where the employee is paid sick pay for absence arising from an injury caused by the negligence of a third party, the employee is required to reimburse the Company any amount recovered from the third party as compensation for loss of earnings (not exceeding the amount of sick pay) and the payment by the Company shall be regarded as an interest-free loan for these purposes.

50 Where the employee or his spouse is confined in a hospital for a period of two weeks or more the company will pay an additional 5 per cent of the employee's gross salary for each complete week of hospitalisation towards the employee's additional out-of-pocket expenses, for up to a maximum of... weeks.

51* Where the employee is on paid sick leave for a continuous period of one week or more the Company will pay the employee an additional amount of 1/52 of the commission earned by the employee during the previous calendar year for each complete week of continuous sick leave so long as the employee remains on full pay; and thereafter 1/104 of that amount of commission for each complete week that the employee remains on half pay. This clause only applies to employees who have completed one year's continuous employment before the incapacity for work begins.

52 It is a condition of engagement by and of continued employment with the Company that the employee's general state of health is maintained at a level satisfactory to the Company. The employee is therefore required as a condition of employment and before taking up employment to undergo a medical examination by a fully qualified medical practitioner appointed for the purpose by the Company, and the Company may cancel this contract if it is not satisfied on the report of the medical examination with the employee's general state of health. The employee is also required to undergo a medical examination as directed by the Company every three years.

53 Nothing in this part of the contract affects or diminishes the right at any time of the Company to give notice to terminate this agreement in accordance with Clause 12.

54 If the employee is given notice to terminate this contract (whether by reason of illness or otherwise) he is entitled to be paid at his full normal rate of salary during the period of the notice notwithstanding any incapacity for work due to illness, but in such a case any state benefit payable shall be deducted from salary. *(In such a case the employee is also entitled to be paid commission at a rate equivalent to the average daily rate of commission payable to the employee over the 12 weeks immediately previous to the week in question.)

K Pension

55 The employee is eligible and required to become a member of the Company's pension scheme on completion of 6 months' continuous employment, or to continue to be a member if already in membership. The full conditions and benefits of the pension scheme are set out in the Pensions Rules, a copy of which is available from the Personnel Office on request; a summary of the benefits is set out in the handbook for monthly paid staff.

56 The Company undertakes to pay its contributions to the pension fund on behalf of the employee, and to deduct the employee's contribution from salary and pay that amount to the pension fund. The employer will pay the employee's contribution when the employee is on unpaid sick leave, but

(Continued)

otherwise the employee is responsible for his contributions even when on unpaid leave.

57 The employee authorises the Company to deduct his pension contributions at the prescribed rate from his salary, and undertakes to comply with the conditions of the pension scheme and the directions of the trustees.

58 The Company pension scheme is contracted out of the state reserve pension scheme.

L Special leave

59 The employee is entitled to one week's additional paid holiday on the occasion of his marriage.

60 The employee may apply for special leave for any purpose, but the grant of special leave other than for marriage and as provided below for certain specific purposes is entirely at the Company's discretion. It is normally the policy of the Company to grant reasonable requests for special leave with pay in the case of the death or serious illness of a close relative, but in other cases special leave is normally without pay.

61 (*Women employees*) The employee is entitled to maternity leave without pay subject to the conditions laid down in *The Employment Protection (Consolidation) Act, 1978*. The employee is not entitled to leave (but may apply for the discretionary grant of special leave) for longer than the period laid down for the time being by law or in a case where she has not completed sufficient continuous employment. It is a condition of maternity leave that the employee gives all the required notices in writing and provides a certificate from a qualified doctor or midwife of the expected date of her confinement.

62 The employee is entitled to maternity pay during maternity leave or on leaving employment to have a baby to the extent only that this is provided for by law.

63 (*Male employees*) The employee is entitled to one week's additional paid holiday on the occasion of the birth to his wife of a child.

M Trade union rights

64 The employee is entitled to be or become a member of any independent trade union, and to take part in its activities at any time other than a time at which he is required to be at work. The employee is not permitted to take part in the activities of a trade union during working hours or make use of the Company's facilities for trade union purposes except as provided for in Clause 65.

65 If the employee is or becomes a member of the . . . Trade Union he is entitled to take part in its activities during working hours and to be given unpaid leave to take part in its activities in accordance with the agreement for the time being in force between the Company and the . . . Trade Union. If the employee is elected or appointed to become an official of the . . . Trade Union, he is entitled to be permitted paid time off to carry out his trade union duties, and the use of the Company's facilities for this purpose, in accordance with the agreement for the time being in force between the Company and the . . . Trade Union. The terms of the agreement as they relate to the calculation of pay shall also apply to this contract.

66 The Company will at the written request of the employee deduct from his salary the monthly amount due of his subscription to the . . . Trade Union and pay this amount each month to the Union.

N Public duties

67 If the employee is or becomes a member of any statutory tribunal, or public authority, or a Justice of the Peace, he is entitled to be permitted to take a reasonable amount of unpaid leave for the discharge of his functions. The amounts and timings of leave are for agreement in each individual case with the Personnel Manager.

(Continued)

68 The employee is entitled to unpaid leave in order to fulfil any obligation to perform jury service or to attend as a witness in proceedings in a court of law or statutory tribunal.

69 If the employee is nominated as a candidate for a bona fide political party in a Parliamentary election he is entitled to unpaid leave for the day of the poll and the three weeks immediately preceding that date. The Company will consider applications for extended unpaid leave for employees elected to Parliament.

O Grievance procedures

70 If the employee has any grievance relating to any aspect of his employment he shall first discuss the matter with his supervisor before raising the matter formally. This does not apply where the grievance relates to the conduct of the supervisor or arises from a failure to agree on any matter which this contract provides is for settlement by agreement, or relates to the exercise by the Company of a discretion established by this contract.

71 If the grievance is not resolved by discussion, or Clause 70 does not apply to it, the employee may pursue the matter by formal application in writing to the Personnel Manager. This must be done within 14 days of the grievance coming to his notice, or of the failure of discussions, as the case may be.

72 A formal grievance application will be dealt with in accordance with the grievance procedure agreed for the time being between the Company and the . . . Trade Union. A copy of the current procedure is set out in the handbook for monthly paid staff. The employee agrees to accept the outcome of his complaint if it is dealt with under this procedure.

P Probation

73 The employee's employment is subject to an initial probationary period of three months. The Company may extend the probationary period by a further month at any time before the end of the three-month period.

74 The provisions of this contract apply equally to the probationary period, except that the grievance and disciplinary procedures do not apply to decisions taken to extend the period of probation or to terminate the employee's services on the ground of inadequate performance or potential.

75 At any time during the period of probation the Company may give at least one week's notice in writing to terminate the employee's employment on the ground of inadequate performance or potential.

76 Promotion within the Company may be made subject to a period of probation and to downgrading or cancellation of the promotion on the ground of inadequate performance or potential in the new post.

Q Employee's general obligations

77 The employee undertakes that he will not disclose any of the Company's trade secrets to a third party either during or after the termination of his employment with the Company.

78 The employee undertakes that he will not disclose any information which he has come to know in the course of his employment, relating to the personal affairs of a fellow employee, to a third party or to the employee concerned, either during or after the termination of his employment with the Company.

79 The employee undertakes that he will not disclose any information about the Company's affairs, whether or not covered by Clause 77, or any information which he has come to know in the course of his employment whether or not covered by Clause 78, to any third party, without prior authority from the Company. A third party does not include a fellow employee who requires the information for the performance of his duties.

(Continued)

80 The employee will at any time if required to do so sign an agreement giving undertakings in the terms set out in Clauses 77 and 78.

81 The employee may not write letters to the press on matters concerning the Company's affairs, or in any way referring to his position in the Company, or using the Company's address, without the prior written permission of the Company.

82 The employee is required to inform the Company immediately if his spouse or a close relative with whom he is living is engaged by any competitor of the Company. The Company reserves the right to give notice to terminate this contract in such a case.

83 The employee may not enter into another occupation or employment, or conduct any trade or business, in his spare time, without the prior written approval of the Company. Approval will not be given for any outside work which might interfere with the proper performance of the employee's duties.

84 The employee will not engage in spare-time activities of such a nature or to such an extent as to impair his fitness to carry out the duties of his employment.

85 The employee will at any time if required to do so sign an agreement undertaking not to work for a competitor of the Company and not to solicit the Company's customers during such period after this contract is terminated as the Company may reasonably specify and within such geographical area and subject to such other provisions as the Company may reasonably specify.

86 The copyright in any written material produced by the employee in the course of his employment shall vest in the Company.

87 Any invention made by the employee, whether or not in the course of his employment, shall be the property of the Company, except to the extent and in the circumstances that Section 39 of *The Patents Act, 1977*, provides otherwise.

88 The employee will at all times while in the course of his employment maintain a neat and tidy appearance and dress in a respectable and sober fashion, and will comply with any reasonable instructions of the Company as to appearance and dress.

89 The employee will reside within reasonable travelling distance of the establishment at which he is for the time being employed, and will notify the Company of any change of address.

90 The employee will notify the employer promptly of any change to his name, marital status or next of kin, or of any circumstances which might affect the Company's insurance cover in respect of the employee.

91 The employee will notify the employer promptly if he is convicted of a criminal offence, giving details of the offence and penalty. This does not apply to motoring offences not involving an endorsement of licence.

92 The employee is permitted to make and receive a reasonable number of telephone calls on the Company's telephone lines; this is a privilege and the Company reserves the right to withdraw it at any time without notice, if it is abused.

93 Unauthorised possession of the Company's property and the unauthorised removal of the Company's property from the Company's premises is regarded as a serious disciplinary offence.

94 The Company reserves the right at any time, through any person authorised to do so, to search the employee's person and personal effects and the vehicle in which he is travelling, before he is permitted to enter or leave the Company's premises. The employee in accepting employment agrees to be searched at any time and to be detained for the purpose of search, and further to be detained for as long as may be required to verify his authority to be in possession of any item found in the course of a search.

(Continued)

(Continued)

R Safety

95 The Company undertakes to observe all duties imposed on it by statute to protect and preserve the health safety and welfare at work of the employee.

96 The employee undertakes to observe all duties imposed on him by statute to protect and preserve the health, safety and welfare of himself and other persons at work.

97 The employee will familiarise himself with all fire and safety precautions and procedures which are laid down for his job and for the premises at which he is required for the time being to work, and will comply with these procedures.

98 The Company undertakes to provide for the employee free of charge any protective clothing or apparatus reasonably required for him to carry out his duties, and the employee undertakes to make use of these at all appropriate times.

99 The employee will not be required to undertake any additional responsibilities for safety not included in his job description as attached to this contract without being given a clear written statement of the nature of those responsibilities, and adequate training in order to discharge them.

100 The employee will report to his supervisor any safety hazard or any hazardous occurrence which comes to his notice in the course of his employment.

S Disciplinary procedure

101 Without prejudice to the Company's general power to terminate this contract by giving the notice required by Clause 12, the Disciplinary Procedure agreed between the . . . Trade Union and the Company on . . . (a copy of which is printed in the Handbook for monthly paid staff) forms part of this contract, and the employee will be dealt with in accordance with the provisions of the Procedure in all cases of alleged misconduct, incompetence or inadequate performance of work.

102 The Company may suspend the employee on full pay during or pending the investigation of any matter under the Disciplinary Procedure.

103 The employee is expected to perform his duties with reasonable efficiency and diligence, to behave towards fellow employees with reasonable courtesy and decorum, not to misuse, damage or misappropriate the Company's property and not to cause offence to customers or potential customers. Any failure to maintain these standards constitutes misconduct. The employee's attention is drawn to the list of offences in the Disciplinary Procedures, but this is by way of illustration only and is not intended to be exhaustive.

104 The Company recognises the employee's right to be represented by a representative of his trade union in any disciplinary proceedings.

105 The penalties which may be imposed for misconduct are as specified in the Disciplinary Procedure.

106 The Company reserves the right of summary dismissal without salary in lieu of notice in cases of gross and wilful misconduct or gross neglect of duties. In such cases the Company gives notice that the penalty will in all cases be summary dismissal.

Signature on behalf of Company: *Signature of Employee:*

Signed: *Date:* *Signed:* *Date:*
Position:

(Both copies to be signed by both parties.)

Form 11 Amendments to contract of employment

XYZ Co. Ltd
The Employment Protection (Consolidation) Act, 1978.

Name of employee: Date:

Works No:

Department/Section:

Location:

This is to give you formal notice that the terms of your contract have been amended as detailed below. Please acknowledge receipt by signing the second copy and returning to the Personnel Office. You should attach the top copy to your main Contract of Employment.

If you have any query or dispute over these changes you should raise the matter with your supervisor in the first instance.

Personnel Manager

Date changes effective:

New wages/salary:

New job title:

New hours of work:

New location:

Other changes:

For signature (Second copy only)

I acknowledge receipt of your notice dated . . . informing me of amendments to the terms of my contract of employment.

Signed: *Date:*

Form 12 Application for payment of wages by cheque

(It is illegal under the Truck Acts to pay wages otherwise than in cash unless the individual employee has agreed in writing to payment by cheque. Agreement cannot be made a condition of employment. The Truck Acts apply to manual workers and shop assistants. For other workers payment by cheque may be made a condition of employment – otherwise the written form of agreement below may be used for all employees.)

XYZ Co. Ltd

The Payment of Wages Act, 1960

Employee's Name:

Department/Section:

Location:

State whether weekly or monthly paid:

I apply to have my wages paid by cheque from (date):

I understand that I can cancel this agreement at any time by giving the Company four weeks' notice. I also understand that I shall continue to receive a written statement of my gross wages, deductions and net wages every time I am paid.

Signed: *Date:*

Please indicate with a tick which method of payment you wish:

Cheque to be given to me personally.

Cheque to be paid into my account no. . . . at my bank: (*name and address of bank*).

Return this form to the Wages Office.

Form 13 Agreement to contract out of statutory rights

(This form is only valid if the contract of employment is for a fixed term.*)*

Re contract of employment between XYZ Co. Ltd and . . .

Date of commencement of contract:

Date of expiry of contract:

I hereby agree to forego such of my statutory rights under *The Employment Protection (Consolidation) Act, 1978* or subsequent similar legislation as it is permitted by the relevant legislation to agree to forego in the event that the contract of employment detailed above expires without being renewed by XYZ Co. Ltd or any associated company.

Signed: *Date:*

Form 14 Employee's undertaking as to confidentiality

XYZ Co. Ltd
Confidentiality

To: Date:

Department/Section:

Location:

In view of the nature of your work and your access to important and confidential information about the Company's affairs, it is important that you should appreciate and accept your legal obligation not to divulge confidential information about the Company. You are therefore asked to sign the declaration below and return it to the Personnel Office, keeping the second copy for reference. If you have any doubts about what information this covers, please consult your supervisor, who will if necessary take the matter up for you.

I must remind you that unauthorised disclosure of confidential information is a disciplinary offence. Also you should not disclose confidential information to your trade union representative. Any information which your trade union is entitled to have disclosed to it will be dealt with through the established negotiating machinery.

Personnel Manager

Declaration

I undertake not to disclose to any person, other than an officer or employee of XYZ Co. Ltd who requires the information in the course of his duties, unless I am required by law to do so, any information to which I have had access in the course of my employment which falls within any of the following categories: secret manufacturing processes; design of machinery and equipment; unpatented designs; marketing arrangements; customer discounts; names of customers; proposals for commercial developments; planning applications, new buildings or plant, or takeovers or mergers; the make-up of tenders; financial data not published in the Company's accounts; information personally relating to individuals; information about defence or other Government contracts.

Signed: *Date:*

Form 15 Employee's restrictive covenant

(**Important.** *A restrictive covenant of this kind will not be valid and enforceable unless it is reasonable in relation to the business of the employer and the public interest. Employers are strongly advised to take legal advice before fixing such matters as the length of time and the area within which competition is to be restricted in their particular circumstances.)*

XYZ Co. Ltd
Working for Competitors

To: Date:

Department/Section:

Location:

The Company is concerned at the possibility that employees may be poached by our competitors, and may take with them valuable commercial information or information about our customers which it could be extremely damaging to the Company to have disclosed. The Company is confident that its employees would not wish to damage its interests in this way. However those employees in a particularly strong position to damage the Company are being asked to give a formal, legally binding undertaking not to do so. In view of the nature of your work I must ask you to sign the attached undertaking and return it to the Personnel Office, keeping the second copy for reference.

In order to make this document legally binding the Company will pay you a nominal sum of £1 to sign it. You may collect this when you return the signed copy to the Personnel Office.

Personnel Manager

Undertaking by employee

In consideration of the payment to me by XYZ Co. Ltd ('the Company) of the sum of one pound (£1) the receipt of which is hereby acknowledged, I hereby give the following formal undertakings:

1 I will not enter into any form of remunerated employment with any person or company which is in direct competition with the Company in the manufacture or sale of products within the United Kingdom, such employment being *anywhere in the United Kingdom/within the following area(s): . . . so long as I remain in the employment of the Company or within . . . years of the termination, in whatever manner and for whatever reason, of my employment with the Company.

2 I will not set up any business *within the United Kingdom/within the following area(s): . . . which will be in direct competition with the Company in the manufacture or sale of products so long as I remain in the employment of the Company or within . . . years of the termination, in whatever manner and for whatever reason, of my employment with the Company.

3 I will not make use of or divulge to any third person or to any further or prospective employer any information which has come into my possession in the course of my employment which relates to the Company's customers or its prices, in such a way as might be detrimental to the Company, at any time while I remain in the employment of the Company or within . . . years of the termination, in whatever manner and for whatever reason, of my employment with the Company.

Signed: *Date:*

Signed for XYZ Co. Ltd: *Date:*

Position:

**Delete as required*

Part Two

Assessment, performance and training

XYZ Co. Ltd

Assessment of Progress of Probationary Employee

Name of employee:

Date of starting:

Length of probation period:

Department/Section:

Location:

1 Supervisor's assessment and recommendation *(To be completed after employee has completed all but one month of probation period.)*

Lenth of period assessed (maximum number of working days):

Attendance:
No. of days late:
No. of days certified sickness:
No. of days uncertified sickness:
No. of days holiday/special leave:
No. of days unauthorised absence:
Total absence:

Training: Has employee completed basic induction/training? Yes/No

Work performance: please assess the following aspects on this rating: 4 good, 3 satisfactory, 2 fair, 1 poor, 0 not known.
Reliability:
Attitude to work:
Quality of work:
Speed of progress:
Ability to work with others:
Responsibilities assumed:
Honesty:
General assessment:
Please comment on any unusual features and any ratings of 1:

Are you satisfied with the potential of this employee? Yes/No

Signed: *Date:*

2 Comments by Section Head

I agree/do not agree with the supervisor's assessment. If you do not agree please give details:

Signed: *Date:*

(Continued)

(Continued)

3 Personnel Manager's decision

Decision (*tick as appropriate*):
Confirmed in permanent employment:
Failed probation: post terminates on:
Probation extended to:
A decision to fail an employee must not be recorded without giving the employee an opportunity to meet the criticisms by interview with the supervisor and section head.

Date of interview and interviewers' comments:

Extension of probation must be accompanied by an interview with the supervisor and section head to explain what is required by way of improvements in performance.

Date of interview and interviewers' comments:

In both cases the employee is entitled to be accompanied by a trade union official.

Signed: *Date:*

Form 17 Notice of decision on probationary employee

XYZ Co. Ltd

Name of employee: Date:

Works No.

Department/Location:

Probationary Assessment

Date of appointment:

Date of expiry of probation period:

Date of expiry of extension of probation (if applicable):

You were appointed to your post with the Company on a probationary basis for three months* (which was subsequently extended to four months). Assessment of your performance has now been completed and the result is given below.

Delete as appropriate:

*Your performance has been satisfactory and I am happy to be able to inform you that you have been appointed to the permanent staff with effect from . . . .

(Your wages/salary from that date will be . . . .)

*Your performance has not been satisfactory and I regret to inform you that it has not proved possible to offer you an appointment on a permanent basis. Your employment with the Company will therefore terminate at the end of your probationary period.

*Your performance has not yet been sufficiently satisfactory for the Company to offer you an appointment on a permanent basis; however, in order to give you an opportunity to reach a satisfactory level of performance and qualify for a permanent appointment, your period of probationary employment has been extended by one month as indicated above. Your supervisor will explain to you the aspects of your work in which the Company will be looking for an improvement during this period.

Personnel Manager

XYZ Co. Ltd
Annual Employee Assessment

Name of employee:

Job title:

Department/Section:

Location:

Part 1 *(This Part to be filled in by supervisor and shown to and discussed with employee)*

General assessment of work performance: please use rating 4 good, 3 satisfactory, 2 fair, 1 poor.
Attendance:
Timekeeping:
Reliability:
Attitude to work:
Quality of work:
Ability to work with others:
Responsibility assumed:
Honesty:
Discipline:
General performance:
Please comment specifically on the following:

Has progress improved during the last year?

Has employee received any training during the year? If so, has he/she benefitted from this?

Is there any training to be recommended for this employee?

Comments on any particularly meritorious aspects of employee's performance:

Comment on any particularly weak or unsatisfactory aspects of employee's performance, and steps you have taken to remedy them:

Other comments:

Signed: *Date:*

The form should now be discussed with the employee.

(Continued)

Part 2 Comments by employee and supervisor after discussion

Employee's comments You are invited to make any comments you wish on the above report. If you wish to make your comments direct to the Personnel Manager you may do so by separate letter. Otherwise please comment below. You are particularly asked to mention any explanations you wish to put forward for any criticism of your performance, or any point on which you want to dispute the accuracy of your supervisor's report:

Signed: *Date:*

Supervisor's further comments Indicate particularly any change you wish to make in the assessments above in the light of discussion and/or employee's comments above:

Signed: *Date:*

Part 3 Section Head's comments

I agree/do not agree with the supervisor's assessment. If you do not agree please give details:

Any other relevant information/comments:

Signed: *Date:*

Part 4 Personnel Manager's record of action taken

Indicate action taken under following heads:
Supplementary training authorised *(give details)*:
Interview with employee (*date*):
Comments:

Letter of commendation sent:
Disciplinary action to be initiated:
Salary review (if appropriate):
Existing salary and grade:
Proposed salary and grade:
Notification to employee:

Signed: *Date:*

Form 19 Employee record card

XYZ Co. Ltd
Employee Record Card

1 Personal Details

Name: D.o.b.:

Place of birth: Sex: M/F

Marital status: Single/married/widowed/divorced/separated.

Changes (with dates):

Address:

Tel. No.:

Changes: 1
(date:) Tel. No.:

2
(date:) Tel. No.:

3
(date:) Tel. No.:

Next of kin: Name:
Address:
Tel. No.: Relationship:

Changed to: Name:
(date:) Address:
Tel. No.: Relationship:

Children:

Names	Sex	Date of birth

(Continued)

(Continued)

Medical Registered disabled? Yes/No
Allergies, illnesses or disabilities that might prejudice safety or restrict range of work that may be undertaken, e.g. asthma, heart weaknesses, haemophilia:

Industrial injuries sustained:

Date:

Nature of accident:

Injuries sustained:

Time off work:

Subsequent outcome — decision on liability/compensation (if known):

Dates of company medical examinations:

Date	Comments and action (if any)

2 Trade union

Membership of union: (if known)

Joined: Left:

Check off authorised: Cancelled:

Offices held:

Agreement as to time off for union duties:

(Date:)

3 Job details

Date started: Date left:

Initial appointment:

Starting pay:

Hours of work:

Place of work:

Overtime arrangements:

(Continued)

(Continued)

Subsequent promotion or transfer (including passing probation):

Date	Details of change	Hours of work

4 Job changes

Date	New rate	Date	New rate

5 Performance of job

Annual job assessment:

Year	Summary of assessment	Action taken

(Continued)

Attendance and sickness:

Year	Times Late	Certified Sickness	Uncertified Sickness	Special Leave	Unauth. Absence

Relevant factors affecting performance of job or attendance:

Training completed:

Date	Training course attended	Qualifications obtained	Remarks

Give details of any new qualifications obtained by employee through private study etc. not recorded above.

(Continued)

(Continued)

6 Disciplinary record

Formal disciplinary record

Date	Nature of complaint	Disciplinary decision	Date to be deleted from file

Notes on disciplinary record:

7 Other information

Include here any matters of importance not specifically dealt with elsewhere:

Form 20 Employee attendance record

XYZ Co. Ltd
Quarterly Attendance Record

Name of employee:

Department/Section:

Location:

Record maintained by:

Dates: from to

Week No. and dates	Lateness: (see key)					Remarks	Absence: to be paid (see key)					Remarks	Absence: not paid (see key)					Remarks
Week 1 to																		
Week 2 to																		
Week 3 to																		
Week 4 to																		
Week 5 to																		
Week 6 to																		
Week 7 to																		

(Continue this layout to week 13.)

Key

Lateness record Top line is for morning, bottom line for afternoon. Numbers signify as follows:

0 = on time or less than 5 min late.
1 = 5 to 20 min late: ¼ hour's pay deducted
2 = 20 to 35 min late: ½ hour's pay deducted
3 = 35 to 50 min late: ¾ hour's pay deducted
4 = 50 to 60 min late: 1 hour's pay deducted
5 = more than 65 min late — referred to supervisor.

(Continued)

Absence record Top line figures — reason for absence; lower line figures — amount of absence in hours. If a whole day, leave blank.

Key to reasons for absence:

Paid *0* = paid holiday
1 = paid sick leave
2 = paid day release/study leave
3 = paid time off for trade union duties
4 = special paid leave

Unpaid 5 = unpaid sick leave
6 = maternity leave
7 = time off for public duties or jury service
8 = special unpaid leave
9 = absent without permission

Summary for quarter ended

Maximum working days:

Days actually worked:

Lateness:
- under 20 min
- 20 - 65 min
- over 65 min
- Total over 20 min

Absences:

Holidays	days
Special/maternity leave (nos. 2,4,6,8)	days
Sickness	days
Paid time off (3)	hours/days
Unpaid time off (7)	hours/days
Unauthorised absence	hours/days
Total sickness and unauthorised absence	days

Signed: *Date:*

Supervisor's comments (if any):

Signed: *Date:*

Form 21 Flexitime attendance record

XYZ Co. Ltd
Flexitime Attendance Record Card

Name:

Department/Section:

Location:

Four weeks from to

Week	Monday	Tuesday	Wednesday	Thursday	Friday	Totals
1						hr min
Total						
2						hr min
Total						
3						hr min
Total						
4						hr min
Total						
						Total hr min

Normal average week by hours:

Total hours required for 4 weeks:

Add any arrears for previous period:	hr	min
Total required hours this period:	hr	min
Total actually worked:	hr	min
Shortfall/excess hours:	hr	min

(Continued)

(Continued)

Credits against shortfall: (count each day as 7 hours)

Holiday:	hr	min
Sickness:	hr	min
Time off for trade union activities:	hr	min
Other paid leave:	hr	min
Credit from previous period:	hr	min
Total credits:	hr	min

Deduct credits from shortfall or *add* to excess

Total shortfall/excess is now:	hr	min

Excess time may be credited against next period or paid as overtime. Please tick which you would prefer:

Credit against next period:

Overtime:

Shortfall will be added to your required hours for the next four-week period. If you have had any *unpaid leave* during this four-week period you may set this against the shortfall, but an appropriate amount will be deducted from your pay.

If you wish to claim for hours of unpaid leave please fill in these details:

Unpaid sick leave:	hr	min
Time off for public duties:	hr	min
Other unpaid leave:	hr	min
Total unpaid leave:	hr	min
Net shortfall for four-week period:	hr	min

Signed: *Date:*

Form 22 Authorisation of overtime working

XYZ Co. Ltd
Authorisation for Overtime

Authority for overtime is required whenever more than 2 man-hours are to be worked on one day in one section/department. A separate copy of this form must be filled in for each day for each department.

Authorisation:
 up to 10 man-hours per day: supervisor
 up to 50 man-hours per day: section head
 above 50 man-hours per day: Personnel Officer
The Personnel Manager may restrict levels of authorisation where substantial overtime occurs regularly.

Department/Section:

Location:

Date:

Person authorising overtime:

Names of employees and number of hours' work each:

Total man-hours authorised:

Work to be done in overtime:

Reasons why this work cannot be done during normal hours?

Authority given — signed:

I confirm that overtime was worked as stated by the individuals listed — signed:

(Return form to Personnel Office on morning of next working day.)

XYZ Co. Ltd
Training Assessment

Name:

Department:

Location:

Works no.:

Job title:

Starting date:

Dates basic training completed:

Induction:

Fire:

Safety precautions:

Basic job routine:

Assessment of quality of employee and aptitude for further training:

Relevant qualifications already possessed by employee:

Details of any evening class/day release courses employee is willing to undertake (or already undertaking):

Assessment of prospects of promotion if further training provided:

(To be completed by head of section, etc., after employee has passed probationary bar, and submitted for discussion by employee and training officer.)

Training Officer's Report (*confidential*)

Assessment of quality of employee and aptitude for further training:

Assessment of employee's willingness to undergo training:

(Continued)

(Continued)

Value to company of further training:

Are the skills needed?

Is employee likely to stay long enough?

Will further training assist in performance of existing job?

Other reasons for training:

Recommendation for training programme

(a) In-company courses

Title of course	Duration	Suggested date for commencement	Rating

Ratings: 0 useful, 1 very useful, 2 essential

(b) Day release, evening and other courses

Institution	Course	Duration	Company commitment		Rating
			Time	Fees	

Training Officer's comments:

Signed: *Date:*

Approved by Personnel Manager:
(Approval required for courses, etc., involving substantial commitments to company.)

Signed: *Date:*

Form 24 Trainer's assessment of progress

XYZ Co. Ltd

Trainer's Assessment of Progress

Name:

Department/Section:

Location:

Dates of training course:

Title of course:

Number of participants:

Trainer:

Assessment of performance

Rate as follows:

0 Poor
1 Unsatisfactory
2 Fair
3 Satisfactory
4 Good
5 Very Good
6 Outstanding

Interest and attendance:

Participation:

Understanding of materials:

Co-operation with group:

General progress:

Assessor's comments (comment on unusually poor or good ratings is particularly desirable):

Assessment of potential for further training:

Signed: *Date:*

Form 25 Employee's appraisal of training

XYZ Co. Ltd
Form of Assessment of Training Course

Name:

Department/Section:

Location:

Title of training course:

Dates:

Venue:

You are asked to give the following answers to assist the Training Department to develop and improve its courses. Please be frank: your comments will be given full consideration and will be treated as confidential.

What do you understand the objectives of this course to have been?

How far did the course meet the objectives?

How might the course have been improved to meet them?

Are there any changes in emphasis you wish to suggest for future courses?

Please assess the following aspects of the course (as applicable) acording to the following rating: 5 very good, 4 good, 3 satisfactory, 2 unsatisfactory, 1 poor.

Venue:
Accommodation:
Catering:
Degree of participation:
Variety:
Timetable:
Quality of tuition:
Use of documentation:
Use of audio visual aids:
Any other comments:

Signed: *Date:*

Form 26 Application for review of grading

XYZ Co. Ltd
Application for Review of Grading

Name:

Department/Section:

Location:

Job title:

Present grade of job:

Basic wages/salary:

Name of supervisor:

Summarise the main duties involved in your work:

How long have you been on your present grade? . . . years When was the last occasion that you asked for your grading to be reviewed?

(Note: an application will not be considered within one year of a previous review unless there are special circumstances.)

Please state any changes in the nature of the job you have been doing since the last review, under the headings given:
Effort:
Skill:
Relevant new qualifications:
Responsibility, e.g. confidentiality, security:
Supervision of other employees:

Volume of work:

Other:

Please state any other reasons which you consider would justify a regrading of your job. (*Note:* the fact that you may do your job particularly well may affect your level within a grade but does not affect the grading of the job itself.)

Please state any other reasons why you consider you personally should be placed higher on the scale of your present grade:

Signed: *Date:*

Give this form to your supervisor who will add his/her comments and transmit it to the Personnel Office.

(Continued)

(Continued)

To be filled in by supervisor

Description of job Is employee's description accurate? Yes/No.

Please comment and give details of any inaccuracies:

Changes in job Please comment under the headings below on the employee's assessment of changes in the nature of the job. Include comments on any changes since last reassessment which employee has not mentioned:

Effort:
Skill:
Relevant new qualifications:
Responsibility, e.g. confidentiality, security:
Supervision of other employees:
Volume of work:
Other:

Comment on other reasons put forward by employee to justify regrading:

Would any other employees doing similar work be affected by regrading in this case?

Do you support this application: Yes/No

If yes, please indicate the grade you consider justified:

Review of position within grade Please indicate any changes, either improvements or deterioration, in employee's performance of job since you last filed an annual assessment of this employee:

Signed: *Date:*

To be filled in by Personnel Manager

Regrading approved/refused.

New grade:

New salary:

Other employees to be reviewed:

Increase of salary within grade approved/refused.

New salary:

Decision letter sent to employee and supervisor: (*date*)

Date: *Signed:*

Form 27 Decision on review of grading

XYZ Co. Ltd

Review of Grading and Pay

To: Date:

Department/Section:

Location:

Copy to supervisor:

Your application for a review of your grading and salary, dated . . . has been very carefully considered, together with comments thereon by your supervisor.

*I regret that there is insufficient justification for a change either in the grading of your job or in your salary within the grade, and your present grade and salary will therefore remain in operation for the time being. You will be able to apply for a regrading again in a year's time if you consider this justified, and your salary will be considered at the next annual assessment of your performance.

*I regret that there is insufficient justification for a change in the grading of your job, and your present grade will therefore remain in operation for the time being. You will be able to apply for a regrading again in a year's time if you consider this justified. However, I am pleased to say that your performance of your job has been sufficiently good for me to be able to increase your point on the salary scale within your existing grade. From . . . your salary will therefore be £ . . . .

You will receive a notice of the formal change in your contract of employment in a few days.

*I am pleased to say that due to changes in the nature of your job since it was last reviewed, I am able to place your job on grade . . . from . . . . This means that your salary scale will now be £ . . and your initial salary will be £ . . . . You will receive a notice of the formal change in your contract in a few days.

Personnel Manager

**Delete as appropriate*

Form 28 Notice of promotion

XYZ Co. Ltd

Name: Date:

Department/Section: Location:

In confirmation of your recent conversation with . . . this is to notify you formally that the Company agreed to offer you promotion from your present post to the post of . . . . . As a result of promotion there will be a number of changes to your contract of employment. I will send you a formal notification of these when I have had your acceptance in writing on the second copy of this form.

The changes in the terms of your contract will be as indicated below. Where no change is indicated, the terms remain the same:

Job title:

Responsible to:

Job description/statement of duties:

Location:

Hours of work:

Overtime requirements:

Grade:

Rate of pay/salary:

Payment for overtime:

Holiday entitlement:

Sick pay entitlement:

Other:

*As you will know, your promotion is subject to an initial probation period of . . . month(s). If, during that period, it is established that you are not suited to the new job, you will be required to revert to your previous position.

*As you will know, your promotion is subject to an initial probation period of . . . month(s). If, during that period, it is established that you are not suited to the new job, the Company will endeavour to place you in suitable alternative employment. Because it is necessary to fill your present job immediately, it will not be possible to restore you to your present position, and it is regretted that in this unlikely situation, the Company would not be able to guarantee your continued employment.

Your acceptance of this offer of promotion will be taken to be acceptance of the conditions indicated above.

Personnel Manager

**Delete as required*

Form of acceptance (2nd copy only)

To the Personnel Manager, XYZ Co. Ltd

I agree to accept the company's offer of promotion as set out above and on the terms and conditions stated.

Signed: *Date:*

XYZ Co. Ltd

Name: Date:

Department/Section:

Location:

This is to notify you formally that the Company has agreed to offer you a transfer of employment as detailed below. As a result of this transfer there will be a number of changes in your contract of employment. I will send you a formal notification of these when I have had your acceptance in writing on the second copy of this form.

The details of the transfer and consequent changes in your contract are indicated below. Where no change is indicated the terms remain the same.

Job title:

Responsible to:

Job description/statement of duties:

Location:

Hours of work:

Grade:

Rate of pay/salary:

Other:

*As this transfer is the result of the redundancy of your present job, I have to warn you that if you unreasonably refuse to accept the transfer you will be made redundant with no right to redundancy pay. You are entitled to try out the new job for a period of up to four weeks before deciding whether to accept the transfer or not.

Personnel Manager

**Delete as appropriate*

Form of acceptance (2nd copy only)

To the Personnel Manager, XYZ Co. Ltd

*I agree to accept the Company's offer of transfer as set out above, and on the terms and conditions stated./ I wish to try out the new job for four weeks before deciding whether to accept it.
**Delete whichever does not apply*

Signed: *Date:*

Part Three

Trade unions

Note on disclosure and participation

The law requires at best participation and at least consultation in four cases:

1 In connection with proposed redundancies (see Part 9 for Forms).
2 On boards of pension funds.
3 Safety committees (details and forms in Part 6).
4 Through disclosure of information during the course of collective bargaining.

Various proposals for increased worker participation are under discussion. Meanwhile: disclosure gives independent, recognised trade unions far more power than either they or their employers commonly recognise. Both fear it — employers because disclosure equals increased power; unions because knowledge shackles bargaining and may impose responsibilities.

The following essentials must be satisfied before disclosure is required by law:

1 The union must be 'independent' (normally: certified as such) and 'recognised' by the employer (normally: to any extent for bargaining purposes).
2 The information must be in the possession of the employer or of any 'associated employer' — which (broadly) means: any company in the group, at home or abroad . . . any company under the same control.
3 The information must be required for the purposes of *collective* (as opposed to *individual*) bargaining.

The employer may legitimately refuse to provide the information if any of the above factors are absent, and/or for any of the following reasons:

1 National security.
2 Illegality.
3 Information concerning an individual who has not given his consent.
4 Information collated for purposes of legal proceedings, i.e. 'privileged'.
5 That revealing of the information would cause serious harm to the employer, for reasons other than its effect on collective bargaining.
6 That the information was communicated to the employer in confidence.
7 That the expense of collating the information would be out of all proportion to its value, when collated.

In addition: the union is not entitled to inspect the employer's books nor to copies of any accounts or other documents, other than those prepared for the purpose of supplying the information.

Rules of practice for disclosure are contained in an ACAS Code, which should be consulted. Wise employers:

1 Provide as much information as they reasonably can.
2 Ensure that disclosure is honest and accurate.
3 Train employees to understand and to interpret the information given.
4 Do their utmost to ensure that supervisors (especially foremen, chargehands and line supervisors) receive as much information as possible, and do not have to discover it from those whom they supervise. In general, communication between top management and union representatives is improving; communication between various levels of management is not.

XYZ Co. Ltd
Trade Union Membership

Name of employee:

Department/Section:

Location:

The Company has agreed with the [*insert name(s) of relevant Union(s)*] that there should be a closed shop for employees including those in your grade and department. The terms of this agreement are that all relevant employees should be or become members of **one of* the Trade Union(s) named above or of *(one of) the following Trade Union(s): . . . .

Our records do not show that you are a member of the/one of these Trade Union(s). The Company sets great store on the value of harmonious relationships with the trade union representatives of its employees and the value of a closed shop. I must therefore ask you to confirm to me that you are in fact in membership, or to take immediate steps to join *(one of) the Union(s).

(May I also remind you that it is now a term of your employment that you become a member of an/the appropriate Union.)

If there is any difficulty over this matter please arrange an appointment for an interview with me as soon as possible.

I am also enclosing a form for you to use, if you are already a member of a union, for authorising your union dues to be deducted directly from your wages. You are not compelled to use this method of payment, but the Company strongly encourages it as it avoids misunderstandings.

Please reply to my main enquiry on the tear-off slip below.

Personnel Manager

**Alternative wording as required.*

To the Personnel Manager
XYZ Co. Ltd

Name:

Works No:

Department/Location:

I am a member of the . . . Trade Union.

I intend to apply to join the . . . Trade Union.
Delete as necessary

Signed: *Date:*

Form 31 Check-off authorisation (deduction of trade union dues)

XYZ Co. Ltd
Deduction of Trade Union Dues

Name:

Trade Union:

Department/Section:

Location:

I authorise the Company to deduct from my wages/salary the sum of . . . p per week/month and pay the same to the above-named trade union. I further agree that the Company may at any time increase the sum to be deducted as requested from time to time by the trade union to meet any change in the rate of subscription. I understand that I may cancel this authority at any time by giving four weeks' notice in writing to the Personnel Office.

Signed: *Date:*

(Give this form to your trade union representative who will forward it to the Personnel Office.)

Form 32 Company's credentials for shop stewards

XYZ Co. Ltd
Approved Shop Steward's Credentials

Name:

Trade Union:

Department/Section:

Location:

The above is a duly appointed shop steward of his/her trade union and represents the following work group:

The trade union is recognised by the Company for collective bargaining on behalf of this work group and . . . as a duly appointed shop steward has the following authorisation:

*Paid time off in accordance with the joint agreement.
*Access to Company telephones for union business.
*Access to union office.
*Access to members as defined above for consultation and collection of subscriptions at reasonable times.
*Representation of members in grievance and disciplinary procedure.
*Convening meetings of members with the permission of the Personnel Manager.
*Consultation with and making representations to supervisors and heads of section concerned with collective problems.
*Attending at safety inspections by union safety representatives.
*Posting union literature on approved notice-boards.

Signed: *(Personnel Manager)* *Date:*

Signed: *(Shop Steward)* *Date:*

Signed: *(TU-authorised signatory)* *Date:*

**Delete as necessary*

Agreement between
XYZ Co. Ltd ('the Company')
and
ABC Trade Union ('the Union')

Preliminary

1 The Company recognise that adequate time off and facilities for the carrying out of trade union duties are essential to the effective functioning of the Union as a representative of its members.

2 The Union recognises that the continued efficiency and profitability of the Company will be materially damaged by unreasonable exercise of rights to take time off causing disruption to the production process.

Trade Union officials

3 All Trade Union officials will be elected or appointed annually by the Union in accordance with its rules and procedures for the time being in force and will be employees with at least one year's service with the Company.

4 The number of Union officials at any one time will be as set out in the Annex to this agreement; any increase or decrease in numbers will be by mutual agreement of the parties. [*This Annex is not included in this book as numbers are a matter for negotiation.*]

5 The Union will notify the Company in writing of the names of all the Union officials for the time being and the workgroups they each represent, and will similarly notify any changes.

Time off

6 Union officials will be permitted by their supervisor to take time off for any of the following purposes:
a to attend a recognised course of training in industrial relations on the nomination of the Union;
b to attend negotiating or consultative meetings with an appropriate level of management, and to meet among themselves to prepare for such meetings;
c to represent members in disciplinary and grievance hearings and appeals, including appeals before an Industrial Tribunal;
d to discuss individual grievances and disciplinary problems with members at the request of the member concerned;
e to report back to members the results of negotiations and consultations with management;
f to consult full-time Officers of the Union about any of the matters in *(b)* to *(e)*;
g to explain to new employees the functions and working of the Union.

7 Union officials will seek permission from their supervisor before taking time off, will give as much notice of such requests as reasonably practicable, and will endeavour to meet reasonable requests to arrange the timing of their absence from work so as to minimise interference with production.

8 Where a supervisor considers that a request for time off is unreasonable he may, after consultation with the Personnel Department, refuse to permit the official to leave work (either unconditionally or at a particular time). The Union agrees that officials will abide by this decision unless in the view of the Convener of Shop Stewards the matter is urgent, in which case the matter will be referred to the Personnel Manager for immediate resolution. In other cases disputes about time off may be referred for settlement to the agreed negotiating procedures.

9 Time off permitted under Para. 7 will be paid for in accordance with Para. 11 below.

(Continued)

(Continued)

10 Union members who are officers of the Branch will be permitted to take reasonable time off without pay to attend Branch meetings. Union Members who are representatives on any other body within the Union constitution or are representatives of the Union on any other body may be permitted to take reasonable time off without pay to attend the meetings of that body.

Payment

11 Where paid time off is permitted, rates of pay will be as follows:

a for time workers — time rates, applicable to that time and shift;

b for workers covered by guaranteed earnings levels — the guaranteed earnings rate applicable to that time and shift;

c for workers on piece rates — average earnings; whichever is the higher in the particular case.

12 Where an official attends the workplace outside his normal working hours either at the request of management or for a purpose recognised under Para. 6 which could not reasonably be carried out during working hours, the official will have the option of being paid at appropriate overtime rates for the time involved, including reasonable travelling time, or being given an equivalent amount of time off on the next shift without loss of pay.

13 Any disputes about the amount of pay due to an official under this agreement shall be resolved through the normal negotiating machinery.

Facilities

14 The Union will be permitted the use of an office with reasonable office equipment and a private telephone line (for which the Union will pay all Post Office rental and usage charges), and the reasonable use of other rooms (subject to availability) for the holding of meetings of officials and private consultations with members.

15 Facilities will be provided for the conduct of Union elections by secret ballot on the premises, and at the discretion of the Personnel Manager a reasonable amount of paid time off will be allowed to members for voting in elections. Facilities and time off for general meetings of the Union members will be given at the discretion of the Personnel Manager where the interests of the Company so require and at a time convenient to the Company. Such time off will be with pay.

16 The Company will deduct Union subscriptions from the pay of Union members who have signed a written authorisation to deduct and while such authorisation remains in force, and will pay the money deducted to the Union with a list of individual deductions. No charge will be made for this service.

Part Four

Illness and incapacity

XYZ Co. Ltd

Entitlement to Payment for Periods of Absence due to Sickness or Injury

1 The provisions of this sick pay scheme apply to all employees of XYZ Co. Ltd and are a condition of employment by XYZ Co. Ltd.

2 In this scheme a reference to 'sickness' is intended to mean any illness, mental or physical, or the effects of any accident or injury to the person, which in either case render the individual incapable of, or unfit for, work. An employee who is incapable of work solely because she is pregnant is not entitled to the benefits of this scheme (but this does not exclude entitlement to any other benefits in accordance with the Company's conditions of employment).

3 An employee who is absent from work by reason of sickness as defined above is not entitled to any remuneration from the company in respect of that absence except as detailed below. All entitlements set out below are *ex gratia* and subject to the discretion of the Company, and may be withdrawn on an individual or collective basis at any time. No entitlement to payment amounts to an enforceable right under the employee's contract of employment.

4 An employee who is absent from work for any reason other than sickness is not entitled to any remuneration under this scheme (but this does not exclude entitlement under any of the Company's other schemes, such as compassionate leave).

5 Any remuneration paid under this scheme is referred to as 'sick pay'.

6 Sick pay entitlement is based on the sick pay year, which is 1 January to 31 December. Entitlement is calculated from the year in which the first day of a period of absence occurred. A period of absence is regarded as continuous for this purpose even if the employee has returned to work, if the duration of the return to work is shorter than the duration of the preceding period of absence.

7 An employee is entitled to be paid for a maximum of four weeks' absence in any sick pay year with full pay, and a further four weeks' absence at half pay. Employees with at least five years' continuous employment at the start of the sick pay year are entitled to up to eight weeks in each category, and those with at least ten years' continuous employment to up to thirteen weeks in each category.

8 An employee who begins work during the year is entitled to up to a week's absence with full pay for each three months of completed service.

9 'Full pay' means the full amount of the basic weekly remuneration for that employee, divided by five, for each day of absence; or, where there is a guaranteed day or week, the guaranteed daily rate or a fifth of the guaranteed weekly rate; or where earnings are calculated by reference to piecework, the average daily rate of earnings for days worked during the preceding 13 weeks, whichever is the higher in the particular case. 'Full pay' does not include any overtime which might otherwise have been worked, unless this is covered by the guaranteed day/week. In each case the amount stated is subject to reduction by the amount of any sickness or industrial injury benefit actually paid to or payable to the employee, including any amounts which could have been claimed by the employee, and in the case of women employees who pay the lower rate of Social Security contributions, any amount which could have been claimed had the individual concerned paid the higher rate.

10 'Half-pay' means half of full pay but without the deduction of Social Security payments referred to above.

11 It is a condition of payment of sick pay that a certificate is produced, signed by a duly qualified medical practitioner, to the effect that the employee was incapable of or unfit for the period in question. The Company will normally waive this requirement for absence of less than three working days, but reserves the right, on giving notice to the individual concerned, to insist for the future on strict compliance with this requirement.

(Continued)

(Continued)

12 The Company reserves the right to require any employee at any time to undergo a medical examination by a duly qualified medical practitioner nominated by the Company for this purpose.

13 An employee who is absent through sickness or injury occasioned by self-neglect, self-inflicted injury or participation in any dangerous sport is not entitled to any sick pay, but payment may in exceptional cases be made at the discretion of the Company, to relieve hardship.

14 If an employee is injured by a third party in circumstances such that a claim may be pursued for compensation for the injury, any payment of sick pay to the employee for an ensuing period of absence shall be regarded as an interest-free loan which shall be repaid by the employee in the event of compensation being recovered for lost earnings.

15 The Company reserves the right in its absolute discretion to withdraw at any time any entitlement to benefit, without giving reasons; and in particular the Company may decline to make further payments to a particular individual, although his entitlement for the sick pay year has not been exhausted, if in the Company's view he has an unsatisfactory record of attendance at work.

Form 35 Notice of requirement to submit to medical examination

XYZ Co. Ltd
Medical Examination

To: Date:

Department/Section:

Location:

*You have been off sick on . . . days during the last . . . weeks/months.

*You were absent on . . . (dates) and stated that the reason was sickness, but did not produce a doctor's certificate.

The Company is concerned to know what are the prospects for your health for the future and whether you will be in a position to continue to work to the standards required by the Company. You are therefore asked to attend for an independent medical examination to be conducted by Dr . . . at . . . on . . . at . . . am/pm. You will be allowed time off work without loss of pay to attend for this examination.

†May I remind you that you agreed as a condition of employment that you would undergo medical examinations when required by the Company.

It is hoped that the doctor will be able to give the Company an assurance that your health will be sufficiently improved in the future that your continued employment will not cause any difficulty. However in view of your recent record of illness I must make it clear that if the medical examination discloses that you will not be in good health for the foreseeable future, the Company will wish to discuss with you the circumstances of your continued employment.

Personnel Manager

**Delete as appropriate*
†Include this paragraph only if there is such a clause in the contract of employment

Form 36 Notice of requirement to submit sick notes

XYZ Co. Ltd
Absence Due to Illness

To: Date:

Department/Section:

Location:

You have been absent from work on the following dates during the last . . . weeks/months:

You have given the reason for these absences as sickness but you have not produced a medical certificate/you have not produced a medical certificate covering the following dates:

You will be aware that you are not entitled to be paid when you are absent from your work unless you show to the satisfaction of the Company that your absence was due to sickness. The Company's agreement to accept short absences without a medical certificate is a concession which may be withdrawn and it is the Company's practice to withdraw this concession in cases of excessive uncertificated absence. I must therefore inform you that with effect from . . . you are to produce a medical certificate for every day's absence other than authorised leave or holiday. Failure to do so without a reasonable explanation will not only disentitle you to sick pay for the days in question but will also be regarded as a breach of discipline.

Personnel Manager

Form 37 Notice of refusal/discontinuation of sick pay

XYZ Co. Ltd
Payment for Absence Due to Illness

To: Date:

Department/Section:

Location:

*You were absent from work on the following dates:

You have given the reason for these absences as sickness.

*You have not produced a medical certificate for these absences.

*You had already been absent through sickness on . . . days since . . . and this is the maximum amount of absence for which the Company is required to pay you under your contract in any one year.

*You have now been absent for a total of . . . days through sickness since . . . . This is the maximum amount of absence for which the company is required to pay you under your contract in any one year.

In these circumstances I regret that I must inform you that your sick pay will be dealt with as follows:

†Payment of sick pay is entirely at the Company's discretion and in view of your record of absence you will no longer be paid sick pay until further notice.

†Payment of sick pay is entirely at the Company's discretion. In view of your record of absence and the fact that you have not produced a medical certificate, you will not be paid sick pay for the following dates of absence:

*Payment of sick pay is dependent on the provision of a medical certificate, and you will therefore not be paid for the absence detailed above for which you did not produce a medical certificate. This rule will also apply to any future absences not covered by a medical certificate.

*You are not eligible for any more sick pay for absences after today until . . . .

*You are not eligible for any more sick pay for absences after today until . . . or for your absence on the following dates:

Personnel Manager

**Delete where not applicable*
†These paragraphs may only be included where the contract of employment provides that sick pay is discretionary.

Form 38 Application for special leave

XYZ Co. Ltd
Application for Special Leave

Name:

Department/Section:

Location:

The Company will grant special leave with pay in the following circumstances as indicated:
Marriage of employee: one week
Paternity: one week
Maternity: special arrangements apply. Consult Personnel Office.
Sickness of close relative: discretionary
Bereavement: discretionary
Study and examinations: discretionary

Special leave without pay will be granted to any employee required to attend a Court of Law or Statutory Tribunal as a witness, or summoned for jury service. A claim for loss of earnings in these cases may be made to the Court authorities.

In other cases special unpaid leave is discretionary. Leave for the performance of public duties is dealt with by law and special arrangements apply: consult Personnel Office.

I apply for special paid/unpaid leave for the following dates:

Reason for application:

If leave is discretionary please give any relevant information that will assist the Personnel Manager to decide whether to approve your application:

Signed: *Date:*

(Now give this form to your supervisor).

Supervisor's comments:

I approve/do not approve this application (discretionary leave only).

Signed: *Date:*

(Form to be sent to Personnel Office)

Personnel Officer's decision:
Paid leave approved — dates:
Unpaid leave approved — dates:
Application refused — state reason:
Note of arrangements for substitute:

Signed: *Date:*

**Delete as appropriate*

Part Five

Maternity rights

Introduction

A mother has two special rights in law:

1 She may claim maternity pay — up to 9/10ths of her normal pay, minus the maximum current maternity benefits (irrespective of whether or not she qualifies for them).

2 The right to return to 'her job' within 29 weeks of her confinement — with a possible additional 4 weeks, either at her option, say, if she is unwell, or at her employers' (if they need time to make her place available).

To qualify for either right, the mother must have been continuously employed for at least two years at the beginning of the 11th week before the date of her expected confinement; and she must stay at work until the end of that week — unless her condition makes it impossible for her to do so. In that case, if she resigns, she loses her rights; but if she is dismissed because she cannot do her job, she retains them.

To qualify for the right to return (but not for maternity pay) the mother must also (where reasonably practicable) give notice to her employer of her intention to exercise that right and (where reasonably practicable) she must do so at least three weeks before she leaves.

XYZ Co. Ltd
Personnel Officer's Record of Maternity Interview

Name of employee:

Department/Section:

Location:

Date of Interview:

Interviewed by:

Part A

Date employment began:

Date baby due:

Has certificate of expected date of confinement been seen? Yes/No

Will employee have completed 2 years' continuous service at least 11 weeks before baby is due? Yes/No.

(If no, fill in only parts B and C.)

Part B

Date employee intends to stop work:

Assess likelihood that she will be reasonably capable of performing her work until then:
(Give reasons for negative answer):

Alternative suitable work (if likely to be required):

Proposals for earlier termination of employment (if applicable):

Confirm that arrangements have been made to notify pensions department: Yes/No.

(Do not fill in this part if employee has statutory *right to return to work.)*

Part C

Does employee wish to return to work if work is available? Yes/No. Part time/Full time

Would employee be suitable for re-engagement if work were available? Yes/No.

If yes, indicate types of work that would be suitable and any special skills of value to the Company:

(Continued)

(Continued)

Is employee likely to be in a position to resume work within the next year? Yes/No

Give details of any information disclosed about child-minding arrangements relevant to this:

Part D *(Fill in this part if employee has statutory right to return to work.)*

Does employee intend to give notice of intention to return to work? Yes/No

Has employee been informed that such notice must be given in writing? Yes/No

Assess the likelihood that employee will in fact wish to return to work at her present job:

Give details of any information disclosed about child-minding arrangements relevant to this:

If return to full-time work is unlikely, would employee be likely to seek part-time work if available? Yes/No

If yes, would she be suitable? Yes/No

Signed: *Date:*

Part E Arrangements for replacement *(to be filled in on receipt of requisition for replacement).*

*Permanent replacement (w.e.f.)
*Temporary replacement (w.e.f.)
*Post suppressed
*Work reallocated
*Work to be covered temporarily by overtime

**Delete as appropriate*

Signed: *Date:*

Form 40 Application for maternity leave

XYZ Co. Ltd
Maternity Arrangements

Employee's name:

Department/Section:

Location:

Date started employment:

I am expecting a baby on . . . (*date*). I have discussed my position with . . . of the Personnel Office, and he has explained to me what my legal rights are with regard to my job under the Employment Protection Consolidation Act. In partic ular it has been explained to me that provided I have the necessary service I am entitled to maternity pay and to come back to work within 29 weeks after the baby is born. I also understand that if I resign my job earlier than 11 weeks before the baby is due, I shall lost both of these rights, and that if I say now that I do not want to come back to work I cannot change my mind later.

I wish to make the following decisions with regard to my job:

*I give notice of resignation with effect from . . . .

*I (do/do not) intend to return to work after the birth of my baby. Provisional date of intended return:

*I have made the following arrangements for the baby to be looked after while I am at work:

*I intend to cease working for the Company on . . . (date) until my return to work and apply for maternity leave for that period.

I attach a certificate from a qualified medical practitioner/midwife of the expected date of my confinement.

Signed: *Date:*

(This form need not be completed if the employee will not have completed two years' continuous employment at least 11 weeks before her baby is due.)

**Delete as required.*

Form 41 Notice to employee replacing woman on maternity leave

(This Notice will only be effective if it is given to the employee at the time of engagement. *It may be convenient to attach it to any written offer of employment.)*

XYZ Co. Ltd
The Employment Protection (Consolidation) Act 1978, Section 61

To: Date:

In accordance with the above Act of Parliament the Company wishes to give you notice as follows:

You are engaged to replace . . . (*name of employee on maternity leave*) who has left work to have a baby, but who has given notice to the Company that she intends to return to work after the baby is born. This lady has the right to return to her previous job if she so wishes, and if she does so the Company will have no alternative but to dismiss you from that job. If at that time there is any alternative employment available within the Company for which you are considered suitable every effort will be made to offer you the alternative, but the Company cannot guarantee to make any offer.

You may wish to know that . . . 's baby is due on . . . . She has the right to return to work at any time within 29 weeks of the birth.

Personnel Manager

Form 42 Application to return to work after confinement

To the Personnel Manager | Date:
XYZ Co. Ltd

Name of employee:

Address:

Telephone No.:

Previous Post:

Date of leaving:

Date of birth of baby:

I hereby give notice that I intend to exercise my right of return to work in my former job on . . . *(put in the date of intended return, giving at least one week's notice).**

I understand that I may postpone my return for not more than 4 weeks from this date on medical grounds but that otherwise if I do not return to work on the date I have given I shall lose my entitlement to return.

Signed:

**The latest date you can exercise your right to return is 29 weeks from the beginning of the week in which your baby was born.*

Form 43 Notice of postponement of right to return

XYZ Co. Ltd

To:

Your application to return to work

With reference to your formal notice that you intend to return to work on . . . you will be aware that the Company is legally entitled to require you to postpone your return to work for a period of up to four weeks for any specified reason. The Company is anxious to avoid any postponement, but regrettably in your case it has proved to be necessary to postpone your return to work until . . . for the reason given below. Will you please report for work to this office at . . . a.m. on . . . . I must also advise you that you will not be paid for the period that your return to work has been postponed.

Personnel Manager

Statement of reasons *(Delete as necessary)*

*Your work has been temporarily reallocated in your absence and time is needed to divide up the work again.

*A temporary employee has been recruited to replace you during your absence, and time is needed to make alternative arrangements for his/her future.

*Other (state):

Form 44 Notification to returning mother of transfer of employment

XYZ Co. Ltd

To: Date:

Your application to return to work

With reference to your formal notice that you intend to return to work after the birth of your baby, I regret to have to inform you that your previous job no longer exists. The post was abolished by reason of redundancy with effect from . . . .

(Delete as appropriate)

*You are therefore entitled to a redundancy payment based on your continuous service up to the date that the job was declared redundant, and a cheque for the appropriate amount will be forwarded to you shortly. I regret that there is no suitable alternative employment available for you.

*I am able to offer you instead employment in the post of . . . , starting on . . .† which is suitable alternative employment.

The duties of this post are briefly as follows:

You would be responsible in this post to . . . . In all other respects except those listed below the terms and conditions of this post would be identical to whose appertaining to your previous post.

Differences in terms and conditions:

If you wish to discuss the details of this offer, please telephone my office for an appointment. I hope you will be able to accept the offer, and I must point out that if you do not accept it the Company will not consider itself liable for a redundancy payment.

Personnel Manager

†*If this date is later than the date notified by the woman a separate notice of postponement (Form 43) must also be sent.*

Part Six

Health and safety

Introduction

Health and safety rights fall into two categories: civil (including the employee's right to sue for damages in a civil court) and criminal (employer or employee or both may be prosecuted for failing to comply with standards necessary for the protection of the community).

The civil law is mainly contained in binding judicial decisions ('common law'). An employer must take reasonable care not to submit an employee to 'unnecessary risk'. He must therefore (among other things) do what he reasonably can: to ensure a safe system of working, a safe place of work, reasonably competent fellow employees, adequate supervision and training and to maintain in good condition any necessary plant, materials or appliances.

The employer must also comply with his statutory duties, e.g. under *The Factories Act, 1961; The Offices, Shops and Railway Premises Act, 1963; The Health and Safety at Work etc. Act, 1974* — and all Regulations. Maximum penalties: if tried by a Magistrates Court, £1,000 (£400 where the offence is triable either summarily or on indictment); if by a Crown Court (jury trial), 2 years' imprisonment and/or unlimited fine. Note: insurers will pay civil damages for you but not your criminal penalties, although they may cover the legal costs of defending a prosecution.

So the employer must avoid negligent acts or omissions which he knew or ought to have known would be likely to cause danger to the employee. For his part, the employee must take reasonable care for his own safety. If he is injured entirely through the employer's negligence or breach of statutory duty, he will get his damages in full. But those damages will be reduced proportionately to the extent (if any) that his own negligence contributed to his own downfall.

Equally: under the 1974 Act an employee must take such steps as are reasonably practicable to protect himself and his colleagues from dangers at work. Note: a safety representative (union-appointed and voluntary) bears neither civil nor criminal liability in respect of acts or omissions committed while he is acting in his capacity as a safety representative.

The main features of the 1974 Act are as follows:

1 It is an all-party statute, emanating from a Conservative Private Member's Bill, but passed (in almost identical form) by a Labour government — therefore it is likely to be permanent.

2 It retained existing legislation (the Factories Act, etc.) but with increased penalties for default (see above).

3 It created *(a)* the Health and Safety Commission, combining safety functions of most Government Departments and taking charge of providing information and advice, conducting enquiries, creating codes and regulations and having control over *(b)* the Health and Safety Executive — in charge of the combined Inspectorate. (There are no private prosecutions under the Act without the consent of the Director of Public Prosecutions — which has been seldom applied for, and never given.)

4 The Inspectorate is given power to issue:

a *Prohibition Notices* — prohibiting the carrying on of an activity or operation, usually immediately; or

b *Improvement Notices*, requiring improvements in safety measures, etc., usually within a stated time. The people served with either notice may appeal to an Industrial Tribunal; an Improvement Notice is suspended until the appeal is heard, a Prohibition Notice is not.

5 The 1974 Act, in effect, codified the civil law on industrial safety and transferred it to the realms of crime — making almost any unsafe industrial or commercial practice a criminal offence. So the same wrong may lead to a civil action by a person who suffers personal injury, loss or damage as a result and/or to a criminal prosecution of any guilty person 'at or below board level'.

6 Personal responsibility (in addition to, or in substitution for, corporate liability) is imposed on any 'director, manager or secretary', who has *consented* to, *connived* at, or caused through his *neglect* the unsafe industrial or commercial practice referred to.

7 All employees 'at work' are now covered and not merely those who work in offices, shops or railway premises — and some 5½ million employees were therefore brought under the protection of the criminal law, e.g. those who work in research establishments, hospitals, schools, parks, hotels or recreational institutions or on the roads.

Indirectly, the criminal law affects the civil because the person convicted of a criminal offence is highly unlikely to escape civil responsibility.

The Act does not impose absolute duties, but only requires people to 'take such steps as are reasonably practicable' — which, as usual, means looking at all the circumstances of the particular case. For example:

1 Employers must take such steps as are reasonably practicable to protect employees 'at work' — which includes providing adequate instruction, supervision and training in safety matters; a safe place of work and system of working; and a working environment which, so far as is reasonably practicable, is adequate as regards facilities for health, safety and welfare at work — 'welfare' meaning non-financial provision, e.g. heating, ventilation and decent working conditions as provided for in other statutes.

2 An employer must take such steps as are reasonably practicable to protect people whom he does not employ but who are 'affected by his undertaking', e.g. contractors, sub-contractors, visitors, neighbours and the general public.

3 Designers, manufacturers, importers and suppliers of articles designed for or substances intended for use at work must take such steps as are reasonably practicable — through research, testing or otherwise — to ensure that articles or substances will not cause danger to health or safety.

Safety representatives and committees

Safety representatives are appointed by 'recognised' trade unions, i.e. trade unions recognised to any extent for bargaining purposes. Independent means free from managerial control — normally: certified as independent by the Certification Officer.

Unions are not bound to appoint representatives. But if they do so, management must inform and consult with them and enable them to perform their functions. These include: representation of those who appoint them; carrying out safety inspections, samples and surveys; informing management of safety complaints; and above all, encouraging co-operation among and between employees and management on health and safety matters.

Any two safety representatives may demand the setting up of a safety committee. While trade unions appoint representatives, management decides on the composition of, and arrangements for, safety committees.

Regulations (with the force of law); a Code of Practice (failure to comply with which may be used in evidence against you); and Guidance Notes, prepared by the Health and Safety Commission, came into force on 1 October 1978. Most of the rules for safety committees are contained in the Guidance Notes.

Form 45 General warning

> **GENERAL SAFETY WARNING**
>
> The safety committee/management/safety officer hereby warn all employees that the practice of smoking in restricted areas/working in hard-hat areas without head protection/working on roofs without crawling boards/(*or as the case may be*) must cease forthwith. Any future violation of this important safety rule will be treated as a serious breach of discipline/unions and management have agreed that any future breach of this important safety rule will/may lead to dismissal.

Form 46 Warning to individual

> As you were informed both in your terms of service/by notices on the board/(*or as the case may be*) and orally by your foreman/safety officer on the . . ./on numerous occasions from . . . to . . . , it is essential that all employees working on . . . wear their safety hats/goggles/(*or as the case may be*).
>
> You have ignored these warnings, thereby causing danger to yourself/and to others.
>
> I must therefore warn you that any further infringement of this rule may/will lead to your dismissal/instant dismissal.
>
> If you have any queries regarding this or any other safety rule, please do not hesitate to contact your safety representative/safety officer/or myself.

Form 47 Final warning to individual

> You have now been warned about smoking in a prohibited area/operating your machine without a guard (*or as the case may be*) on the following occasions:
>
> 1 Orally, by your foreman on several occasions during the month of . . . .
>
> 2 Orally, by your shop steward, alone or in the company of management representatives, on several occasions between . . . and . . . .
>
> 3 In writing, by notice/letter dated . . . .
>
> In spite of these warnings and in spite of explanations carefully given to you by your shop steward as well as by your foreman/and safety officer/and safety representative (*or as the case may be*) you have persisted in breaking this safety rule which has been accepted as necessary for your protection/and that of your colleagues/by a safety committee by all union/staff representatives (*or as the case may be*). I must therefore inform you that if you are again in breach of this rule/or of any other safety rule, your contract of employment will be terminated/forthwith.
>
> It is most earnestly hoped that it will not become necessary to terminate your service with the company, but strict compliance with safety rules — and in particular with the requirement that . . . — is essential, for your safety and for that of your colleagues at work and so as to ensure that the company itself complies with its obligations under the Health and Safety at Work Act and other industrial safety statutes and regulations.

Form 48 Notice to visitors

TAKE NOTICE THAT THE FOLLOWING INFORMATION AND WARNINGS ARE ISSUED TO YOU PURSUANT TO SECTION 3 OF THE HEALTH AND SAFETY AT WORK ACT, 1974.

We welcome you to the company's premises/works/site at . . . , but ask you to comply carefully with the company's safety rules and regulations, and in particular to pay heed to notices which you will see exhibited. You will be issued with safety clothing and headgear, as appropriate, and are required to wear it at all times as instructed.

Please pay special attention to the following safety hazards:

1 No smoking is permitted in the following areas: the stores; the . . . shop; the filling station (*or as the case may be*). (*Alternatively:* Smoking is permitted only in the canteen/dining room.) In these areas there is particular danger from explosions caused by naked lights.
2 Hard hats must be worn on all construction sites (*or as the case may be*), because of the danger of objects falling from above/of your striking your head against obstructions.
3 White coats/sanitary headgear (*or as the case may be*) must be worn in all areas where food is under preparation.
4 . . . .

Your strict compliance with these rules will not only be appreciated by the Company but will minimise any risk to your own safety, as well as to that of others.

Form 49 Notice to contractors, sub-contractors, etc.

TAKE NOTICE THAT THE FOLLOWING INFORMATION AND WARNINGS ARE GIVEN TO COMPLY WITH SECTION 3 OF THE HEALTH AND SAFETY AT WORK ACT, 1974.

While you are working in our factory/on our site (*or as the case may be*), you are expected to follow all those safety precautions necessary for the minimising of the hazards of your own work. You must guard against those risks ordinarily incidental to your own employment, for your own protection and that of your colleagues as well as that of this Company and its employees and of others working on or visiting this factory/works/site.

In addition, your special attention is drawn to particular hazards which you must take special care to guard against:

1 . . . .
2 . . . .
3 . . . .

Should you have any queries regarding these or any other health or safety matters, please contact the Company's safety officer, Mr . . . at . . . or Mr . . . , Chairman of the Company's safety committee at . . . .

Form 50 Hazard report

NOTE: It may be desirable that this form should be signed by the immediate supervisor and by the departmental manager or supervisor concerned.

Date: Department:

Reported by:

Nature of unsafe working practice/hazard:

Action required:

Suggested time limit/urgency:

Work commenced:

Work completed:

Date: *Signed:*

Form 51 Accident report

NOTE: It may be desirable that this form should be signed by the immediate supervisor and by the departmental manager or supervisor concerned.

To be completed by departmental manager/supervisor

Name: Age: Male/Female:

Department:

Date and time of accident:

Nature of work/activity being carried out at time of accident:

Details of accident:

Details of any equipment/machinery involved:

Recommendations to avoid recurrence:

Signature: *(Department Manager/Supervisor)*

Form 52 Report of medical action on accident

Name of employee:

Date and time when report received:

Treatment given, i.e. returned to work after treatment/sent home/sent to hospital/referred to own doctor:

Date and time sent to hospital/home/own doctor:

Details of injuries:

Was employee off work for more than 3 days?

Entry for general register:

Total lost time:

Action taken by personnel manager or officer:

Completion of insurance company accident report form:

Completion of factory inspectorate form F43:

Copy sent to safety officer/safety representative/safety committee.

Form 53 Notice — appointed safety representatives

The management is pleased to inform you that the . . . union/unions/all recognised unions in this works/factory/unit/organisation have now appointed safety representatives. Please be sure that you know your representative and that you consult him on any matter regarding your health, safety or welfare or that of other employees. Arrangements for the setting up of a safety committee are in hand and you will be informed as soon as these are completed.

For my part, I shall continue as before to be at your service and at that of the company in connection with health and safety matters. Please do not hesitate to contact me as and when you wish.

Signed: *(Safety Officer)*

Details of Safety Representatives

Name	*Union*	*Unit/shop/category of employee represented*
1		
2		
3		

Form 54 Notice of safety inspection

A safety inspection of . . ./your shop/office/site (*or as the case may be*) will be carried out by . . ., from about . . . to . . . on . . . . Please give them every assistance and co-operation in helping to achieve the highest possible standards of safety in our work.

Signed:

On behalf of the Safety Committee/trade union (*or as the case may be*).

Form 55 Advance notice of safety committee meeting

A meeting of the . . . safety committee/of the safety committee covering the following unit/units/shops (*or as the case may be*) will be held at . . . am/pm in the Boardroom/canteen (*or as the case may be*). A detailed agenda will be circulated and put on all notice boards nearer the date.

Signed:

Chairman, Safety Committee

Form 56 Agenda for first meeting of safety committee

1 Welcome by company chairman/managing director.
2 Election of (provisional?) chairman.
3 Future composition of committee.
4 Officers of committee.
5 Functions of committee:
   a General;
   b Particular to unit/site/company (*or as the case may be*).
6 Urgent safety matters requiring immediate attention.
7 Date of next meeting/date of future meetings.

Form 57 Agenda for normal meeting of safety committee

1 Minutes of previous meeting having been circularised and exhibited on notice board, to be corrected as necessary, and agreed.
2 Matters arising from previous Minutes, not covered by specific items later on agenda.
3 Apologies for non-attendance.
4 Correspondence.
5 Reports of safety inspections/audits/surveys/sampling since last meeting.
6 Consideration of accident book and of additional safety measures required to avoid recurrence.
7 Consideration of any major accident, and safety recommendations arising therefrom.
8 Reports from safety officer/hygienist/company doctor/. . . .
9 Special occurrences, eg. prohibition notices, improvement notices, visits by Inspectorate, recommendations for change, etc.
10 Announcements of future changes in composition of committee, e.g. resignation/new appointments, and/or consideration of co-options or other changes.
11 Any other business.
12 Date of next meeting/future meetings.

Form 58 Minutes of safety committee

MINUTES of the . . . Safety Committee of the site/unit/office (*or as the case may be*), held from . . . am/pm to . . . am/pm on . . . day, the . . . 19 . . , at . . . .

1 Minutes of previous meeting approved, subject to the following changes:
a . . . .
b . . . .
c . . . .
2 Apologies for absence were received from: . . . .
3 Correspondence from . . . and . . . was circulated and read.
4 The resignation of Mr . . . from the committee was accepted with regret, as he is leaving the company/being transferred to . . . . The committee thanked him for his outstanding service and wished him good fortune in the future. The . . . union has appointed Mr . . . as its representative on the committee, as from the next meeting.
5 It was agreed that the following be co-opted as additional members of the committee: . . .
6 Reports were presented as follows:
By Mr . . . on a safety inspection held by . . . at . . . on . . . . Recommendations arising therefrom:
a That . . . .
b That . . . .
c That . . . .
By Messrs . . . and . . . of a safety survey carried out by . . . at . . . on . . . . Recommendations:
a That . . . .
b That . . . .
c That . . . .
By safety officer. His recommendations as follows were accepted:
a That . . . .
b That . . . .
c That . . . .
His following recommendations were discussed but put back for further consideration and study and for discussion at a future meeting, namely:
d
e
The company doctor reported on . . ./requested that. . . . All employees are urged to take note and to follow the doctor's advice/attend at the sick room, as suggested.
Agreed that all employees be urged to wear hard hats in the . . . area/wear safety boots, whenever . . ./report all accidents, however minor to . . . .
7 The date of the next meeting was fixed for . . ./future meetings were fixed for . . . .

Form 59 Alternative agenda — safety committee

Agenda of Safety Committee of XYZ Co. Ltd
To be held at . . . am/pm at . . . on . . . .

1 Minutes of previous meeting to be read, amended as necessary and approved.
2 Matters arising from Minutes, not dealt with later in Agenda.
3 Apologies for non-attendance.
4 Correspondence and matters arising therefrom.
5 Report on accidents, occurring since previous meeting, and consideration of recommendations for corrective action.
6 Examination of safety audit reports and recommendations for corrective action.
7 Consideration of reports and factual information provided by Inspectors, since last meeting.
8 Consideration of reports which safety representatives may wish to submit; and recommendations arising therefrom.
9 Safety officer's report: with recommendations for improvements or developments of works safety rules and safe systems of work.
10 Report of personnel/training officer concerning effectiveness of safety content of employees' training; and recommendation arising therefrom.
11 Report by . . . on adequacy of safety and health communication and publicity in work places; and recommendations arising therefrom.
12 Consideration of possible inspections by safety committee itself.
13 Membership of safety committee; including consideration of possible co-options.
14 Consideration of report by . . . on safety committee procedures; and recommendations arising therefrom.
15 Any other business.
16 Date of next and future meetings of safety committee.

Part Seven

Grievance and disciplinary procedures

XYZ Co. Ltd
Employee Grievance Procedure

1 The Company has established, after consultation with the appropriate trade unions, the following grievance procedure. The purpose of this procedure is to ensure that machinery exists for the speedy resolution of individual grievances, but the procedure itself cannot guarantee the resolution of any particular grievance. This depends on all concerned adopting a reasonable attitude to problems.

2 Where the procedure has been followed through all its stages and you are not satisfied with the outcome, then if you are a member of a trade union recognised by the Company, the trade union may raise the matter through the agreed negotiating procedures as a dispute. Apart from this, the decision of management at the last stage of the grievance procedure is final.

3 If you have a grievance you should in the first instance discuss the matter informally with your immediate superior, who is . . . . Only if this informal discussion fails to produce a mutually acceptable solution should you move to the next stage in the procedure.

4 The next stage in the procedure is for you formally to raise your grievance in writing with your immediate superior, who will arrange a meeting to discuss the grievance within five working days of your request. You are entitled at this formal meeting and at the subsequent stages in the procedure to be assisted or represented by a fellow employee of your choice or a lay representative of your trade union. Your superior may at his/her discretion arrange for another representative of the management to be present as an observer. A formal written note of this meeting and of any agreed conclusions will be made and a copy given to you or your representative (if any) within five working days of the date of the meeting.

5 If you are dissatisfied with the outcome of this formal meeting you may appeal in writing to your departmental manager within five working days of receiving the written note of the meeting. Your departmental manager will arrange a formal meeting to hear your grievance within five working days of receiving your appeal. A member of the Personnel Department will attend this meeting in an advisory capacity, and you are entitled to be assisted or represented as at the earlier stage. You will be notified in writing of the manager's decision on your appeal, and a copy of this decision will be sent to your representative. The manager's decision will be final.

6 Where your grievance relates to the conduct of your immediate superior and you do not feel able to discuss the matter formally with him/her, you should raise your grievance in writing with the Personnel Manager, who will arrange for the matter to be considered by a suitable member of the management with a member of the Personnel Department present as an observer. Similarly where the grievance relates to your Departmental Manager, you may appeal to the Personnel Manager instead of to the Departmental Manager; the Personnel Manager will then arrange for your appeal to be heard by another appropriate manager.

7 If your grievance relates to a change in your terms and conditions of employment, or your duties or conditions of work, your immediate superior has discretion, after consulting the Personnel Manager, to suspend the effect of the changes pending consideration of your grievance, but this is not done automatically. If the change is not suspended you will be expected to work normally under the new arrangements. However this will not be taken as indicating an acceptance by you of a variation in your terms of employment.

8 This grievance procedure is intended for the raising of individual grievances only. Where a group of employees together wish to raise the same grievance that should be done by the appropriate trade union through the normal negotiating machinery.

9 The procedure is designed to resolve problems speedily, and it is your responsibility in turn to ensure that grievances are raised without undue delay, at a time when it is more likely to be possible to arrange a solution than may be the case if the problem has been allowed to drag on.

10 This procedure in no way restricts your right to consult at any time the appropriate representatives of your trade union, nor is it intended to deprive you of your legal rights under your contract of employment.

11 The provisions of this procedure form part of your contract of employment.

Form 61 Application for formal consideration of grievance

XYZ Co. Ltd
Formal Grievance

This form is not to be issued to employees unless the grievance has been informally discussed with the supervisor and has not been resolved at that stage.

Name: Location:

Department/Section: Job title:

Trade Union:

Nature of grievance

Please state briefly the grievance you wish to pursue:

Steps taken to resolve grievance:

What action do you wish to be taken to rectify this complaint?

Name(s) and position(s) of individual(s) at whom your complaint is directed:

I apply for the grievance stated above to be formally investigated by the Personnel Office. If it is not resolved at that stage I agree that it will be referred in accordance with the Company's grievance procedure to a joint management/trade union committee for settlement, and I agree to accept any settlements reached through the joint committee.

I do/do not wish to be represented at interviews or meetings by my trade union representative.

I nominate . . . of . . . trade union to be my representative (if applicable).

Signed: *Date:*

(Now give this form to your supervisor, or if your grievance is about him/her, to your section head.)

Supervisor/Section Head's comments

Name:

What do you understand the employee's real grievance to be?

Give an assessment of its validity:

Any comments on employee's written complaint?

Any suggestions for the resolution of this complaint?

Signed: *Date:*

Form 62 Personnel manager's report on investigation of grievance

XYZ Co. Ltd

Report on Formal Grievance

Name of employee: Date:

Department/Section:

Location:

Job title:

Trade union:

Name of representative:

Date formal grievance tendered:

Summary of grievance and supervisor's comments:

(Employee's full statement and supervisor's comments to be attached.)

Statement of action taken by Personnel Manager:

Persons interviewed, with dates:

Other action taken:

Reasons for non-resolution:

Personnel Manager's comments on merits of grievance:

Proposals (if any) for consideration for resolution of grievance:

List of other relevant documents attached:

Signed: *(Personnel Manager)*

This form and attachments to be sent to management and union members of joint committee investigating grievances, and copies to be supplied to aggrieved employee and his/her representative.

XYZ Co. Ltd

Statement of Outcome of Formal Grievance

To: *Date:*

Department/Section:

Location:

Copy to trade union representative:

Your formal notice of grievance dated . . . has now been fully investigated and I now give you formal notice of the outcome of that investigation.

*After discussion with yourself and others concerned, it was agreed that your grievance could be mutually resolved in the following terms:
Any necessary steps to implement this settlement are now being taken.

*It was not possible to resolve your grievance by discussion and it was therefore referred in accordance with the agreed grievance procedure to a meeting of the joint management/trade union committee which sat on . . . .

*The unanimous decision/decisions, reached by a majority of both management and trade union representatives, was that no action would be taken on your grievance/the following steps would be taken in settlement of your grievance:

(This decision is the last stage in your grievance procedure and I regret that if you are dissatisfied with the outcome there is nothing more that can be done.)

*Any necessary steps to implement this decision are now being taken.

*The committee recorded a failure to agree on your grievance. In the terms of the agreed grievance procedure this means that no action will be taken by management. However, it is open to your trade union to apply for arbitration by an independent arbiter appointed by ACAS, whose decision would be binding on you and the Company. You are advised to discuss this possibility with your trade union representative.

Signed: *(Personnel Manager)*

**Delete as appropriate*

XYZ Co. Ltd
Disciplinary Procedure

1 Discipline rests on two basic principles. The first is that the Company is entitled to expect employees to maintain reasonable standards of conduct, reliability, efficiency and competence. The second is that employees are entitled to know what standards are expected of them, and to be given a fair hearing before any disciplinary decision is taken against them. This disciplinary procedure has been drawn up after consultation with the appropriate recognised trade unions on the basis of these principles.

2 This disciplinary procedure forms part of the terms and conditions of employment of all employees to whom it applies.

Disciplinary rules

3 Specific rules as to timekeeping, conduct and working arrangements are set out in detail in the *Working Handbook* given to every employee. Rules which apply to a particular group of employees are posted on the appropriate notice board and copies are given to each employee concerned. Any significant changes in disciplinary rules or the Company's policy in enforcing the rules will be communicated in writing to employees concerned.

4 It is important that employees should read these disciplinary rules carefully and, if in any doubt as to what they mean, should consult their immediate superior. If employees do not understand the rules, which lay down what the company expects of its employees, there is a greater risk that they will fail to maintain the required standard.

Disciplinary procedure

5 Minor lapses in behaviour or performance, or failures to comply with required standards, will normally result in an informal oral warning being given to the employee concerned by his supervisor. The purpose of this warning is to explain to the employee the way in which he is not complying with expected standards, and to assist him in complying with them in the future by explaining what is required, and arranging for other steps such as additional training to be undertaken. An informal warning of this kind is not recorded on the employee's file and is not a prerequisite to formal disciplinary procedure should that prove necessary.

6 In more serious cases, or where an informal warning has not resulted in improved behaviour or performance, the following procedure will apply:

a The employee's immediate supervisor will request the holding of a formal disciplinary hearing before the section supervisor (or in the case of an employee in a supervisory grade, the Departmental Manager).

b The Departmental Manager will notify the employee in writing of the time and place of the hearing and the nature of the matters complained of. At least one full working day's notice will be given of the hearing. The notice will also inform the employee of his rights of representation and to call witnesses as set out below.

c The employee's immediate superior, or the person convening the hearing, may in any case where it is considered necessary suspend the employee on full basic pay for a period up to five working days pending the disciplinary hearing. This period may be extended if the employee is under police investigation or has been charged with a criminal offence, pending completion of the investigation and/or trial.

d The employee is entitled to be assisted or represented at the disciplinary hearing by a fellow employee or a lay representative of his trade union. If the facts are in dispute the employee or his representative is entitled to put questions to any witnesses called by the Departmental Manager, and to ask for additional witnesses to be called. Fellow employees called as witnesses are entitled to time off without loss of pay for this purpose. The employee will be given an opportunity to draw attention to any mitigating circumstances before any decision as to the appropriate disciplinary penalty is taken.

e A member of the Personnel Department will attend the formal disciplinary hearing in an advisory capacity and will make a written record of the proceedings. The employee will be told the decision and the reason for it at the end of the hearing, and this will be confirmed in writing.

(Continued)

(Continued)

Penalties

7 The penalties which may be imposed after a formal disciplinary hearing are as follows:
a A formal verbal warning.
b A first written warning.
c A final written warning.
d Suspension without pay for up to five working days.
e Dismissal with notice or pay in lieu of notice.
f Instant dismissal.

8 In less serious cases the penalty will normally be on the first occasion a formal verbal warning; if the employee again fails to comply with the Company's requirements, this would be followed by a first and then a final written warning, and, if matters still do not improve, dismissal. A warning may be accompanied by a period of suspension without pay.

9 A written record of any disciplinary warning will be kept on the employee's file for a period of six months from the date of the disciplinary decision, and will then be removed and not taken into account in any subsequent disciplinary proceedings. This does not apply where a further penalty is imposed during the six-month period; in such a case the original warning remains valid until six months after the later warning has expired.

10 The Company reserves the right of instant dismissal in cases of proven serious misconduct as defined in the disciplinary rules. Where dismissal would otherwise be justified but there are mitigating circumstances, a warning at any level in the procedure may be given instead of dismissal.

Appeals

11 An employee who is aggrieved at any formal disciplinary decision adverse to him may appeal in writing to the appropriate Director within five working days of receiving written confirmation of the decision.

12 The Director will hear the appeal within ten working days of notification. The same procedure will apply as for disciplinary hearings (set out in Para. 6 above). The Personnel Director will attend the hearing in an advisory capacity.

13 Where the employee has been dismissed, he will be regarded as suspended without pay pending the decision on his appeal. If the appeal is successful the Director will decide whether any or all of the period of suspension is to be paid. If the appeal is unsuccessful the dismissal will be regarded as having taken effect in accordance with the original decision.

14 On an appeal, the Director may allow the appeal by setting aside the penalty in whole or part, or substituting a less severe penalty, or he may dismiss the appeal. A more severe penalty may not be imposed on appeal.

15 The Director's decision on an appeal is final; but this does not affect the employee's legal rights under statute or any other terms of the contract of employment, or the right of a recognised trade union of which he is a member, to pursue any issue arising from the disciplinary decisions through the established negotiating machinery.

Trade union representatives

16 In the event of a trade union representative being disciplined the Personnel Director will inform the representative's full-time District Officer, and the representative will be entitled to have his District Officer represent him at the disciplinary hearing.

Substitution

17 Where a Departmental Manager or Director is not available to conduct a disciplinary hearing or appeal, the Personnel Director may nominate a suitable substitute.

Form 65 Formal application for disciplinary action

XYZ Co. Ltd
Application for Disciplinary Action

Name of employee: Date:

Department/Section:

Location:

Name of supervisor:

Name of complainant (if not supervisor):

Position of complainant (if not supervisor):

(A copy of this form should be given to the relevant supervisor if not filed by him/her.)

Nature of complaint:

Date and time of incident:

Names of witnesses:

Statement of any action taken at time of complaint or since (including sending home or suspension of employee):

Has employee been informed of this application? Yes/No.

Has employee admitted conduct complained of? (Give brief details of the circumstances of any admission.)

Give details of any previous relevant complaints about employee including warnings given orally (disregard incidents more than a year ago):

Has employee committed misconduct of this kind previously? (Disregard incidents more than a year ago):

Are there any reasons why employee should be suspended/continue to be suspended pending hearing?

Other observations:

Signed:

To be sent to the Personnel Manager.

Form 66 Notice to employee of disciplinary hearing

XYZ Co. Ltd

Notice of Formal Disciplinary Hearing

To: Date:

Department/Section:

Location:

A formal complaint has been made to me about your conduct as detailed below:

Statement of complaint:

Name of complainant:

Date and time of alleged incident:

*I have been informed that you have made the following admissions:

I propose to consider the question of disciplinary action against you in accordance with the Company's disciplinary procedure. For the purpose of considering this matter you are required to attend a formal disciplinary hearing on . . . at . . . am/pm at . . . . You are entitled if you wish to be accompanied by a representative of your trade union. If you do wish to make use of this facility you should give the enclosed copy of this form to your representative. You are also entitled to the assistance of witnesses. If there are any witnesses you wish to call please let me know their names and I will arrange for them to be released from their duties for the hearing.

The following have already been asked to attend the hearing as witnesses:

If I am satisfied after hearing the evidence that you are guilty of misconduct I shall wish to consider the penalty to be imposed. I shall wish to take into account the following matters which appear on your record/which have been notified to me by your supervisor:

You will be entitled to make representations about any penalty to be imposed and also to appeal against it.

*Your suspension on full pay will continue until the date of the hearing.

Signed: *(Personnel Manager)*

**Delete as appropriate*

Form 67 Disciplinary record form

XYZ Co. Ltd

Record of Disciplinary Action Against Employee

Name:

Department/Section:

Location:

Statement of complaint:

Date and time of incident complained of:

Employee's representative:

Date and time of hearing:

Persons present:

Findings on complaint:

Admissions made by employee:

Other matters taken into account in considering outcome:

Disciplinary penalty to be imposed:

Employee notified of right of appeal against penalty/decision: Yes/No. Date:

Other action to be taken in consequence of complaint:

(Continued)

(Continued)

Notice of appeal received? Yes/No. Date:

Outcome of appeal, if any:

Date of appeal hearing:

Persons present:

Findings on appeal if different from above:

Date disciplinary record to be removed from employee's file:

Signatures:

Date:

Chairman of Appeal Board: *Date:*

Countersigned by management representatives at hearing

Signatures

Personnel Manager *Date:*

Chairman of Appeal Board: *Date:*

Countersigned by management representatives at hearing:

Signed: *Date:* *Position:*

Signed: *Date:* *Position:*

Signed: *Date:* *Position:*

Countersigned by management representatives at appeal:

Signed: *Date:* *Position:*

Signed: *Date:* *Position:*

Form 68 Formal warning to employee

XYZ Co. Ltd
Formal Warning

To: Date:

Department/Section:

Location:

Copy to union representative:

A formal complaint was made to me about your conduct as detailed below:

Statement of complaint:

Name of complainant:

Date and time of incident:

A disciplinary hearing was held by me on . . . . I established that you were guilty/you admitted that you were guilty of misconduct in the terms of the complaint. After hearing your representations on this matter, and taking into account the following matters relating to your conduct in the past:

I decided on this occasion that it was not necessary to dismiss you.

However, your conduct on the occasion in question and on previous occasions has been seriously below the standard required by the Company. *I therefore now give you formal warning that if your conduct again falls below a satisfactory standard in any respect you will be liable to immediate dismissal.*

If you maintain a satisfactory standard of conduct for . . . months from today, this formal warning will be cancelled and the record of your disciplinary hearing will be removed from your file.

I enclose a separate notice of your rights of appeal.

You are required to acknowledge that you have received this formal warning, and I shall be obliged if you will do so by signing the second copy of this notice and returning it to me.

I must also inform you that if you dispute the accuracy of any statement in this notice you are entitled under the disciplinary procedure to write a letter setting out your view of the matter, which will be attached to the record of the disciplinary hearing in your personal file.

Signed: *(Personnel Manager)*

Receipt *(second copy only)*

I acknowledge receipt of the formal warning of which the above is a copy.

Signed: *Date:*

Form 69 Notice of right of appeal from disciplinary decision

XYZ Co. Ltd
Disciplinary Procedure: Right of Appeal

To: Date:

Department/Section:

Location:

Copy to union representative:

Following disciplinary proceedings against you on . . . I decided to impose on you the following penalty:

In accordance with the agreed disciplinary procedure you have a right of appeal against my decision that you were guilty of misconduct and/or against the penalty imposed. If you exercise your right of appeal the appeal will be heard by a board consisting of three senior managers of the Company who have not been involved in your case at this stage. Their decision will be final.

*Your suspension/demotion will remain in effect pending the hearing of any appeal.

You are entitled to be accompanied by your trade union representative at the hearing of your appeal. You are also advised to discuss with him/her the question whether you should appeal. In this connection may I draw your attention to the fact that under the disciplinary procedure it is open to the appeal board to increase as well as decrease the penalty I have imposed.

If you wish to appeal you should do so by filling in the form below and returning it to me.

Signed: *(Personnel Manager)*

To the Personnel Manager
XYZ Co. Ltd

Name:

Trade union:

Name of trade union representative:

I give notice of appeal from the disciplinary decision dated . . . . I wish to appeal against the finding that I was guilty of misconduct/against the penalty imposed/against both (*delete whichever does not apply*). I do/do not wish to be accompanied by my trade union representative.

State briefly the grounds of your appeal:

Signed: *Date:*

Part Eight

Dismissal

Introduction

When you hire, you create a contract of employment. When you dismiss, you terminate that contract. Dismissal means termination by the employer. It may be:

1 *Actual* — 'the sack' — or refusing to keep the employee working on the same basis as before, e.g. you reduce his pay or status or insist upon changing his hours or place of work without his consent. Or:

2 *Constructive* — you force him out of his job — you 'repudiate' (or smash) the contract by behaving in a way that makes it really impossible for the employee to stay on. So when he does leave, he has not destroyed the contract but merely accepted the situation which you have created. Or:

3 By not re-engaging the employee when a fixed-term contract comes to an end 'by effluxion of time'.

Until an employee qualifies for unfair dismissal protection (in the main, after 26 weeks' service), his only right is to receive his proper notice or pay in lieu. He is entitled to:

a *Agreed notice* — see his contract of employment or written particulars; or, in the absence of agreement, to

b *Reasonable notice* — such period as is reasonable in all the circumstances of the case, including his status, responsibilities, length of service, etc.; and in any event to

c Not less than the statutory minimum period, which is: after 4 weeks, 7 days; after 2 years, 2 weeks; after 3 years, 3 weeks; and so on up to 12 weeks after 12 years' service.

An employee may be dismissed 'summarily', i.e. with neither notice nor pay in lieu, if he has 'repudiated', i.e. smashed, his contract, which he may do by:

1 One really serious act of contractual breach, e.g. normally stealing or some other criminal offence affecting his work; or

2 By persistent or habitual minor offences.

An employee who does not receive his proper notice or pay in lieu is said to be dismissed 'wrongfully' (NB: *not* 'unfairly'). A wrongfully dismissed employee sues for damages for breach of contract — he claims what he has lost as a result of his employer's breach, which will normally be:

a The remuneration which he should have received during the period of notice; plus

b The value of any fringe benefits for that period, e.g. use of company car, canteen facilities and/or additional pension payments, but minus

c Anything earned by the employee during the notice period (as he must 'mitigate his loss').

In addition to the above rights, the employee is entitled not to be dismissed 'unfairly'. To qualify, he must:

1 Be continuously employed for at least 26 weeks (but, note, a 'week' means any week during any part of which the employee worked); and if you dismiss an employee instantly (with or without pay in lieu), then the statutory minimum of seven days is added to the presumed period of service. So '26 weeks' may actually equal '23 weeks and 2 days' — so assessment of performance should be carried out after a much shorter period.
2 He must not be a 'part-timer', i.e. one who normally works for less than 16 hours a week or if he has worked continuously for 5 years, for less than 8 hours a week; and
3 He must not be a pensioner — above the national (or your normal) retirement age.

There are other but less important exceptions, e.g. employees who 'normally work' overseas who according to their contracts of service are 'based' outside the UK.

A qualified employee must prove that he was 'dismissed'. The burden of proof then shifts onto the employer, to show:

a That he dismissed for one of the statutory reasons.
b That he acted 'reasonably' in treating the reason concerned as one sufficient to warrant removing the employee's livelihood.
c That he followed a fair system.

The statutory reasons are: lack of capability; lack of academic or technical qualifications; conduct; redundancy; illegality; or some other 'substantial reason', e.g. engagement for a temporary purpose which has terminated.

To estimate what is or is not 'fair' or 'reasonable', you must look at all the circumstances of the case. Especially: that dismissal should be a last resort.

A fair system means following the ACAS Disciplinary Code and in particular, giving the employee the opportunity to state his case and (where practicable) to appeal to a higher level of management. Dismissal for a first offence will only be 'fair' in exceptional circumstances: normally, an employer should give at least one written warning of intended dismissal — which will itself 'go stale', usually after about six months.

Current maximum awards for 'unfair dismissal':

1 *Compensatory award* — up to £5750, which covers the actual loss suffered; but it may be reduced to reflect the employee's own conduct, which contributed to his dismissal.
2 *Basic award* — up to £220 (two weeks' pay at £110 per week), even if no actual loss; or (more important) the total lost redundancy entitlement (maximum: £3,300 after 20 years' service at appropriate remuneration and age).
3 *Additional award* — where the employer unreasonably refuses to comply with a Tribunal 'order' for the reinstatement or re-engagement of the unfairly dismissed employee — maximum: £2,860, or double if dismissal for 'discrimination' — sex, race or trade union. This award is exceedingly rare.

* * *

An employee who can prove 'discrimination' need not wait 26 weeks before claiming unfair dismissal. And if he can produce a certificate from a trade union official that the discrimination was for wishing to join or take part in the activities of an independent trade union (or not to join or take part in the activities of a non-independent organisation), a tribunal has power to order the employer not to dismiss the employee until the tribunal hearing.

Form 70 Warning of intended dismissal — general

You have received oral warnings of disciplinary offences as follows:

1 On . . . , by Mr/Mrs/Miss . . . about:

2 On . . . , by Mr/Mrs/Miss . . . about:

3 On . . . , by Mr/Mrs/Miss . . . about:

Despite these warnings, you have committed the following further disciplinary offences:
1 On . . . .
2 On . . . .
3 On . . . .
I must therefore warn you that if you are again guilty of any of the above offences, your employment will/may be terminated.

Form 71 Warning of intended dismissal — referring to previous written warning

On the . . . 19 . . , I/Mr/Mrs/Miss . . . gave you written warning concerning . . ./disciplinary offences, fully detailed in that warning.

On the . . . you again . . . . This is therefore your final warning that any further misconduct/repetition of . . . will result in your dismissal.

Form 72 Warning of dismissal — absenteeism

The Company's records show that you have been absent from/late for work on the following occasions:
1 . . . .
2 . . . .
3 . . . .
On each of these occasions, you have been asked to comply with your terms of service and to attend for work as you have agreed.

In addition, on . . . 19 . . , you were handed a written complaint concerning the same matter.

Despite the above, you were again absent/late on . . ./from . . . to . . . . If, therefore, there is any further repetition of this absenteeism/lateness, your employment will be terminated.

Form 73 Final warning

This is your final warning that if you are guilty of any further disciplinary offences/if you again are/if you continue to ignore the Company's Safety Rules, as specified in the written warnings handed to you on . . . and . . . you may be dismissed. I most strongly urge you to comply with the Company's Rules so that your employment with the Company may continue.

Form 74 Written reasons — previous warnings

We acknowledge receipt of your written request for reasons for your dismissal, dated . . . . We refer you to the Company's Notice dated . . . in which you were given a Final Warning that if you persisted in breaking the Company's Disciplinary Rules, you would be dismissed. The matters complained of in that Notice were the following:
1 . . . .
2 . . . .
3 . . . .
You failed to heed this warning, in that on the . . . you again . . . . In addition, you were dismissed because of . . . .

Form 75 Written reasons for dismissal

We thank you for your letter dated . . . seeking written reasons for your dismissal. You were dismissed for the following reasons:

1 Because of your persistent absenteeism/failure to comply with instructions/flouting of Safety Rules (or as the case may be). Particular instances were the following:
   a . . . .
   b . . . .
   c . . . .
2 The incident which occured on . . . when you . . . . Details of many of the above complaints/of the complaints in (1) above are contained in warning notices handed to you on . . . and . . . .

Form 76 Written reasons — suspected stealing

In response to your written request for written reasons for your dismissal, you were dismissed because of your conduct, as follows:

1 On the . . . you were found with the following items belonging to the Company/your colleague Mr/Mrs/Miss . . . on your person/in your handbag/case/in your locker/in the boot of your car, namely:

2 On the . . . the following items belonging to the Company/the Company's customers/clients were found in your home:

3 On the . . . you were seen rummaging through the contents of Mrs/Miss . . . handbag/shopping basket, without her permission.

4 At about . . . p.m. on the . . . you were challenged by the Company's Security Officer/Personnel Officer, Mr . . . and you admitted having the following items belonging to the Company/the Company's customers/clients on your person/in your possession, namely:

You admitted to Mr . . . and later to Mr . . . that you did not have prior consent from . . . to take possession of the above property or any of it, and you apologised/admitted that you intended to keep it/offered no explanation/no acceptable explanation.

As you well know and knew, such behaviour cannot be tolerated and is regarded by the Company as a serious disciplinary offence, justifying instant dismissal. I refer you in particular to paragraph . . . of the Company's Disciplinary Rules/of the written particulars of your terms of service/and to notices on the Company's notice boards, warning that such behaviour would lead to dismissal.,

Yet nevertheless: the Accounts Department have been instructed to pay you . . . weeks' wages/salary in lieu of notice, without prejudice to its rights to dismiss summarily.

Form 77 Written reasons — single incident

In compliance with the request contained in your letter dated . . . we confirm (as you were/your client was informed by me/Mr/Mrs/Miss . . . on the . . .) the reason for your/your client's dismissal was the following:

On the . . . at . . . , he . . . .

You were/he was immediately suspended for investigations. His explanation was considered by . . . on . . . and was found totally unsatisfactory. In accordance with the Company's disciplinary rules, he was given the opportunity to appeal to a higher level of authority, namely Mr/Mrs/Miss . . . , but he did not avail himself of that opportunity/and he did so on . . . but the original decision was upheld.

Form 78 Dismissal — with explanation of notice

Your Contract of Employment provides that you are entitled to . . . period of notice/the statutory minimum period of notice, which in your case is . . . weeks. I hereby give you notice of termination in accordance with that Contract, to terminate on . . . .

Please ensure that the following property is returned to Company HQ *(or as the case may be)* by not later than . . . p.m. on that date:

1 The Company's car, registration number . . . .
2 Any samples belonging to the Company which may be in your possession.
3 Any stationery or other property belonging to the Company which may be in your possession.
4 All relevant books of account, receipts or other documents.

When the above items have all been handed in, the Accounts Department will make all final payments due to you.

Form 79 Dismissal with notice — explanation of statutory reason

I regret that I have been instructed to give you notice in accordance with the terms of your Contract of Employment, to terminate your employment as from the end of work on . . . the . . . 19. . . Your dismissal is for the following reason/ reasons *(delete as necessary)*:

*That you do not have the necessary qualifications/technical ability/skill to carry out your job/the job in its reorganised form.

*That you have reached the normal/the Company's retirement age/that your age/health has rendered you unable to perform your job in an adequate or satisfactory manner.

*That you are a foreigner whose work permit has expired.

*That the Company was unable to obtain an extension; and that it would therefore be illegal for the Company to employ you further.

*That as you were told at the time when you were taken on, your job was temporary because:

a You were replacing Mrs . . . who was away having a baby and who had given notice of her intention to return to her job after childbirth.
b You were engaged only for the duration of the summer/winter season.
c You were employed to carry out a specific task, namely . . . , and that your employment would terminate when the task was completed.
d You were replacing Mr . . . who was suspended on medical grounds and who has now given notice of his intention to return to work once the suspension has been lifted.

*That your job became redundant/and that the Company was not able to offer you suitable alternative employment

*Your conduct — and in particular:

a That you failed to heed the warnings contained in notices/warnings dated . . . , . . . and . . . .
b That you have persistently failed to comply with the Company's Safety Rules.
c That you have been guilty of persistent absenteeism.
d That you were found to have property belonging to the Company/Company customers/clients in your car/home/handbag/possession, without prior consent.
e That you smoked in a forbidden area, thereby causing grave risk to the health and safety of everyone employed in the works/stores.
f That you assaulted Mr . . . .

Form 80 Written reasons — with additional complaint form reducing compensation

We thank you for your letter dated . . . in which you ask for the reasons for your dismissal to be put into writing. You were given these reasons orally by me/Mr/Mrs/Miss . . . on . . . . They were and remain the following:

1 . . . .
2 . . . .
3 . . . .

It is right that we should also inform you that other matters have come to light since your departure and which were therefore not reasons for your dismissal, but which the Company will if necessary place before a Tribunal as reasons why even if (which will be denied) your dismissal was in any way unfair, the award of compensation would be inappropriate:

1 The examination of the accounts has revealed claims for expenses (details of which are set out in the sheet enclosed herewith), which were claimed in respect of items not in fact incurred.
2 Despite assurances given on . . . and . . . to Mr/Mrs/Miss/your . . . , you did not carry out the following work/obey instructions in the following respects:
   a . . . .
   b . . . .
   c . . . .
3 You treated Mr/Mrs/Miss . . . in an intolerable manner in that on the . . . , the . . . and the . . . , and other dates, you . . . .

Form 81 Dismissal with regret

I regret that I am instructed to give notice to terminate your Contract of Employment on . . . , because of your continued ill-health/unfortunate absence due to ill-health/your reaching the Company's normal retirement age/due to the return of Mrs . . . , she having given birth to her baby and there being no reasonably suitable alternative position which we are able to offer to you (*or as the case may be*).

On behalf of the company, I thank you for the excellent service which you have given to it and I wish you health and happiness in your retirement/and I hope you will soon be fully recovered — in which case, please contact me and I will be pleased to try to find a position for you with the Company/and I hope that you will be very happy in your marriage/new home (*or as the case may be*).

Form 82 Dismissal with reason

I am instructed that your Contract of Employment with the above Company is terminated forthwith. The reason is the following:

*You hazarded the lives of others by your conduct in . . . .

*You were discovered with the Company's property in the boot of your car, without the consent of your superiors or other lawful excuse.

*You attacked Mr . . . with a weapon/gun/knife.

*You assaulted Mr . . . causing him to suffer severe/bodily injuries.

As the Company has no wish to cause hardship to your family/you have served the Company for an extended period (*or as the case may be*), you will shortly receive your pay in lieu of notice, without prejudice to the Company's rights to dismiss you summarily without either notice or payment in lieu.

**Delete as required*

Part Nine

Redundancy

Introduction

In broad terms, an employee is 'redundant' if his job has gone, along with him. A redundant employee now has three main rights:

1 If he has served for two years after reaching the age of 18, i.e. at a minimum age of 20, he qualifies for redundancy pay. The amount is assessed on a sliding scale, rising to £3,000 after 20 years' service at appropriate ages and salaries.

2 He is entitled to reasonable paid time off work to seek *(a)* other employment and *(b)* training for new employment.

3 If he is qualified (see above) through service, etc., he must not be made redundant 'unfairly'. An employer must act 'fairly' in choosing whom to make redundant.

In addition, employers must inform any recognised, independent trade union if they intend to make redundant even one member or one employee affected by its bargaining. In any major proposed redundancies (10 or more) employers must notify both the union and the Department of Employment. Criteria: 10 or more proposed redundancies at one establishment within a period of 30 days — required notification: 60 days; 100 or more within 90 days, 90 days.

Failure to notify the union gives it the right to claim a 'protective award' on behalf of its members and other workers affected. The Tribunal will give this award to compensate employees affected by the redundancies, not to punish employers. Maximum: pay for the period during which consultation should have taken place. For failure to notify the Department, the maximum fine is: £400, or loss of 10 per cent of the redundancy rebate — which at present is 41 per cent of the statutory redundancy payment. It does not cover any additional redundancy pay that may have been negotiated by the union, which employers pay from their own resources.

An employee who can prove that he was 'dismissed' (see above) is presumed to have been both dismissed 'unfairly' and as 'redundant'. The burden of proving both fairness and some reason other than redundancy rests on the employer. All redundancy disputes are heard by Industrial Tribunals — redundancy pay; unfair redundancies; time off work; and claims for protective awards.

* * *

No Appeal Court will dislodge an Industrial Tribunal's finding of fact, provided that it was one to which, on the evidence before it, it could have come. Appeals on points of law go to the Employment Appeal Tribunal; from the EAT to the Court of Appeal; and then (at the leave of the Court of Appeal or of the House of Lords — and on a point of public importance) to the House of Lords.

Form 83 Applications for voluntary redundancies invited

Due to the recession in trade/the company's decision to close the . . . department/the need to reduce its work force in order to remain viable/to remain competitive in the teeth of fierce competition, the following redundancies will have to be made by not later than . . . , namely:

1 . . . in the . . . department.
2 . . . in the . . . workshop.
3 . . . in the office/maintenance engineers/machine operatives.

(*Or as the case may be.*)

Applications are invited from employees who would wish to use this occasion to retire from work or from the service of this company. Generous redundancy payments have been negotiated with and agreed by all unions concerned.

The company must retain the right to decide which applications to accept and which to reject.

Applications should be made in writing to Mr . . . (Personnel Manager), not later than . . . . Any special reasons for wishing to accept voluntary retirement/redundancy should be stated.

Closing date for applications:

Form 84 Redundancy with reasons

The Company greatly regrets that your job will become redundant as from . . . . The reason is the following:

*That the demand for the goods manufactured by the Company has greatly diminished so that the Company has no alternative other than to reduce its workforce.

*That due to the need for the Company to remain . . . competitive, it has been forced to reduce overheads and to manage with a smaller staff/workforce.

*That we are closing down our works at . . . and transferring our undertaking to . . . .

*That the Company is selling its business to . . . who will not be retaining the current workforce/who have stated their intention of closing your department.

*That the installation of new capital equipment has reduced the need for workers with your particular skills.

On the . . . your union was notified of this proposed redundancy and the Department of Employment was informed on the . . . .

We greatly regret having to take this step; we thank you for the services which you have given to the Company; and we trust that you will succeed in finding alternative employment. Arrangements have been made for officers from the Local Department of Employment/Job Centre to call at our works on . . . and if you require help in finding alternative employment, please consult them — or your Personnel Manager/Department Head.

**Delete as required*

Form 85 Redundancy — offer of trial in alternative job

As you were informed by notice/letter dated . . . your current employment as a . . . in the . . . department/workshop/office will terminate on . . . , whereupon you will become redundant.

However: the Company is now able to offer you the following alternative positions, all or any of which it considers would represent reasonably suitable alternative employment for you:

We ask you to consider these offers carefully, and would remind you that an unreasonable refusal to accept a suitable alternative offer may result in an employee forfeiting his right to redundancy pay. And we remind you of your legal right to accept an alternative job offered for a trial period of up to four weeks.

In the circumstances, please complete the form attached hereto (*Form 86*) and return it to . . . , not later than . . . .

Form 86 Acceptance or rejection of alternative employment

Name:

Place of work (unit and shop):

1 I acknowledge that I will become redundant on the . . . .
2 I do not wish to accept your offer of alternative employment, as listed in your notice dated . . . .

OR: I do wish to accept your offer of alternative employment, namely: (*specify which alternative is preferred, or if more than one are acceptable, state order of preference*):

I wish to accept the above employment on a trial basis and I understand that if I wish to reject this employment and to retain those rights which I would otherwise have had, I must inform you within four weeks of the start of that employment.

OR: I am pleased to accept the above appointment on a permanent basis. I do not wish to do so merely for a trial period of up to four weeks.

Signed: *Date:*

Form 87 Employee's notice — leaving before due date

I refer to your notice dated . . . informing me that I would be dismissed from . . . by reason of redundancy. I have now found alternative employment and I wish to leave on the . . . . I trust that you will have no objection.

Form 88 Employer's notice — objecting to early leaving

We thank you for your notice dated . . . stating your wish to terminate your employment prior to the date when you would become redundant. We regret that we are unable to agree to your request because it is essential that the work which you and your colleagues are undertaking should be completed/we are hoping that it will prove possible to remove the redundancy notices, as further work is likely to become available *(or as the case may be).*

Form 89 Redundancy — notifying union

(Note: there are no reasons laid down by statute for refusing an employee's request to leave before the expiry of his notice. If the employee does *leave early where his employer has asked him to withdraw his notice, the employer may dispute having to pay redundancy pay. An industrial tribunal will consider the reasons for wanting to leave early and their reasons for refusing to let the employee leave early and may reduce the amount of redundancy pay.)*

I regret to have to inform you that the Company expects to make the following redundancies, among your members and/or others affected by your Union's negotiations:

1 By . . . , . . . men/women/workers from the . . . Department.
2 By . . . , . . . men/women/workers from the office.
3 By . . . , . . . men/women/workers in each of the following categories:
   a . . . machine operatives;
   b Maintenance/. . . engineers;
   c Clerks/typists/office staff.

The company will be pleased to consult with you concerning these redundancies. Kindly contact me/the personnel manager/industrial relations officer at your earliest convenience.

As you know, the above redundancies have been necessitated by . . . .

Form 90 Redundancy notice — Department of Employment

I hereby give you notice in accordance with *The Employment Protection Act, 1975*, that the company proposes to make the following redundancies:

1 On or after the . . . , between 10 and 30 employees at its establishment at . . . .
2 On or after the . . . , between 31 and 60 employees from its establishment at . . . .
3 On or after the . . . , over 100 employees from its establishment at . . . .

Part Ten

Miscellaneous

XYZ Co. Ltd
Time Off for Public Duties

Employees are entitled to reasonable unpaid leave to serve on certain public and statutory bodies as defined in Section 29 of the Employment Protection (Consolidation) Act. This right is subject to the reasonable requirements of the Company that its works shall not be interrupted unnecessarily. Permission is required as to the times and dates of leave, once an overall amount has been approved. Permission should be sought in the first instance from your superior, who will not refuse requests unreasonably. Difficulties may be referred to the Personnel Officer.

Name:

Department/Section:

Location:

Office or position in respect of which this application is made:

Dates of service (if you have been elected give the period up to the time you will be liable for re-election):

Give the name and address of an appropriate official of the body concerned whom the Company can approach for confirmation of the duties involved in your membership:

Name:

Position:

Address:

Amount of time off required (indicate in hours per week or per month, or days per year):

How much notice can you give of particular requirements?

Signed: *Date:*

(Now give this form to your supervisor)

(Continued)

(Continued)

Supervisor's comments

Comment on any problems that would be caused by employee's absence:

What arrangements can be made to cover the work that employee would normally be doing?

What is the maximum time off which could be authorised without a need for additional staff?

Signed: *Date:*

Personnel Manager's decision

Application refused [outside Employment Protection (Consolidation) Act]/granted.

Time off to be allowed: . . . hours/days per week/month/year.

Conditions imposed on time off:

Arrangements for cover/additional staff resources:

Duration of authorisation:

Signed: *Date:*

XYZ Co. Ltd
Report of Employee Leaving Job or Resigning

This report form should be filled in and sent to the Personnel Officer in any case where an employee is absent for 3 or more days without explanation or previous warning, or where the employee has stated his intention to resign or walked off the job in circumstances suggesting he may intend to resign. In case of absence, check with personnel office whether they have been notified, e.g. of illnss, before filling in form.

Name of employee: Date:

Department/Section:

Location:

Supervisor/section head filing report:

A Unexplained absence

Date employee last attended work:

Do you know of any circumstances which may explain this absence?

Have enquiries been made of others as to possible explanation?

If so what was outcome?

Has the employee previously been absent for a long period without prior warning or explanation? Yes/No.

(If yes give details):

(Continued)

B Resignation

Date and time of incident:

Witness:

Nature of incident:

Did employee threaten to resign/offer his resignation? Yes/No.

If yes, do you think this was intended seriously? *(Give details of reasons).*

Did you accept resignation offer (if made)? Yes/No/Not applicable

Are there any circumstances which would suggest that employee may claim to have been constructively dismissed?

Signed: *Position:*

Note of action by Personnel Manager

Letter sent to seek explanation of absence (date):

Reply received:

Medical certificate received:

Employee returned to work:

Resignation confirmed:

Action taken to avert claim for constructive dismissal (specify):

Signed: *Date:*

Form 93 Notice of lay-off

XYZ Co. Ltd

To: Date:

Department/Section:

Location:

Owing to:

it will not be possible to provide you with your normal work

*on the following days: . . . .

*from . . . until further notice.

*from . . . on the following days each week until further notice: . . .

*Alternative work will be provided for you as indicated:

Although you cannot be required to do this work under your contract, the Company will only pay you if you agree to do so.

*You will not be required to report for work until . . ./until further notice/on the days stated.

*Under the terms of the guaranteed week agreement you will be paid . . . . You should call to collect this on the normal pay days/this will be included in your wage packet.

*You are not entitled to be paid under the guaranteed week agreement because . . . .

*You are entitled to a statutory guarantee pay of £ . . . per day for the first . . . days you are laid off. You should call to collect this on the normal pay day/this will be included in your wage packet.

*You are not entitled to statutory guarantee pay because the layoff is due to a strike at . . . .

Please note that you may in certain circumstances be eligible for unemployment pay for days when you are laid off and not paid (disregarding the first three days). You should enquire about this at your local unemployment benefit office.

Personnel Manager

**Delete as appropriate*

Book Two

ACTUAL COMPANY FORMS

Introduction

Parts 1-3 include some of the employment forms most frequently used by three leading companies. My warm thanks to my friends in Marks and Spencer, Amoco and the Johnson Matthey Group for their generous help in providing these forms, which I am confident will be of considerable value to readers. Part 4 contains a procedural agreement between Unigate Foods Ltd, the Transport and General Workers' Union and the Union of Shop, Distributive and Allied Workers for the provision of facilities to safety representatives. I should like to thank the Company and these Trade Unions for their kind permission to reproduce this agreement.

Part One

Marks and Spencer Ltd

Form 1 Application form — non-management staff

CONFIDENTIAL **MARKS AND SPENCER APPLICATION FORM**

POSITION APPLIED FOR:

SURNAME (Block Letters)
Mr. Mrs. Miss

Date of Application

MAIDEN NAME (if married)

Date of Birth

FORENAMES

Nationality

Please tick as applicable

SINGLE MARRIED

WIDOWED DIVORCED

ADDRESS

Age of Children:

Telephone No.

EMPLOYMENT
Reference to present employer will not be made without your permission.

NAME AND ADDRESS OF PRESENT EMPLOYER:

Date Started Salary:
Nature of Work
Reason for Wishing to Leave

NAME AND ADDRESS OF PREVIOUS EMPLOYER	DATES FROM/TO	NATURE OF WORK	REASON FOR LEAVING	SALARY

PERSONAL REFERENCE - Please give the names and addresses of two people unrelated to you, who would give you a personal reference.

Name
Address

Occupation

Name
Address

Occupation

(Continued)

(Continued)

If you are still at, or have just left school/college, please give the name and initials of your Head Teacher/Tutor and the name and address of your school/college.

If you have passed any examinations give details:

Have you been employed with this Company before: YES/NO
If YES - give details:-

Store etc. Position Held:

Dates employed:

HEALTH

Have you suffered any serious illness? YES/NO

Are you willing to undergo medical examination by the Company's Doctor? YES/NO

Are you a registered disabled person? YES/NO

TO BE COMPLETED BY APPLICANTS AS REQUIRED

Add the following:

27p	£1.99
15p	24p
18p	£7.33
___	___
22p	£2.18
7p	37p
46p	£5.42
39p	£1.15
___	___

Subtract the following:

£9.99	£10.00
- £7.50	- £3.99
___	___
£7.50	£6.99
- £2.75	- £1.45
___	___

Convert into dozens and singles -

	Dozens	Singles
47 =		
91 =		
113 =		
78 =		
62 =		

FOR MARKS AND SPENCER USE ONLY

SOURCE OF APPLICATION: Advertisement (name newspaper), Window Board, Random.

Interview Report

Holiday Arrangements:

References taken up: Date Sent Date Returned Comment

Medical: Date Time Letter Sent

Conditional offer sent:

Present employers reference: Date Sent Date Returned Comment

Offer Confirmed: Date Sent Category Salary

Employment Commence:

Training Arrangements:

Hours of Work: Monday Tuesday Wednesday Thursday Friday Saturday Total

Uniform Size:

Form 2 Invitation to interview

Marks & Spencer Ltd

Registered Office
Michael House Baker Street
London W1A 1DN
Registered No. 214436 (England & Wales)

Dear

Thank you for your application for employment with the Company.

We have arranged an interview for you at the above address on

at

Would you please confirm that this arrangement is convenient to you and bring this letter with you to the interview.

Yours sincerely,
MARKS & SPENCER LIMITED

STAFF MANAGERESS

Z40/252 - 3/77

Form 3 Store interview report

STORE INTERVIEW REPORT

Date: ______________________ Applicant's Name: ______________________

Commercial Management
Departmental Management
Warehouse Management

Store Staff Management
Office Management
Junior Management

	TICK			POINTS FOR THE FINAL SELECTION BOARD TO PROBE.
	OUT-STANDING	SATIS-FACTORY	UNSATIS-FACTORY	
1. APPEARANCE Bearing Speech				
2. VITALITY/ENTHUSIASM				
3. DRIVE/DETERMINATION				
4. SELF RELIANCE				
5. AMBITION Competitive Spirit				
6. RESILIENCE Ability to overcome difficulties and to tolerate stressfull situations				
7. LEADERSHIP Keen to accept responsibility and to organise.				
8. ADAPTABILITY Willing to: Work as part of a team Accept new ideas and methods Start at the bottom of the management ladder				

Please summarise your impressions of the candidate, commenting on particularly relevant aptitudes (e.g. Commercial Management should be sales orientated; Staff Management approachable and sensitive; Office Management numerate and analytical).

Please give dates **NOT** convenient for further interview: ________

____

Interviewer(s) ______________________

____

Store ______________________

Vote

YES/NO

Form 4 Letter of regret — after interview

St Michael®

Marks and Spencer Ltd

Registered Office
Michael House Baker Street
London W1A 1DN

Registered No. 214436 (England & Wales)
Joint Secretaries: F.C.Hirst, F.C.A. · J.H.M.Samuel, F.C.A.

Dear

We are writing to thank you for giving us the opportunity of considering your application for employment with us.

We have considered your application and regret to inform you that we are unable to offer you a suitable position.

May I take this opportunity to wish you every success in the future and to thank you for your interest in the Company.

Yours sincerely,
MARKS & SPENCER LIMITED

STAFF MANAGERESS

Form 5 Request for medical examination

Marks and Spencer Ltd

Registered Office
Michael House Baker Street
London W1A 1DN

Registered No. 214436 (England & Wales)
Joint Secretaries: F.C Hirst, F.C.A. · J.H.M Samuel, F.C.A.

Dear

In connection with your recent interview for employment we would like you to have a medical examination which will be carried out by the Store Doctor.

We have arranged an appointment for you

on at at

Would you please confirm that you will be able to attend for this medical. Please bring your spectacles if you wear them and a specimen of urine with you to this examination.

Yours sincerely,
MARKS & SPENCER LIMITED

STAFF MANAGERESS

Form 6 Medical examination report

MARKS & SPENCER LTD. HEALTH SERVICES

Store ______________________________

To: ______________________________

M ______________________________

Job applied for ______________________________
is attending for a pre-employment medical examination as arranged with you.

Date ____________________ Time ____________

Signed ____________________

- -

TO : MARKS & SPENCER LTD.

Store: ______________________________

I have examined M ______________________________

Job Applied for ______________________________

and certify him/her as being of ____________ category

Comments ______________________________
____
____
____
____
____
____

Signed ____________________

Z40/154-2/77 Date ____________________

Form 7 Letter of regret — no vacancies

St Michael®

Marks and Spencer Ltd

Registered Office
Michael House Baker Street
London W1A 1DN

Registered No. 214436 (England & Wales)
Joint Secretaries: F.C.Hirst, F.C.A. - J.H.M.Samuel, F.C.A.

Dear

Thank you for your letter enquiring about employment with this Company.

We regret that we have no vacancies at present and as we do not foresee any in the immediate future we are unable to help you with your request.

Thank you, however, for writing to us.

Yours sincerely,
MARKS & SPENCER LIMITED

STAFF MANAGERESS

Form 8 Letter of regret — no vacancies at present

Marks and Spencer Ltd

MARBLE ARCH, 458 OXFORD STREET,
LONDON, W1A OAP.
Telephone: 01-486 6151 & 01-935 7954

Registered Office
Michael House Baker Street
London W1A 1DN

Registered No. 214436 (England & Wales)
Joint Secretaries: F.C.Hirst, F.C.A. - J.H.M.Samuel, F.C.A.

Thank you for your application for a position with this company.

We regret we do not have a suitable vacancy at the present time to offer you, but will file your application for future reference.

Yours faithfully

STAFF MANAGERESS

Form 9 Reference for school leaver requested

St Michael®

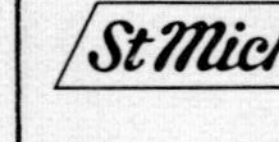

Marks and Spencer Ltd

Registered Office
Michael House Baker Street
London W1A 1DN

Registered No. 214436 (England & Wales)
Joint Secretaries: F.C.Hirst, F.C.A. - J.H.M.Samuel, F.C.A.

Dear

The above has applied to us for employment as a
after leaving school, and has given your name as a referee.

It would be helpful if you would let us have your opinion of the applicant's ability and character, together with any additional comments, including one about attendance, which would assist us in considering his/her application for employment with us and in determining possible future development.

Thank you for your assistance. Your reply will be treated in the strictest confidence.

A stamped addressed envelope is enclosed.

Yours faithfully,
MARKS & SPENCER LIMITED

STAFF MANAGERESS

Form 10 Personal reference requested

St Michael®

Marks and Spencer Ltd

Registered Office
Michael House Baker Street
London W1A 1DN

Registered No. 214436 (England & Wales)
Joint Secretaries: F.C.Hirst, F.C.A. - J.H.M.Samuel, F.C.A.

Confidential

Dear Sir/Madam,

The above named has applied to us for a position as a
and has given us your name as a personal referee.

We should be grateful if you would let us know how long you have known the applicant, whether you know him/her to be honest, reliable and hardworking, and whether you know of any reason why we should not employ him/her.

Please use the back of this letter for your reply, with the enclosed stamped addressed envelope.

Thank you for your assistance. Your reply will be treated in the strictest confidence.

Yours faithfully,
MARKS & SPENCER LIMITED

STAFF MANAGERESS

Form 11 Reference requested and questionnaire

St Michael®

Marks and Spencer Ltd

Registered Office
Michael House Baker Street
London W1A 1DN

Registered No. 214436 (England & Wales)
Joint Secretaries: F.C.Hirst, F.C.A. - J.H.M.Samuel, F.C.A.

CONFIDENTIAL

Dear Sir/Madam,

The above-named person has applied to us for employment as a
and has given us your name as a referee.

We should be grateful if you would answer the questions set out on the reverse of this letter and return it to us in the enclosed stamped addressed envelope.

Thank you very much for your assistance. Your reply will be treated in the strictest confidence.

Yours faithfully,
MARKS & SPENCER LIMITED

STAFF MANAGERESS

Are the following particulars correct?

Name
Employed at
From
To
As
Salary
Reason for Leaving

Is the applicant to the best of your knowledge

Honest

Reliable

Hard-working

Punctual

Do you know of any reason why we should not employ her/him?

Any general comments you may care to make -

Date

Signed ....

Position Held ....

Form 12 Conditional offer — subject to reference

/St Michael®/

Marks and Spencer Ltd

Registered Office
Michael House Baker Street
London W1A 1DN

Registered No. 214436 (England & Wales)
Joint Secretaries: F.C.Hirst, F.C.A. - J.H.M.Samuel, F.C.A

Dear

With reference to your recent interview for employment at this store we are pleased to make you a conditional offer of employment as a

at a salary of £ per
of £ per . This offer is subject to our receiving a satisfactory reference from your present employer.

Would you please confirm that we may contact your present employer for a reference.

Yours sincerely,
MARKS & SPENCER LIMITED

STAFF MANAGERESS

FROM:

I confirm that you may approach my present employer for a reference in connection with this conditional offer of employment.

Signed .... Date ....

Form 13 Conditional offer of part-time employment — subject to reference

Marks and Spencer Ltd

Registered Office Registered No. 214436 (England & Wales)

MICHAEL HOUSE BAKER STREET LONDON W1A 1DN

Telephone 01-935 4422
Telegrams Marspenza London
Telex Number 267141

Joint Secretaries: F.C.Hirst, F.C.A.- J.H.M.Samuel, F.C.A.

Dear

With reference to your recent application for employment at this store we are pleased to make you a conditional offer of employment as a
at an hourly rate of p, plus a supplement of p per hour.
As discussed with you we wish you to work the following hours:-

Monday
Tuesday
Wednesday
Thursday
Friday
Saturday

giving a weekly total, exclusive of refreshment breaks, of hours.

This offer is subject to our receiving a satisfactory reference from your present employer.

Would you please confirm that we may contact your present employer for a reference.

Yours sincerely,
MARKS & SPENCER LIMITED

STAFF MANAGERESS

FROM :

I confirm that you may approach my present employer for a reference in connection with this conditional offer of employment.

Signed ______________________________ Date __________

St Michael®

Marks and Spencer Ltd

Registered Office
Michael House Baker Street
London W1A 1DN

Registered No. 214436 (England & Wales)
Joint Secretaries: F.C.Hirst, F.C.A.- J.H.M.Samuel, F.C.A.

Dear

We are now pleased to confirm our offer of employment as a

for hours per week at an hourly rate of
of per hour. Your agreed minimum hours will be per week exclusive of refreshment breaks. Initially your hours of work will be:-

Monday	Thursday
Tuesday	Friday
Wednesday	Saturday

giving a weekly total of hours exclusive of refreshment breaks.

It may be necessary, on occasions, to ask you to work extra hours but these would be arranged with you on a week to week basis.

Your employment will commence on
at

I would be grateful if you would sign and return the perforated section of this letter informing us whether or not you wish to accept this offer of employment. If you accept please bring your National Insurance number and, if you have one, your P.45 Tax form when you report to the store.

I look forward to meeting you and would like to take this opportunity to welcome you to the Company.

Yours sincerely,
MARKS & SPENCER LIMITED

STAFF MANAGERESS

- -

FROM:

I accept/do not accept the offer of employment detailed in your letter
of and will commence employment on
at

Signed ______________________________ Date ______________

If you accept this offer please state your Dress/Jacket/Trouser size.

Form 15 Offer of full-time employment

Marks & Spencer Ltd

Registered Office
Michael House Baker Street
London W1A 1DN
Registered Number 214436 (England)

Dear

We are now pleased to confirm our offer of employment as

at a salary of £ per , plus £ supplement per
Your employment will commence on
at

I would be grateful if you would sign and return the perforated section of this letter informing us whether or not you wish to accept this offer of employment. If you accept please bring your National Insurance number, and if you have one, your P.45 Tax form with you when you report to the store.

I look forward to meeting you and would like to take this opportunity to welcome you to the Company.

Yours sincerely,
MARKS & SPENCER LIMITED

STAFF MANAGERESS

FROM:

I accept/do not accept the offer of employment detailed in your letter of and will commence employment on
at

Signed ______________________________ Date ____________

If you accept this offer please state your Dress/Jacket/Trouser size.

Form 16 Management application form

CONFIDENTIAL

MARKS & SPENCER LTD.,
PERSONNEL GROUP,
MICHAEL HOUSE, BAKER ST.
LONDON, W1A 1DN.

Application Form

Please state Marks & Spencer career(s) applied for:

Please complete this form fully and carefully. It will be used in making an initial assessment of your application

Surname (BLOCK CAPITALS)	*Maiden name (if applicable)*
Forenames	
Address *Telephone*	*Dates available at this address* *From* *To*
Permanent address (if different from above) *Telephone*	*Dates available at this address* *From* *To*

Date of birth	
Nationality	
National Insurance No.	
Please tick as applicable *SINGLE ENGAGED MARRIED* *WIDOWED SEPARATED DIVORCED*	
Children	
Sex	*Date of birth*
Are you willing to undergo a medical examination? YES/NO	

EDUCATION

Secondary Schools	*Dates* *From*	*To*	*Examinations taken or to be taken. Please list the subjects/options with grades attained.*	*Dates*
Further Education (University/Polytechnic/College)			*(Please give details of any higher qualifications obtained or to be taken)*	
If you are proficient in any Foreign Language please give details.				

(Continued)

(Continued)

EMPLOYMENT

Employer's name and address and type of business.	Dates From	To	Positions held and nature of responsibility	Reasons for wishing to change employment	Salary and emoluments
(Include vacation employment) Present (A reference will be taken up, but only with your permission)					
Previous					

REFEREE

Please give the name and address of your Tutor/Principal if you are about to, or have recently, completed your education. If you are employed, the name and position of your Referee.

LEISURE INTERESTS

Sports/Social/Artistic/Intellectual - with attainments or official positions held.

SOURCE OF APPLICATION

Please indicate the source of your application

Press Advertisement Name and Date:

Marks and Spencer Employee

Name: Position:

Other Sources

Have you applied to Marks and Spencer before? YES/NO

If yes please give details

Please state your nearest Marks and Spencer Store

Signature ______________________ Date ______________________

(Continued)

MARKS AND SPENCER LIMITED **NAME** ____________________

1. *What have been your major achievements in recent years and why do you consider them to be significant?*

2. *To be successful in Management, you must be able to accept responsibility, to lead, organise and innovate. In what way have you been able to demonstrate these abilities?*

(Continued)

(Continued)

3. *How are you approaching the question of a future career, and what attracts you to Marks and Spencer?*

4. *A progressive career generally requires that you are free to take up promotional opportunities wherever they occur. Will this be feasible for you? If not, give details of the degree of your personal mobility.*

Signature ______________________ *Date* ______________________

Form 17 Store management final selection board report

STORE MANAGEMENT FINAL SELECTION BOARD REPORT

PRE-SELECTION STORE ____________ DATE ____________ NAME ____________

	OUTSTANDING	SATISFACTORY	UNSATISFACTORY
VITALITY/ENTHUSIASM			
DRIVE/DETERMINATION			
SELF RELIANCE			
AMBITION			
RESILIENCE			
LEADERSHIP			
ADAPTABILITY			

COMMERCIAL
DEPARTMENTAL
STAFF
OFFICE
WAREHOUSE
JUNIOR
CATERING

REPORT OF FINAL INTERVIEW

INTERVIEWER(S) :

PLACEMENT RECOMMENDATION

STARTING SALARY	AREA OF PREFERENCE

B/F DATE ____________

PERSONAL REFERENCES	AVAILABILITY DATE
BUSINESS REFERENCES	
MEDICAL	
CONDITIONAL OFFER/OFFER	STARTING DATE
WITHDRAWAL/ACCEPTANCE	
REFERENCE FROM PRESENT EMPLOYER	STORE

Form 18 Appraisal form — sales floor

CONFIDENTIAL

APPRAISAL FORM

SALES FLOOR

DATE OF ENGAGEMENT ______________________ NAME ______________________

DATE OF APPOINTMENT ______________________ CATEGORY ______________________

DATE OF REPORT ______________________ DEPARTMENT ______________________

ANALYSIS OF PERFORMANCE

- Tick only where appropriate to the individual.
- 'Satisfactory' is a level of performance acceptable to the Company
- 'Comments - Recommendations' may be used at the discretion of the writer
- Criticism must be detailed in 'Comments' to explain an 'Unsatisfactory' rating.

SERVICE	OUT-STANDING	VERY GOOD	SATIS-FACTORY	UNSATIS-FACTORY
Positive attitude to selling				
General helpfulness to customers				
Dealing with customer problems and complaints				

COMMENTS – RECOMMENDATIONS

COMMERCIAL KNOWLEDGE AND APPLICATION				
Knowledge of merchandise				
Knowledge of departmental sales				
Ability to react to sales and stock position				
Are the displays proportionate ?				
Attention to quality control				

COMMENTS – RECOMMENDATIONS

SHRINKAGE CONTROL				
Attention to correct cash, till, refund and receipt procedures				
Alertness to security and theft				
Control and recording of known losses				
Accuracy of pricing, I/DLs etc.				
Attention to Checking List compilation				

COMMENTS – RECOMMENDATIONS

ORGANISATION OF SECTION				
Attention to stock ordering				
Control of stock collection				
Organisation of staffing				
Ability to plan ahead/establish priorities				

COMMENTS – RECOMMENDATIONS

(Continued)

(Continued)

HEALTH AND SAFETY	OUT-STANDING	VERY GOOD	SATIS-FACTORY	UNSATIS-FACTORY
Accident Prevention				
Maintenance of Hygiene standards				
Attention to Fire Precautions				

COMMENTS – RECOMMENDATIONS

COMMUNICATION AND LIAISON				
Communication				
Awareness of current developments within store				
Communication to Head Office, e.g. memos, trial lines				
Liaison with other Sections				

COMMENTS – RECOMMENDATIONS

TRAINING AND DEVELOPMENT				
Ability and interest in training others				
Ability to appraise staff and assess training needs				
Follow up of training needs				
Ability to plan and take training sessions				

COMMENTS – RECOMMENDATIONS

OTHER QUALITIES				
Personal relationships				
Ability to work effectively under pressure				
Ability to work unsupervised				
Punctuality and Attendance				
Management attitude				
Judgment and decision making				
Drive and determination				
Ability to motivate staff				

COMMENTS – RECOMMENDATIONS

SUMMARY OF ASSESSMENT – using the completed analysis section

SUMMARY OF DISCUSSION

Report written by: ______________________ Report read by: ______________________

Interviewed by: ______________________ Date: ______________________

Form 19 Appraisal form — management and supervisory staff

CONFIDENTIAL

APPRAISAL FORM

MANAGEMENT AND SUPERVISORY STAFF

DATE OF ENGAGEMENT (Stores – Trainee Cats. Only)

NAME

DATE OF REPORT

CATEGORY

STORE/DEPARTMENT

SUMMARY OF ASSESSMENT

Summarise the individual's performance from the completed Analysis section overleaf.

RECOMMENDATIONS

How can performance be improved?
What further training is required?

SUMMARY OF INTERVIEW

Report written by: ______________________

Report read by: ______________________

Date ______________________

A copy of this appraisal may be given to the individual, on request.

For Divisional comment on Head Office Administered Store Staff

(Continued)

(Continued)

ANALYSIS OF PERFORMANCE

This section should be completed before writing the summary and used as a check list to ensure that no aspect of performance is overlooked.

JUDGEMENT AND DECISION MAKING
DRIVE AND DETERMINATION
PERSONAL RELATIONSHIPS
ABILITY TO (a) PRODUCE CONSTRUCTIVE IDEAS
(b) PLAN
(c) ORGANISE
(d) MOTIVATE
(e) COMMUNICATE
(f) WORK UNDER PRESSURE
(g) TRAIN AND DEVELOP STAFF
(h) ASSESS PEOPLE

Part Two

Amoco (UK) Ltd

Introductory notes to AMOCO contracts of employment

These Amoco (UK) Ltd contracts of employment contain certain references to company policy statements — including: Holiday Policy; Sickness and Disability Benefits Policy; Disciplinary Procedures; Conflicts of Interest; Use of Company Information; and Safety Policy. These contracts of employment should be read in conjunction with the policy statements which follow. In the case of part-time employees the contract of employment is varied in accordance with the terms of Form 8.

Form 1 Requisition for personnel

REQUISITION FOR PERSONNEL

REQUISITION

Department ______ Section ______ Location ______

Title Classification of Job to be filled ______

☐ New Job ☐ Replacement Cost Centre ______ Date Required ______

Duties and Responsibilities: ______

______

Reason not filled by promotion: ______

Reason for new job or replacement: ______

Maximum Starting Rate recommended per annum: £ ______

Approved Salary Rate Range Minimum: £ ______ Maximum: ______ per annum

Salary Classification Number : ______ Date employment will terminate (if for definite period) ______

Person who last filled job (omit if new job)

______ Title Classification: ______

Basic salary rate per annum £ ______

Requested by: Approved by:

______ ______ ______ ______

AUTHORIZATION

Authorized Maximum Starting Salary - Basic Salary per annum £ ______

Authorized by: ______ ______ ______

Title Date

REPORT OF HIRING

Position Filled by: ☐ Married ☐ Single

______ ______

Surname First Middle Title Classification

Home address: ______

Telephone Number: ______ Date of birth : ______

Date commenced work: ______ Salary per annum: ______

If rate is above minimum for salary range, or is greater than that paid to previous employee please explain: ______

______

Person hired informed that employment is ☐ Permanent ☐ Temporary ______ ☐ Full Time ☐ Part Time ______

______ ______ ______

Supervisor Date hours p.w.

AUTHORIZATION

Authorized by:

______ ______

______

Date

Form 2 Application for employment

Name of Applicant______________________________

Position Applied for______________________________

Surname	Christian Name(s)				Mr. Mrs. Miss
Address					Heigh
					Weigh
Telephone Number	Nationality	Date of Birth		Married Single	No. of Children
Trade/Profession/Occupation	Salary Expected	Current U.K. Driving Licence?	Class of Licence	Details of Endorsements	
Date of Availability	Would you be prepared to move if necessary	Languages Spoken, (other than English)			

Employment History (give full address of last employer, as, if position is accepted, references will be applied for)

Dates		Name and Address of Employer	Type of Business	Position Held
From	To			

Full Time Education – After age 11

Dates		School/College/University	Subjects Studied	Exams Passed/Diploma/Degre
From	To			

ave you any Relations nployed by this Company?	If Yes, give name & work location	
ame of next of kin		Relationship
ddress		
ave you been required to be bonded y a Fidelity Guarantee Company?	If Yes, give details	
etails of any major operations		
re you a Registered Disabled Person Yes/No		
so state Registration No. and Date		

Attach Recent Photograph If Available

Brief Statement of Duties	Salary		Reason for Leaving	Name & Title of Supervisor
	Joining	Leaving		

rt-Time Education/Courses Attended

Dates		Organisation	Subject of Course	Course Result
From	To			

I understand that any offer of employment made by Amoco (UK) Limited is subject to the receipt of satisfactory references, and a medical examination to be carried out by an appointed Doctor.

I certify that the information given on this application is true and correct.

Applicant's Signature ______________ Date ______________ 197

(Continued)

(Continued)

THIS PAGE IS FOR USE BY AMOCO

Remarks

Interviewed by: ______ Date: ______

Position Offered ______

Commencement Date ______ Commencing Salary £ ______ Class ______

Authorised by: ______

Salary Range

Min. £ ______

Date: ______ Mid. £ ______

Max. £ ______

Form 3 Pre-employment medical examination

Amoco (U.K.) Limited
Registered Office:
1 Olympic Way
Wembley Middlesex HA9 0ND
Telephone: 01-902 8820
Cables: Amointe Wembley
Telex: 264433
Registration No: 233067—England

Directors:
J. A. Parker (U.S.A.)
A. W. Lyckman (U.S.A.)
E. C. S. Northcote
F. G. Andrusko (U.S.A.)
G. W. Skinner
W. P. Havers

Dear

PRE-EMPLOYMENT MEDICAL EXAMINATION

Arrangements for the above have been made with our Company Doctor, Dr ______________________ Wimpole Street, London, W1., and we should appreciate your attending at the time and date indicated below:

For convenience, a map of the area is printed on the reverse of this letter.

Yours sincerely,

V. A. HOLLOWAY (Mrs.)
Employee Relations Department

Form 4 Previous employer's reference

Amoco (U.K.) Limited
Registered Office:
1 Olympic Way
Wembley Middlesex HA9 0ND
Telephone: 01-902 8820
Cables: Amointe Wembley
Telex: 264433
Registration No: 233067— England

Directors:
J. A. Parker (U.S.A.)
A. W. Lyckman (U.S.A.)
E. C. S. Northcote
F. G. Andrusko (U.S.A.)
G. W. Skinner
W. P. Havers

PRIVATE & CONFIDENTIAL

The above named has applied to us for employment as a

and states that he has been employed by you as follows:-

Position:

From:

To:

Salary:

It will greatly assist us in assessing the suitability of this applicant if you will kindly answer the questionnaire overleaf as frankly as possible and return it to us in the enclosed stamped addressed envelope. The duplicate copy is for your records. Any information which you give us will, of course, be treated in confidence.

Yours sincerely,

B. E. Mills
Personnel Officer

BEM/prl
Encs.

(Continued)

(Continued)

QUESTIONNAIRE

In Confidence and Without Responsibility

Name: ______________________________

1. Can you confirm the information given overleaf?

2. Reason for leaving?

3. How do you rate the applicant in regard to:-

	Very Good	Good	Average	Poor	Very Poor
(a) Ability					
(b) Character					
(c) Conduct					
(d) Attention to duties					
(e) Initiative					

4. Was applicant honest?

5. Did applicant co-operate well with all staff?

6. Was applicant's health good?

7. Would you re-employ?

8. Is there any other information that a prospective employer should know?

Signature: ____________________ Position: ____________________

Date: ____________________

Form 5 Contract of employment for 'twice monthly' (Head Office, etc.) Staff

Amoco (U.K.) Limited
Registered Office:
1 Olympic Way
Wembley Middlesex HA9 0ND
Telephone: 01-902 8820
Cables: Amointe Wembley
Telex: 264433
Registration No: 233067—England

Directors:
J. A. Parker (U.S.A.)
A. W. Lyckman (U.S.A.)
E. C. S. Northcote
G. M. Nickson
F. G. Andrusko (U.S.A.)
G. W. Skinner

Dear

CONTRACT OF EMPLOYMENT

This confirms your position on the staff of Amoco (U.K.) Limited and supersedes any previous Contract of Employment issued. Your terms and conditions of employment are as follows:

1. Present Job Title:

The position for which you are engaged is entitled but Amoco may at its discretion require you to undertake other duties which in its opinion you are capable of discharging.

2. Effective Date of Job Title:

3. Continuous Service Date:

You will be deemed to have continuous service (which includes service with any other Amoco Company) from

4. Location:

5. Hours of Work:

Your normal hours of work are hours per week spread over five days from Monday to Friday

These normal hours may be varied at the discretion of the Company to suit local practice.

6. Remuneration:

Your salary is at the rate of £ per annum payable semi-monthly in arrears. The Company effects payment by credit transfer direct into your bank account. If you have not already supplied the Company with details of your bank, please complete and return the attached Credit Transfer Slip. You will be provided with an itemised pay statement showing inter alia gross pay, all allowances, all deductions and the full net amount payable.

7. Luncheon Vouchers:

a) Luncheon Vouchers are issued to eligible employees at

(Continued)

the rate of £1.00 per day worked of which 85p is taxable under present Government regulations.

b) If your post is such that you work from home you are permitted to claim £1.00 per day worked within your Monthly Expense Report (Form 36).

When an employee is transferred to another location or to other duties the Company may suspend the issue of Luncheon Vouchers or the payment or luncheon allowances in respect of periods when the employee is being otherwise provided with meals.

8. Overtime:

Due to the nature of our business you may be required to work a reasonable amount of overtime.

You are/are not eligible for payment of overtime hours worked in accordance with the Company's overtime policy.

9. Probationary Term:

During the first three months of service with the Company your employment will be probationary and during this period the contract may be terminated by one week's notice on either side.

10. Company Car:

If your post is such that you are to be provided with a Company motor vehicle for use in connection with Company business, you should forward your valid driving licence to this office for perusal. An advance will be paid to you as soon as you take up your duties to cover approved expenses incurred on Company business and in connection with the Company car. The amount of this advance will be determined by your Divisional Manager.

11. Notice of Termination of Service:

a) Period of Notice

Notice of termination of service by either party shall be given in writing. The length of such notice shall depend on the length of continuous service. The employee shall be entitled to the following notice:-

Length of Continuous Service	Notice Period
Less than 3 months	1 week
3 months - 4 years	1 month
4 years - 8 years	2 months
8 years and over	3 months

The employee shall give the Company one month's notice or one week if his service is less than 3 months.

i) The period of notice may be waived either in whole or in part by mutual arrangement.

ii) Payment of salary in lieu of notice may be made at the Company's discretion.

iii) Subject only to any statutory requirements or restrictions to the contrary, the service of the employee may be summarily terminated by the Company without notice or payment in lieu of notice by reason of any conduct on the part of the employee which, in Amoco's opinion, justifies summary dismissal.

b) Retirement:

An employee on attaining normal retirement age (65 for men, 60 for women) is subject to automatic retirement effective the last day of the calendar month in which that birthday occurs without the giving or receiving of any notice to this effect.

12. Maternity:

A pregnant employee who has been employed for two years or more and who continues to work until the 11th week preceding the expected date of confinement is entitled to reinstatement in the same or a similar position up to a maximum of 29 weeks following the confinement. Any employee who wishes to exercise the right to reinstatement must notify Amoco in writing of her intention to return to work at least 3 weeks before the beginning of her maternity leave, and at least one week before the day on which she proposes to return to work. A medical certificate stating the expected date of confinement may be required by Amoco. The date of returning to work may be delayed for a maximum of 4 weeks on provision of a medical certificate by the employee, or by notification in writing specifying the reasons for the postponement by Amoco.

13. Pension Plan:

The Company provides a contributory pension plan as described in the booklet enclosed with these conditions of service.

14. Term of Contract:

The Contract of Employment is for an indefinite term, subject to paragraph 11(b) above (automatic retirement).

15. Occupational Accident Insurance:

The Company maintains an insurance policy under which a payment of three times basic annual salary will be made in the event of death or permanent disability, (i.e. loss of hand or foot or use thereof, or sight of

(Continued)

one eye) or any total and permanent disablement, as a result of an accident occuring whilst the employee is engaged in or travelling on company business. However, normal travel between home and place of work is not covered under this policy. This payment will be in addition to any sum which becomes due as a result of membership of the Amoco Pension Plan, but must be taken into account in any claim against the Company arising from the accident. The Company reserves its discretion as to keeping up such insurance.

16. Holidays:

Your entitlement to holidays is as laid down in the Holiday Policy, a copy of which is attached to this letter.

17. Sickness:

Whilst it is not the Company's policy to pay salary or wage as of right during absence, the Company nevertheless makes payment on an ex gratia basis, according to length of service, in accordance with the Company's Sickness and Disability Benefits Policy a copy of which is attached to this letter.

18. Disciplinary Procedures:

A copy of the Company's policy on disciplinary procedures is attached to this letter and forms part of your Contract of Employment.

19. Conflicts of Interest:

A copy of the Company's policy on conflicts of interest is attached to this letter and forms part of your Contract of Employment.

20. Health and Safety at Work etc. Act 1974:

The Company's policy statement on safety at work is attached to this letter and forms part of your Contract of Employment.

21. Grievance Procedure:

Employees shall have the right at any time within 21 working days after an incident out of which any grievance arises to seek redress. The procedure which the Company will continue to operate is as follows:-

a) The employee shall first make his grievance known to and discuss it witn his immediate supervisor.

b) If the grievance is not satisfactorily resolved within five working days from the date it has been taken up, a written statement recording the facts of the grievance and the outcome of the discussion shall be prepared by the employee, agreed by his immediate supervisor and referred by the employee to the next ranking supervisor. In the event of any disagreement as to the content of the written statement, separate versions shall be prepared and referred to that supervisor.

c) If no satisfactory settlement is reached within five working days after taking the action described in (b), a similar record (or records) shall be prepared for reference by the employee to the Department Head concerned.

d) If the grievance remains unsatisfied under (c), within a further period of five working days, a further record shall be prepared and the employee may appeal with such records to the Employee Relations Manager.

e) If the grievance remains unsatisfied under (d) within a further period of five working days of stating the case, the employee may appeal in writing to the Managing Director of the Company or in the event of his absence, his designated deputy, whose decision or award shall be final and conclusive.

22. Your appointment is subject to:-

a) The receipt by the Company of a satisfactory medical report from its Medical Advisor.

b) The receipt of satisfactory references from the companies and persons named on your Application for Employment Form.

23. You should report for duty to
at a.m. on

24. Will you please sign and date the attached copy of this Contract as your acceptance of these terms and conditions and acknowledgement that you have received the attachments.

Should you require further information on or explanation of the foregoing you should request it from either your Supervisor or the Employee Relations Department.

Yours sincerely,

B. E. MILLS
Personnel Officer Signed:........................

Encs: (7) Date:..........................

1. Credit Transfer Authority Form
2. Pension Plan Booklet + attachments
3. Amoco Holiday Policy
4. Amoco Sickness and Disability Benefits Policy
5. Disciplinary Procedures - Amoco Policy Statement
6. Amoco Conflicts of Interest Policy
7. Health & Safety at Work - Amoco Policy Statement

Amoco (U.K.) Limited
Registered Office:
1 Olympic Way
Wembley Middlesex HA9 0ND
Telephone: 01-902 8820
Cables: Amointe Wembley
Telex: 264433
Registration No: 233067—England

Dear

CONTRACT OF EMPLOYMENT

This confirms your position on the staff of Amoco (U.K.) Limited and supersedes any previous Contract of Employment issued. Your terms and conditions of employment are as follows:

1. Present Job Title:

   The position for which you are engaged is entitled but Amoco may at its discretion require you to undertake other duties which in its opinion you are capable of discharging.

2. Effective Date of Job Title:

3. Continuous Service Date:

   You will be deemed to have continuous service (which includes service with any other Amoco Company) from

4. Location:

5. Remuneration:

   Your rate of pay is per hour payable weekly. You will be provided with an itemised pay statement showing inter alia gross pay, all allowances all deductions and the full net amount payable.

6. Hours of Work:

   You are required to work 42 hours per week in shifts as arranged by your Service Station Manager spread over 7 days.

7. Overtime:

   Due to the nature of our business you may be required to work a reasonable amount of overtime.

(Continued)

(Continued)

You are eligible for payment of overtime hours worked in accordance with the following:

First 2 hours worked in excess of 42 hours will be paid at 1 1/3 times your basic hourly rate of pay. Hours worked in excess of 44 hours will be paid at 1½ times your basic hourly rate of pay.

Hours worked on a Sunday which is outside of your normal shift pattern will be paid at twice your basic hourly rate of pay.

8. Probationary Term:

During the first three months of service with the Company your employment will be probationary and during this period the Contract may be terminated by one week's notice on either side.

9. Notice of Termination of Service:

a) Period of Notice

Notice of termination of service by either party shall be given in writing. The length of such notice shall depend on the length of continuous service. The employee shall be entitled to the following notice:-

Length of Continuous Service	Notice Period
Less than 2 years	1 week

Then 1 week's notice for each completed year up to a maximum of 12 weeks notice.

The employee shall give the Company 1 week's notice.

i) The period of notice may be waived either in whole or in part by mutual arrangement.

ii) Payment of wages in lieu of notice may be given at the Company's discretion.

iii) Subject only to any statutory requirements or restrictions to the contrary, the service of the employee may be summarily terminated by the Company without notice or payment in lieu of notice by reason of any conduct on the part of the employee which, in the Company's opinion justifies summary dismissal.

b) Retirement:

An employee on attaining normal retirement age (65 for men, 60 for women) is subject to automatic retirement effective the last day of the calendar month in which that birthday occurs without the giving or receiving of any notice to this effect.

(Continued)

10. Maternity:

A pregnant employee who has been employed for two years or more and who continues to work until the 11th week preceding the expected date of confinement is entitled to reinstatement in the same or a similar position up to a maximum of 29 weeks following the confinement. Any employee who wishes to exercise the right to reinstatement must notify Amoco in writing of her intention to return to work at least 3 weeks before the beginning of her maternity leave, and at least one week before the day on which she proposes to return to work. A medical certificate stating the expected date of confinement may be required by Amoco. The date of returning to work may be delayed for a maximum of 4 weeks on provision of a medical certificate by the employee, or by notification in writing specifying the reasons for the postponement by Amoco.

11. Term of Contract:

The Contract of Employment is for an indefinite term, subject to paragraph 9(b) above (automatic retirement).

12. Occupational Accident Insurance:

The Company maintains an insurance policy under which a payment of three times basic annual wage will be made in the event of death of permanent disability, (i.e. loss of hand or foot or use thereof, or sight of one eye) or any total and permanent disablement, as a result of an accident occuring whilst the employee is engaged in or travelling on company business. However, normal travel between home and place of work is not covered under this policy. This payment must be taken into account in any claim against the Company arising from the accident. The Company reserves its discretion as to keeping up such insurance.

13. Holidays:

Your entitlement to holidays is as laid down in the Holiday Policy a copy of which is attached to this letter.

14. Sickness:

Whilst it is not the Company's policy to pay salary or wage as of right during absence, the Company nevertheless makes payment on an ex gratia basis, according to length of service, in accordance with the Company's Sickness and Disability Benefits Policy a copy of which is attached to this letter.

15. Pension Plan:

You are not eligible to join the Amoco Pension Plan.

16. Disciplinary Procedures:

A copy of the Company's policy on disciplinary procedures is attached to this letter and forms part of your Contract of Employment.

17. Conflicts of Interest:

A copy of the Company's policy on conflicts of interest is attached to this letter and forms part of your Contract of Employment.

18. Health & Safety at Work etc. Act 1974:

The Company's policy statement on safety at work is attached to this letter and forms part of your Contract of Employment.

19. Grievance Procedure:

Employees shall have the right at any time within 21 working days after an incident out of which any grievance arises to seek redress. The procedure which the Company will continue to operate is as follows:-

a) The employee shall first make his grievance known to and discuss it with his immediate supervisor.

b) If the grievance is not satisfactorily resolved within five working days from the date it has been taken up, a written statement recording the facts of the grievance and the outcome of the discussion shall be prepared by the employee, agreed by his immediate supervisor and referred by the employee to the next ranking supervisor. In the event of any disagreement as to the content of the written statement, separate versions shall be prepared and referred to that supervisor.

c) If no satisfactory settlement is reached within five working days after taking the action described in (b), a similar record (or records) shall be prepared for reference by the employee to the Department Head concerned.

d) If the grievance remains unsatisfied under (c), within a further period of five working days, a further record shall be prepared and the employee may appeal with such records to the Employee Relations Manager.

e) If the grievance remains unsatisfied under (d) within a further period of five working days of stating the case, the employee may appeal in writing to the Managing Director of the Company or in the event of his absence, his designated deputy, whose decision or award shall be final and conclusive.

(Continued)

(Continued)

20. Your appointment is subject to the receipt of satisfactory references from the companies and persons named on your Application for Employment Form.

21. You should report for duty to
    at a.m. on

22. Will you please sign and date the attached copy of this Contract as your acceptance of these terms and conditions and acknowledgement that you have received the attachments.

Should you require further information on or explanation of the foregoing you should request it from either your supervisor or the Employee Relations Department.

Yours sincerely,

B.E. Mills
Personnel Officer

Signed ....

Date ....

6 Encl:

1. Amoco Holiday Policy
2. Amoco Sickness and Disability Benefits Policy
3. Disciplinary Procedures - Amoco Policy Statement
4. Amoco Conflicts of Interest Policy
5. Health & Safety at Work - Amoco Policy Statement
6. Personnel Record Form (to be completed & return to Employee Relations Department)

Amoco (U.K.) Limited
Registered Office:
1 Olympic Way
Wembley Middlesex HA9 0ND
Telephone: 01-902 8820
Cables: Amointe Wembley
Telex: 264433
Registration No: 233067—England

Directors:
J. A. Parker (U.S.A.)
A. W. Lyckman (U.S.A)
E. C. S. Northcote
G. M. Nickson
F. G. Andrusko (U.S.A.)
G. W. Skinner

Dear

CONTRACT OF EMPLOYMENT

This confirms your position as an employee of Amoco (UK) Limited and supersedes any previous Contract of Employment issued to you.

1. Present Job Title:

   The position for which you are engaged is entitled

2. Effective Date of Job Title:

3. Continuous Service Date:

   You will be deemed to have continuous service (which includes service with any other Amoco Company) from

4. Location:

5. Renumeration:

   Your pay and allowances are at the rate established for operatives under the Agreement between Amoco (UK) Limited and the Transport and General Workers Union (hereinafter referred to as the Union Agreement). A copy of this Agreement is available for reference in the Depot/Terminal office.

6. Hours of Work:

   Hours of work and basic week are in accordance with the Union Agreement.

7. Overtime:

   In recognition of the fact that the demand for petroleum products fluctuates seasonally and that emergencies can occur which may entail overtime work, an employee will if required, work a reasonable amount of overtime and shall be paid at the rate as described in the Union Agreement, Section D1.

8. Probationary Term:

   During the first three months of service with the Company,

(Continued)

your employment will be probationary, and during the period, the Contract may be terminated by one week's notice on either side.

9. Notice of Termination of Service:

a) Period of Notice

Notice of termination of service by either party shall be given in writing. The length of such notice shall depend on the length of continuous service. The employee shall be entitled to the following notice:-

Length of Continuous Service	Notice Period
Less than 2 years	1 week

Then 1 week's notice for each completed year up to a maximum of 12 weeks notice.

The employee shall give the Company 1 week's notice.

i) The period of notice may be waived either in whole or in part by mutual arrangement.

ii) Payment of wages in lieu of notice may be given at the Company's discretion.

iii) Subject only to any statutory requirements or restrictions to the contrary, the service of the employee may be summarily terminated by the Company without notice or payment in lieu of notice by reason of any conduct on the part of the employee which, in the Company's opinion justifies summary dismissal.

b) Retirement:

An employee on attaining normal retirement age (65 for men, 60 for women) is subject to automatic retirement effective the last day of the calendar month in which that birthday occurs without the giving or receiving of any notice to this effect.

10. Pension Plan:

The Company provides a contributory Pension Plan, as described in the booklet enclosed with these conditions of service.

11. Term of Contract:

The Contract of Employment is for an indefinite term subject to paragraph 9b (automatic retirement).

12. Occupational Accident Insurance:

The Company maintains an insurance policy under which a payment of three times basic annual wage will be made in the event of death or permanent disability, (i.e. loss of

(Continued)

hand or foot or use thereof, or sight of one eye) or any total and permanent disablement, as a result of an accident occuring whilst the employee is engaged in or travelling on company business. However, normal travel between home and place of work is not covered under this policy. This payment will be in addition to any sum which becomes due as a result of membership of the Amoco Pension Plan, but must be taken into account in any claim against the Company arising from the accident. The Company reserves its discretion as to keeping up such insurance.

13. Holidays:

Your entitlement to holidays and holiday pay is as stated in the Union Agreement.

14. Sickness:

Whilst it is not the Company's policy to pay salary or wage as of right during absence, the Company nevertheless, makes payment on an ex-gratia basis in accordance with Clause D4 of the Union Agreement.

15. Conflicts of Interest:

A copy of the Company's policy on conflicts of interest is attached to this letter.

16. Trade Union Membership:

In this respect you should refer to Clause A.1 of the Union Agreement.

17. Health & Safety at Work etc. Act 1974:

The Company's policy statement on safety at work is attached to this letter.

18. Discipline:

The disciplinary rules applicable to you are specified in Clause D.10 of the Union Agreement. If you are dissatisfied with any disciplinary decision affecting you, you should follow the procedure set out in Clause A.6 of the Union Agreement.

19. Disputes Procedure:

The procedure to follow if you have a grievance is as set out in Clause A.6 of the Union Agreement.

20. Your appointment is subject to:-

a) The receipt by the Company of a satisfactory medical report from its Medical Advisor.

b) The receipt of satisfactory references from the companies and persons named on your Application for Employment Form.

(Continued)

(Continued)

21. You should report for duty to
    at a.m. on

22. Will you please sign and date the attached copy of this Contract as your acceptance of these terms and conditions and acknowledgement that you have received the attachments.

Should you require further information on or explanation of the foregoing, you should request it from either your supervisor or the Employee Relations Department.

Yours sincerely,

B. E. Mills
Personnel Officer

Encl:

1. Amoco Conflicts of Interest Policy
2. Health & Safety at Work - Amoco Policy Statement
3. Amoco Pension Plan Booklet

Form 8 Variation of contract of employment for part-time employees

Amoco (U.K.) Limited
Registered Office:
1 Olympic Way
Wembley Middlesex HA9 0ND
Telephone: 01-902 8820
Cables: Amointe Wembley
Telex: 264433
Registration No: 233067—England

Dear

PART TIME EMPLOYMENT

The detail in the attached Contract of Employment relates to full-time employees. As you are employed for less than 42 hours per week, the Company defines your employment as part-time. The following amendments to the attached Contract of Employment apply in your case.

Hours of Work

Your hours of work will be as arranged and agreed with your Service Station Manager.

Overtime

The overtime rates indicated in Section 7 will not be applicable to you until such time as you have worked a minimum of 42 hours in one week.

Holidays

Your entitlement to paid holidays will be pro-rated down to the average number of hours you work each week but will be based on the entitlement indicated in the Holiday Policy (e.g. if your average working week is 16 hours, your annual paid entitlement would be 3 x 16 hours).

Sickness

The Company's policy on sick pay is attached to the Contract of Employment but where reference is made to full pay and half pay, part-time employees will receive pay on a pro-rated basis relative to the average number of hours worked each week.

Can you confirm your acceptance of these revisions and signify this in the space provided below, along with acceptance of one copy of the Contract of Employment.

Yours sincerely,

B.E. Mills
Personnel Officer

Signed ....

Date ....

Amoco (U.K.) Limited
Registered Office:
1 Olympic Way
Wembley Middlesex HA9 OND
Telephone: 01-902 8820
Cables: Amointe Wembley
Telex: 264433
Registration No: 233067— England

Directors:
J. A. Parker (U.S.A.)
A. W. Lyckman (U.S.A.)
E. C. S. Northcote
G. M. Nickson
F. G. Andrusko (U.S.A.)
G. W. Skinner

HOLIDAY POLICY

Effective 1st January, 1978

PUBLIC HOLIDAYS

Employees are entitled to the following public and customary holidays with pay each year.

New Year's Day	Spring Bank Holiday
Good Friday	Late Summer Bank Holiday
Easter Monday	Christmas Day
May Day	Boxing Day

Other holidays will be recognised under special proclamation by the Queen.

ANNUAL HOLIDAY

1. Employees are entitled to 4 weeks paid holiday every calendar year. One week is equivalent to five work days.

2. New Employees:

   a. New employees holiday entitlements will be as per the attached scales.

3. Employees Leaving Company Service:

   a. Employees who leave the Company will be entitled to the number of days pay shown in the attached scales in lieu of holidays not taken for each month of service completed in the year of termination.

   b. Employees retiring from the Company as annuitants will receive their full holiday entitlement on retirement, less any holidays taken during that calendar year.

(Continued)

(Continued)

GENERAL RULES

Employees may take their annual holiday at any time during the current calendar year with their supervisor's approval; subject to operational requirements.

Holidays shall not be cumulative from year to year.

When a recognized public holiday occurs during an employee's annual holiday, his entitlement shall be extended by one day.

No payment will be allowed for holidays not taken, unless employment is terminated before the employee has had the opportunity of taking his holiday.

HOLIDAY SCALES

MONTH OF	JOINING	LEAVING (provided employees did not join in same calendar year)
January	20 days	0 days
February	18	2
March	16	4
April	14	6
May	12	8
June	10	10
July	8	12
August	6	14
September	4	16
October	2	18
November	0	20
December	0	20

LEAVERS IN SAME CALENDAR YEAR AS JOINING

MONTHS COMPLETED SERVICE		MONTHS COMPLETED SERVICE	
0	0 days	6	10
1	0	7	12
2	2	8	14
3	4	9	16
4	6	10	18
5	8	11	20

Amoco (U.K.) Limited
Registered Office:
1 Olympic Way
Wembley Middlesex HA9 OND
Telephone: 01-902 8820
Cables: Amointe Wembley
Telex: 264433
Registration No: 233067— England

Directors:
J. A. Parker (U.S.A.)
A. W. Lyckman (U.S.A)
E. C. S. Northcote
G. M. Nickson
F. G, Andrusko (U.S.A.)

SICKNESS AND DISABILITY BENEFITS POLICY

Effective 1st June 1976

COMPANY MEDICAL EXAMINATION

Amoco may require any employee to submit to medical examination at Amoco's expense at any time and at its absolute discretion. In any case of absence from work arising out of illness or accident, Amoco reserves the right to have its medical advisor consult the employee's Doctor in confidence concerning the disability. Where absence from work exceeds a period of one week, the employee may be required to undertake a medical examination before returning to work.

SCALE OF BENEFITS

Any employee absent from work as a result of sickness or injury will, subject to Company medical examination when required and as hereinafter provided, receive benefits in accordance with his continuous service date (which for the purpose of this condition, includes service with any of the Amoco Companies) at the full and reduced rates as detailed below:-

Period of Continuous Service	Weeks at Full Pay	Weeks at Half Pay
Less than 6 months	2	4
6 months to 5 years	13	13
5 years and over	26	26

The benefits mentioned above are provided for permanent full-time employees and are in substitution for and not in addition to salary. No benefits are payable to an employee absent from work as of right.

Full pay means pay at the employee's hourly rate including supplements, effective on the day prior to the day of absence less the amount of any benefits the employee is entitled to receive under the National Insurance or Industrial Injuries Acts, or any subsequent amendments.

(Continued)

Half pay means pay at half the employee's hourly rate including supplements effective on the day prior to the day of absence less one half of any benefits the employee is entitled to receive under the National Insurance or Industrial Injuries Acts, and any subsequent amendments.

At the expiry of eligibility to receive benefits, the employee, at the discretion of Amoco, may be placed on authorised leave of absence without pay.

When an employee has returned to work and completed six months service since the preceding period of absence, the employee shall again become eligible for maximum benefits as set forth above for any subsequent sickness absence.

A qualifying period of six months is not required following an absence due to sickness or an accident when a further absence is due to an occupational accident.

When periods of absence are intermittent and are due to the same accident or injury, such periods shall be added together in determining the period during which benefits shall be payable.

TERMINATION OF SERVICE

Nothwithstanding the foregoing, eligibility to receive sickness and disability benefit shall not affect the rights respectively of the Company to terminate the employment and the employee to resign from the Company service under the terms of paragraph 9 of the Contract of Employment.

PROCEDURES

An employee who is absent from work through sickness or injury must advise his supervisor immediately.

Before any benefits is payable, a medical certificate may be required by Amoco. Where absence is for more than three days, the employee must produce a medical certificate dated not later than the fourth day of absence and at weekly intervals thereafter. A final certificate when the employee is fit to resume work may also be required. However, a medical certificate for the first three days of absence will be required by the Department of Health and Social Security in order to qualify for the full National Insurance Sickness Benefit. It will also be the responsibility of the employee to claim any National Insurance benefit due, since the appropriate deduction will automatically be made from wages in the following pay period. If a National Health medical certificate is produced, the Company will, without accepting liability for failure to do so, pass it on to the National Insurance authorities.

(Continued)

Initial deductions from wages from an employee who is sick will be made in accordance with the flat rate benefits, plus maximum earned income supplement ruling at that date, according to the employee's family circumstances (if married or single). The employee will be required to forward to Payroll Form BS12 or covering letter which the Ministry supplies with the first sickness benefit payment setting out the weekly rate of flat rate benefits and Form BF168 or covering letter which will usually be received with the first payment of earnings related supplement after thirteen days waiting period, setting out the weekly rate of earned income allowance to be paid. Total sickness benefits for the period of sickness will be recalculated using the weekly rates shown on the Forms BS12 and BF168 (if applicable) and the total deductions from the employee's wages adjusted as necessary.

In cases of absence directly due to intoxication or to the improper use of stimulants, drugs or narcotics, or to the employees unlawful acts, or to fighting unless in self defence against unprovoked assaults, or to wilful intent of the employee to injure himself or another, disability benefits shall not be paid.

Benefits will only be payable to an employee for a disability incurred while such employee is in the service of the Company. These benefits are non-assignable, and any attempt to transfer or pledge them will not be recognised by the Company. However, any amount due to the Company from the employee or payable under an attachment of earnings order may be deducted from the above benefits.

Amoco (U.K.) Limited
Registered Office:
1 Olympic Way
Wembley Middlesex HA9 0ND
Telephone: 01-902 8820
Cables: Amointe Wembley
Telex: 264433
Registration No: 233067—England

Directors:
J. A. Parker (U.S.A.)
A. W. Lyckman (U.S.A.)
E. C. S. Northcote
G. M. Nickson
F. G. Andrusko (U.S.A.)
G. W. Skinner

POLICY STATEMENT: DISCIPLINARY PROCEDURES

The willing and active co-operation of all employees in accepting certain rules is essential if the organisation is to function as smoothly and efficiently as possible. The procedure detailed below will be used in the handling of all disciplinary matters. Although discipline may imply sanctions against the employee its primary purpose is the improvement in standards of performance. The exact nature of the offence will determine the appropriate course of action in any particular situation. All employees will be treated impartially and no acts of favouritism or discrimination will be permitted.

An employee will render himself liable to disciplinary action if, for example -

1) he persistently fails to perform his work satisfactorily
2) he is involved in a breach of conduct which may include, for example:
   a) disregarding the rules
   b) interrupting the work of the organisation
   c) causing danger to life or property or inconvenience to fellow employees
   d) persistent lateness or bad time-keeping
   e) unauthorised absence without good reason
   f) unauthorised use of Amoco property.

The employee will be informed of the nature of the breach of discipline laid against him as soon as possible, and will have the opportunity and the right to state his case before any decision regarding the appropriate disciplinary action is taken. The employee may be accompanied by a representative of his choice at any stage.

When the facts have been established and responsibility is clear, disciplinary action can comprise one of the following:-

i) Verbal warning
ii) Written warning
iii) Lateral transfer or redeployment
iv) Demotion
v) Suspension without pay
vi) Termination with notice or pay in lieu.

(Continued)

(Continued)

Except where the offence justifies summary dismissal, that is termination without notice or pay in lieu, the employee's previous record will be taken into account in determining the appropriate course of disciplinary action. A first breach of conduct will normally be verbally reprimanded, and only if the breach of conduct recurs or if conduct does not improve, will a written warning be issued and a copy placed on the employee's personal file for a maximum period of one year. Any breaches of conduct which lead to disciplinary action other than a verbal warning will be confirmed in writing to the employee, and should be acknowledged in writing by the individual, unless the letter is handed to him in the presence of his representative. A series of written warnings can render the employee liable to dismissal. Except in the case of gross misconduct no employee shall be dismissed for any offence without a written warning stating that a repetition will be cause for dismissal. However, where the offence is considered grave enough, the employee may be suspended with pay, pending investigation of all the circumstances. In any instance of disciplinary action other than a verbal reprimand, no action should be taken without prior consultation between the employee's supervisor, his Head of Department and Employee Relations.

Certain offences are so serious as to warrant summary dismissal with no previous warning. Where an offence warrants summary dismissal the employee may be suspended with pay while the case is being investigated and no action will be taken until the employee has had the opportunity of stating his case, and the appropriate course of action has been determined after suitable consultations by the Company management. The employee will receive a written statement of the reason for dismissal, and a final record of the disciplinary action taken will be retained.

Without limiting the general nature of such offences, the following breaches of conduct may warrant summary dismissal:-

1. Fighting or causing or attempting to cause or threatening injury to another while on duty or on Amoco property.
2. Causing damage to Amoco property intentionally or through gross negligence.
3. Acting in such a way as to prejudice industrial safety or hygiene.
4. Unauthorised disclosures of confidential Amoco information.
5. Dishonesty in the performance of duties, including:
   a) Falsifying of Amoco documents.
   b) Wilful failure to report and account for all monies, materials and equipment.
   c) Obtaining Amoco property on fraudulent orders.
   d) Accepting or effecting any bribe or secret commission in cash or in kind.
   e) Knowingly making false statements in connection with Company business or investigations.

(Continued)

(Continued)

6. Introducing, possessing, using or causing others to use habit-forming drugs, or intoxicating liquor, or being under the influence of such drugs or liquor while on duty or on Amoco property to such an extent as to affect work performance.
7. Sleeping whilst on duty.
8. Smoking where smoking is prohibited.
9. Intentionally making false statements when accidents are being investigated, when applying for employment, transfer or reinstatement, or in connection with medical examinations.
10. Failure to report to his supervisor any accidents or personal injuries in which the employee is involved.
11. Failure to report to the Company any contagious or infectious diseases which may endanger the health of other employees.
12. Conviction under Court proceedings which in the Company's opinion render the employee unsuitable to continue the duties for which he was employed.
13. Failure to obey a reasonable instruction issued to the employee by a person in authority.
14. Any other breach of discipline not covered above which at common law justifies summary dismissal.

Any employee who is dissatisfied with any disciplinary action applied to him should refer to the person identified in the Grievance Procedure (Section 21 of the Conditions of Service).

Form 12 Statement of policy on conflicts of interest and use of company information

Amoco (U.K.) Limited
Registered Office:
1 Olympic Way
Wembley Middlesex HA9 0ND
Telephone: 01-902 8820
Cables: Amointe Wembley
Telex: 264433
Registration No: 233067—England

Directors:
J. A. Parker (U.S.A.)
A. W. Lyckman (U.S.A.)
E. C. S. Northcote
G. M. Nickson
F. G. Andrusko (U.S.A.)
G. W. Skinner

STATEMENT OF POLICY ON CONFLICTS OF INTEREST AND USE OF COMPANY INFORMATION

The Company expects that its employees will behave ethically as a matter of course. But even the most conscientious employee may from time to time need to be particularly alert in order to avoid becoming involved in a situation in which his own interests are in conflict with those of his company.

The purpose of this statement of policy is to help you avoid these troublesome situations and possibly unpleasant consequences. Aside from this there is no intent to interfere with your personal interests or activities.

As with any statement of policy, the exercise of judgement is required in determining its applicability to each individual situation. In an effort to be helpful, some examples of the policy's applicability are given below, but it should be remembered that these are simply examples, and are not intended to be exclusive.

CONFLICTS OF INTEREST

An employee's interest conflicts with that of his company when he profits, or places himself in a position to profit, directly or indirectly, through a misuse of his company position. It is immaterial whether the profit ensues directly to the employee or to a relative or friend, or whether the company is adversely affected financially by the action.

No employee who is in a position to make or influence a decision regarding a business transaction between the company and a third party should accept anything of substantial value from that party. What is "substantial" is obviously relative, and would include even the most nominal or insignificant items if offered in the expectation of influencing the employee's judgement.

Some of the types of company transactions that could be affected adversely to the company's interest are:

1. purchasing of equipment, supplies or services;
2. awarding construction or other contracts; and
3. the purchase, sale or lease of properties.

(Continued)

The kinds of benefits that should be declined, if offered, by or through someone with whom the Company has dealings, include:

1. gifts of substantial value;
2. lavish entertainment;
3. loans of money or facilities; and
4. preferred investment opportunities.

Such inducements to favoured treatment should be refused by the employee; he should also refuse to permit their acceptance by his family.

CONFIDENTIAL COMPANY INFORMATION

Confidential company information belongs to the company. Use of it by an employee for his own gain or for gain to his relatives or friends is a misuse of the company's property. Even if the company does not suffer an obvious monetary loss it can be injured in other ways.

An employee who makes use of his knowledge of the company's interest in certain property in order to obtain for himself a profit in the transaction is obviously guilty of a gross impropriety. It is immaterial that his position in the company gives him no influence concerning the acquisition by the company or that the price may be a fair one or even a bargain. To the extent of his profit he has converted company property to his own use.

CONCLUSION: GENERAL PRINCIPLES

In summary, an employee must not, by making any investment, by engaging in any activity, by creating any relationship with others, or by accepting any gifts or other benefits, put himself in a position in which he may be tempted to act for the benefit of himself or others in some degree, rather that solely for the benefit of the company. Any confidential information which an employee obtains by reason of his employment is the property of the company, must be kept confidential, and must be used solely for the benefit of the company, not the employee or others.

Any employee who believes that he may be involved in a conflict of interest situation or who has any questions regarding these principles or their application with respect to his own situation should discuss the matter with his department head, or Managing Director. All new regular employees, on commencing work, will be given a company statement on conflicts of interest and use of company information, setting out the above principles. The employee will be required to acknowledge receipt of, and signify his agreement to, the statement.

Amoco (U.K.) Limited
Registered Office:
1 Olympic Way
Wembley Middlesex HA9 0ND
Telephone: 01-902 8820
Cables: Amointe Wembley
Telex: 264433
Registration No: 233067—England

Directors:
J. A. Parker (U.S.A.)
A. W. Lyckman (U.S.A.)
E. C. S. Northcote
F. G. Andrusko (U.S.A.)
G. W. Skinner
W. P. Havers

AMOCO (UK) LIMITED

Company Safety Policy

(PETROLEUM OPERATIONS)

1. GENERAL

Under the Health and Safety at Work etc., Act, 1974:-

a) The Company must take any reasonably practicable steps to ensure:-

   i) the health, safety and welfare at work of all Company employees,

   ii) the health and safety of all persons, other than Company employees, who might be affected by Company operations, whether they are at work or not.

   iii) that products marketed by the Company are safe, and without risks to health of persons who use them, when properly used.

b) All Company Employees must:-

   i) take reasonable care for the health and safety of themselves, their colleagues, and of all other persons who could be affected by their acts or omissions at work.

   ii) co-operate with the Company and all other persons so far as is necessary to enable them to fulfil their obligations under the Act.

c) No person "shall intentionally or recklessly interfere with or misuse" anything provided in the interests of health, safety or welfare under current legislation.

d) In this policy, the term "safety" is defined to include:-

   i) prevention of injuries and/or adverse effects on physical and/or mental health of all persons who might be affected by Company operations.

   ii) control of all conditions which could result in damage to property, plant and/or equipment, whether or not it is Company owned.

(Continued)

2. SAFETY ORGANISATION (PETROLEUM OPERATIONS)

a) Management Responsibilities

While each Manager and Supervisor is responsible for maintaining and furthering safety within and throughout his own area of operations, the ultimate responsibility for ensuring safety and the observance of safety legislation rests with the Managing Director. To assist Management in the implementation of its responsibilities, the Managing Director has appointed:-

b) The Company Health and Safety Co-ordination Committee

This Management Body is directly responsible to the Managing Director, and will meet each month to receive and review reports from, and minutes of safety committee meetings held at Company offices, storage installations, distribution terminals, and Milford Haven Refinery. It is responsible for:-

Recommending action in response to changes in safety legislation;

Review and revision of safety policies;

Monitoring the establishment and maintenance of safe working practices;

The provision of safe equipment and working environment;

The review of incident reports;

The conduct of safety audits;

The development of safety training programmes to suit the needs of all levels and classifications of employees throughout the Company's petroleum operations.

c) Field Safety Committees

To provide the Company with effective channels of consultation and communication the following series of field safety committees, constituted as shown in Appendix I to this policy, has been created within the Company. Their constitution will be reviewed from time to time after appropriate consultation.

i) Principal Office Safety Committee

Will meet as often as required, but at least quarterly.

ii) Storage Installation Safety Committees

Will meet monthly, at locations where the Company is 100% responsible for health and safety.

iii) Distribution Terminal Safety Committees

Will meet, at least during every alternate month, at locations where the Company operates from installations

(Continued)

managed by other companies who impose their own health and safety regulations.

d) Refinery Safety Organisation

Due to differences between distribution and refining operations, the Refinery needs to maintain more specialised health and safety organisation.

The Refining Director will publish a separate Safety Policy to suit local needs, under which departmental safety committees including employee representatives will operate.

3. RESPONSIBILITIES OF FIELD SAFETY COMMITTEES

All field committees will be concerned with health and safety matters within their sphere of operation, and will keep under review the measures taken to ensure safety, including:-

Accident prevention;

Accident and "near miss" investigations;

Fire prevention and control;

Hazards of Company products;

Hazards of the various working environments (i.e. offices, storage plants, road vehicles, vehicle maintenance shops, customers' premises etc.,).

Housekeeping;

Legal obligations of employees;

Protective clothing and equipment;

Safety audits and other reports;

Safety regulations and practices;

Safety training, instruction and supervision.

4. MINUTES OF FIELD SAFETY COMMITTEES

These will be reviewed and signed by representatives of both management and employees, then forwarded to the Distribution Safety Officer for review at the next meeting of the Company Health and Safety Co-ordination Committee, whose decisions on matters which cannot be resolved locally will be given by letter, in time for the next meeting of the field committee concerned. Urgent matters which arise between meetings will be referred to the Distribution Safety Officer who will arrange for essential remedial action to be taken.

5. ACCIDENT AND "NEAR MISS" REPORTING

All such incidents must be reported without delay to the immediate supervisor concerned. Supervisors will, in turn,

(Continued)

(Continued)

pass on the reports, in accordance with Company procedures, so that they will be reviewed, among other matters:-

a) to obtain legal advice

b) at the Refinery, by the Refining Director, through channels established by the Refinery Safety Policy, or

c) at all other locations, by the Distribution Safety Officer, and the Chairman of the Company Health and Safety Co-ordination Committee.

If the nature of the incident is severe, either the Managing Director or the Refining Director may appoint a working party, varying in composition according to the expertise required, to investigate and, as soon as possible, report on the causes of the incident and give recommendations to prevent recurrence. This report will be reviewed by the Company Health and Safety Co-ordination Committee, with copies to the local safety committee.

6. TRAINING

Local Safety committees, and the Distribution and Refinery Safety Officers, will endeavour to identify all hazards and advise management of the training and information needed to minimise the effects of those hazards. Safety training to meet the needs of each job classification will be developed in co-operation with the Training Supervisor, with special emphasis on fire prevention and control essential to the petroleum industry.

7. HAZARD INFORMATION

Written operating instructions or procedures will be provided to all employees whose jobs bring them into contact with potentially dangerous substances, processes or equipment, and must be observed. Information about the hazards of Amoco's petroleum products which must be available for customers and at each workplace so that all employees should be aware of such hazards, is summarized in Appendix II.

8. MEDICAL

Before employment, every prospective full-time permanent employee is required to pass a medical examination by a Doctor designated by the Company. Periodic examinations will be offered to employees throughout their employment.

9. PROTECTIVE CLOTHING AND EQUIPMENT

Where essential protective clothing and equipment is provided by the Company without charge to employees, the Company requires that all employees concerned shall wear and/or use it, in their own interest.

10. VISITORS TO COMPANY PREMISES

Local managements are responsible for ensuring that all visitors, while on Company premises, observe the safety regulations and practices laid down for Company employees.

AMOCO (UK) LIMITED 4th August, 1978.

(Continued)

(Continued)

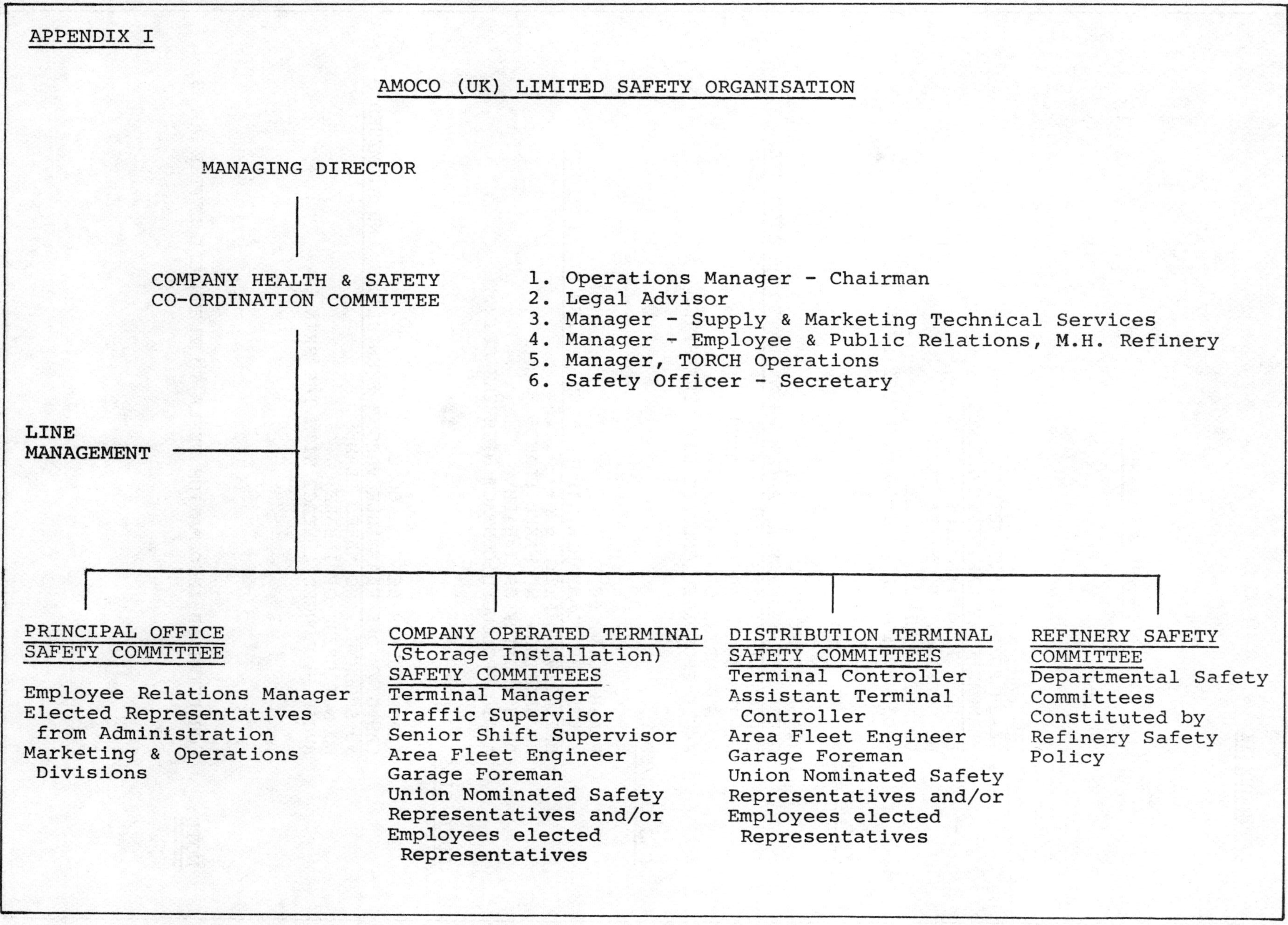
APPENDIX I
AMOCO (UK) LIMITED SAFETY ORGANISATION
MANAGING DIRECTOR
COMPANY HEALTH & SAFETY CO-ORDINATION COMMITTEE
1. Operations Manager - Chairman
2. Legal Advisor
3. Manager - Supply & Marketing Technical Services
4. Manager - Employee & Public Relations, M.H. Refinery
5. Manager, TORCH Operations
6. Safety Officer - Secretary
LINE MANAGEMENT
PRINCIPAL OFFICE SAFETY COMMITTEE
Employee Relations Manager
Elected Representatives from Administration
Marketing & Operations Divisions
COMPANY OPERATED TERMINAL (Storage Installation) SAFETY COMMITTEES
Terminal Manager
Traffic Supervisor
Senior Shift Supervisor
Area Fleet Engineer
Garage Foreman
Union Nominated Safety Representatives and/or Employees elected Representatives
DISTRIBUTION TERMINAL SAFETY COMMITTEES
Terminal Controller
Assistant Terminal Controller
Area Fleet Engineer
Garage Foreman
Union Nominated Safety Representatives and/or Employees elected Representatives
REFINERY SAFETY COMMITTEE
Departmental Safety Committees Constituted by Refinery Safety Policy

(Continued)

APPENDIX II

PRODUCT HAZARDS

GASOLINE

FLASH POINT MINUS 40°C
FLAMMABLE AT ALL TEMPERATURES
EXPLOSIVE LIMITS 1.3% - 7.6%
NO SMOKING. NO NAKED FLAMES
DO NOT DRINK OR INHALE
AVOID PROLONGED CONTACT WITH THE SKIN.

KEROSINE

FLASH POINT 38°C
GIVES OFF FLAMMABLE VAPOUR WHEN HEATED OR ATOMISED
EXPLOSIVE LIMITS 0.7% - 6.0%
NO SMOKING. NO NAKED FLAMES
DO NOT DRINK OR INHALE
AVOID PROLONGED CONTACT WITH THE SKIN.

GAS OIL/DERV

FLASH POINT 66°C
GIVES OFF FLAMMABLE VAPOUR WHEN HEATED OR ATOMISED
EXPLOSIVE LIMITS 6.0% - 13.5%
NO SMOKING. NO NAKED FLAMES
DO NOT DRINK OR INHALE
AVOID PROLONGED CONTACT WITH THE SKIN.

FUEL OILS

FLASH POINTS 66°C - 100°C
CAN GIVE OFF FLAMMABLE VAPOUR WHEN HEATED AND ATOMISED
NO SMOKING. NO NAKED FLAMES
DO NOT DRINK OR INHALE
AVOID PROLONGED CONTACT WITH THE SKIN.

NOTE: FOR DETAILED INFORMATION REFER TO TECHNICAL LETTER NO. 3.

Form 14 Personnel record form

PERSONNEL RECORD FORM

SURNAME .... DATE OF BIRTH ....

CHRISTIAN NAME(S) .... MARITAL STATUS ....

PRESENT ADDRESS ....

.... TELEPHONE NUMBER ....

....

NEXT OF KIN ....

NAME & ADDRESS ....

....

....

TEL. NUMBER ....

CHILDREN AND DATES OF BIRTH

FEMALE ....

MALE ....

NAME & ADDRESS OF FAMILY DOCTOR ....

(FOR EMERGENCY PURPOSES ONLY) ....

TELEPHONE NUMBER ....

EDUCATION AFTER AGE OF ELEVEN

DATES	SCHOOL/COLLEGE/UNIVERSITY	SUBJECTS STUDIED	EXAMS PASSED DIPLOMA, DEGREE ETC.

Signature ....

Date ....

Form 15 Credit transfer authority

CREDIT TRANSFER AUTHORITY

To Messrs. ....

....

I/We hereby authorise you to remit to the undermentioned Bank for the credit of my/our

.... account, all amounts due to me/us from time to time.

Bank .... Code No. [ ]

Name of Branch ....

Address of Branch ....

Date .... *Signature:* ....

Account No. (if known) [ ]

Form 16 Application for temporary employment

1. Personal Details

Surname	Mr/Mrs/Miss	Address
First Name(s)		
Date of Birth		
Married/Single	'Phone No.	

2. Proposed Employment

(a)

Service Station No.	
Service Station Name & Address	
Location (if other than Service Station	

(b)

Position Applied For	
Proposed Wage Rate	£ per Hour/Week
Hours of Employment	
Commencement Date	
Applicant's Signature	Date

3. Other Employment (To be completed if applicable)

If accepted for employment by Amoco (U.K.) Limited, I shall remain in regular employment with: ____________________

of: ____________________

who holds my National Insurance Card, No. ____________ You may apply to the above employer for verification and I will inform you of any future changes in my employment status.

Applicant's Signature ____________ Date ____________

4. Reason For Recommended Employment

(a) New Position ☐	Explain:	
(b) Replacement ☐		
Details of Person Replaced:	Name	Wage Rate £ per Hour/Week

5. Wage Review (Sections 1 & 2(a) also to be completed)

Date of Joining		Proposed Date of Change	
Present Wage Rate £ per Hour/Week		Proposed Wage Rate £ per Hour Week	
Position - Present:		Proposed:	
Explanation:			

Supervisor's Signature ____________

Job Title ____________

Date

Wage Review Recommended:

____________ ____________

Approved: ____________ ____________

Signature Date

Amoco (U.K.) Limited
Registered Office:
1 Olympic Way
Wembley Middlesex HA9 0ND
Telephone: 01-902 8820
Cables: Amointe Wembley
Telex: 264433
Registration No: 233067—England

Directors:
J. A. Parker (U.S.A.)
A. W. Lyckman (U.S.A.)
E. C. S. Northcote
G. M. Nickson
F. G. Andrusko (U.S.A.)
G. W. Skinner

Dear

Terminal:
Basic Rate:
Commencement Date:

This confirms your employment with this Company under the job title of Temporary Driver at the above Terminal with effect from the commencement date shown at the basic rate of pay per week (payable weekly in arrear) as shown above.

This employment is not continuous with any previous periods of temporary employment that you may have had with the Company and is temporary and necessitated by increased seasonal demand for our products. Whilst we hope that employment will be available throughout the winter months, this cannot be guaranteed, particularly when a reduction in product demand occurs.

You are obliged to give and entitled to receive one week's notice to terminate this employment.

When your employment is terminated, you will be paid accrued holiday pay at the rate of one and two-thirds days basic rate for each completed month of employment. When calculation results in a fraction, this will be rounded up to the next whole day. You will not normally be permitted to take paid holiday during your period of temporary employment. There are no terms or conditions of your employment relating to pensions or pension schemes.

The terms and conditions of your employment relating to hours of work and sick pay and the disciplinary rules, grievance procedure, and the person to whom you may apply for redress are set forth in Clauses B4, D4, D11 and A6 of the Agreement between this Company and the Transport and General Workers' Union, a copy of which is available to you on request from your Supervisor for perusal and subsequent return.

A copy of the Company's Policy Statement on Health and Safety at Work is attached to this letter.

Would you please confirm your acceptance of the above by dating and counter-signing the copy of this letter in the space provided and return it to me.

Yours sincerely,

Accepted: ....

B. E. Mills
Personnel Officer

Date: ....

BEM/prl

Form 18 Temporary appointment as trainee cashier (summer vacation employment, etc.)

Amoco (U.K.) Limited
Registered Office:
1 Olympic Way
Wembley Middlesex HA9 0ND
Telephone: 01-902 8820
Cables: Amointe Wembley
Telex: 264433
Registration No: 233067—England

Directors:
J. A. Parker (U.S.A.)
A. W. Lyckman (U.S.A.)
E. C. S. Northcote
G. M. Nickson
F. G. Andrusko (U.S.A.)
G. W. Skinner

Dear

This letter will serve to confirm to you that you are employed on a temporary basis as a Trainee Cashier at

for the period

Your weekly hours of work will be in shifts as agreed with the Service Station Manager.

Should you work any hours in excess of 42 per week you will be paid overtime at the rate of one and a third times your basic rate for the first 2 hours worked and one and a half times your basic rate for the remainder.

Yours sincerely,

B. E. Mills
Personnel Officer

Date: ....

BEM/prl

Signed: ....

Form 19 Notice of changes in terms and conditions

Amoco (U.K.) Limited
Registered Office:
1 Olympic Way
Wembley Middlesex HA9 0ND
Telephone: 01-902 8820
Cables: Amointe Wembley
Telex: 264433
Registration No: 233067—England

Directors:
J. A. Parker (U.S.A.)
A. W. Lyckman (U.S.A.)
E. C. S. Northcote
F. G. Andrusko (U.S.A.)
G. W. Skinner
W. P. Havers

Dear

This letter will serve to confirm details of changes in the terms of your employment with us. All other terms and conditions previously advised to you in your Contract of Employment remain the same.

Job Title:

Effective Date of Job Title Change:

Salary/Wage:

Effective Date of Salary/Wage Change:

Location:

Effective Date of Location Change:

Would you please signify receipt of this letter by signing the attached copy and return it to us.

Yours sincerely,

B. E. Mills
Personnel Officer

BEM/prl
Encs.

Accepted: ....

Date: ....

Amoco (U.K.) Limited

To: Date:

From: J.R.M. Cairns

TRIENNIAL MEDICAL EXAMINATION

Amoco's medical policy provides the opportunity for you to have a routine medical examination every three years, if you wish. This examination includes an X-Ray, blood tests and, if over the age of 40, an E.C.G.

According to our records, you are eligible to take up this option and in this connection, we would appreciate your completing and returning the lower half of this memorandum to indicate whether or not you wish us to arrange an appointment for you with Dr. ______ .

It would be of great assistance to this office if you could indicate whether a morning or afternoon appointment would be preferred, and if any particular dates should be avoided.

J.R.M. Cairns
Employee Relations Manager
JRMC/vah

- -

Name: ____________________

* I do not wish to have a routine medical examination at the present time.

* I would like the Company to arrange an appointment for me with Dr. ______ and I would prefer to attend in the * morning/afternoon. The following dates should be avoided ____________________________.

Signature __________________

Date ______________________

Location __________________

* Delete as necessary

Amoco (U.K.) Limited

To:

ROUTINE MEDICAL EXAMINATION

As requested, arrangements have been made for you to see
Dr. ______ at:-

Dr. ______ 's new address is ______
Wimpole Street, London, W.1.

Valerie Holloway (Mrs.)
Employee Relations Dept.

JULY 1976

Amoco (U.K.) Limited

EMPLOYEE PERFORMANCE APPRAISAL MANUAL

CONTENTS:

(Continued)

EMPLOYEE PERFORMANCE APPRAISAL SYSTEM

A. INTRODUCTION

This manual contains instructions and guidelines for conducting employee performance appraisal interviews.

It is intended for use by Supervisors who are responsible for the appraisals. Use of the manual by all supervisors will help to achieve the goal of uniform assessment of employees throughout the Company.

The Employee Performance Appraisal System ensures that each of the Company's salaried employees is regularly assessed by their Supervisor. This assessment is made at an interview when, by two-way communication, a course of action can be agreed for the employee's future improvement and development.

Performance appraisals are an effective means of systematically obtaining information which will enable a Supervisor to evaluate past effort, assist the employee to improve his performance and assess potential, which will assist with manpower planning.

In order that sufficient time is allowed for consideration of the factors involved, it is imperative that the interview, together with the necessary forms, should be completed during the month preceding the employee's anniversary date.

Salary review will not be a part of the appraisal interview. This will be discussed between the Supervisor and employee at a separate interview.

B. THE APPRAISAL

1. Anniversary Appraisals

Supervisors should maintain a diary recording the anniversary date of each of their employees. (Employee Relations Department should be contacted if confirmation of dates is required). The diary should also note that, approximately thirty days prior to each anniversary date, Supervisors should arrange an appraisal interview date with the employee. When the date is arranged, sufficient time must be allowed for the appraisal forms, and Form 27 (if applicable), to be completed, authorised, and returned to Employee Relations Department no later than the employee's anniversary date.

(Continued)

B. 2. Other Appraisals

Other times when an appraisal interview will be conducted are:

a. when a new employee joins his department, so that his manager can promptly agree and record tasks/objectives and review with the employee the appropriate job description;

b. shortly before an employee is promoted or transferred to another department, provided that three months has elapsed since the completion of a formal appraisal. In this event a formal appraisal should be carried out by the transferring manager, except that new tasks/objectives should be left for the new manager to complete with the employee. The transferring manager should send the semi-complete appraisal form to the new manager when or before the transfer is made;

c. when an employee is promoted or transferred to another department within three months of his last appraisal, so that his new manager can promptly agree and record tasks/objectives and review with the employee the appropriate job description.

3. Salary Review

Salary review will always be discussed with the employee some days after the appraisal interview.

4. Appraisal Forms - General

Guidelines for the completion of appraisal forms are given in Section C, which also includes samples of the forms.

Performance Appraisal Interview Preparation Sheet, Form 1011, should be given to the employee 7 days prior to the date when the interview is to be conducted. The form can be used as a means of confirming to the employee the date agreed for the interview. The purpose of the form is to clarify the employee's thoughts and provide a basis for discussion.

The appraisal interview will be recorded by the Supervisor and the employee on a set of appraisal forms. The type of forms to be used will vary according to the employee's class, Division and type of work.

The table on the facing page shows the type of form to be used for the various categories:

(Continued)

	Position/Type of Work	Management/Sales (1011/M)	Clerical (1011/C)	Operating (1011/O)	Refinery Technician and Clerical (1011/R)
ALL DIVISIONS					
Class 8 to 11 (incl.)	All	X			
ADMINISTRATION DIVISION					
Class 7	All	X			
Class 6 and below	All		X		
MARKETING DIVISION					
Class 7	All	X			
Class 6 and below	Selling	X			
Class 6 and below	Other		X		
OPERATIONS DIVISION					
Class 7	All	X			
Class 6 and below	Clerical/Secretarial		X		
Class 6 and below	Operating			X	
REFINERY DIVISION					
Class 7 and below	Technician (Operations, E&M, Tech. Services and E.&PR.)				X
Class 7 and below	Clerical/Secretarial				X
Class 7 and 6	Professional & Administrative (e.g. Scheduling Clerk, Nurse, Accountant, E.R. Assistant, Assistant Engineer)	X			

Completed forms are confidential, and as such should be kept in a secure place. They must not be left where there is a chance that they will be seen by a third party. Transmission of the completed forms by post must always be under 'Confidential' cover.

The forms should be used to record the appraiser's judgement on overall performance rating. If it is felt that the forms do not adequately cover a particular situation, any additional helpful comments can be written on a separate sheet of paper, which should be attached to the form.

Prior to the interview, the future Main Tasks/Objectives and Standards of Achievement should be drafted for agreement with the employee.

(Continued)

B. 4. The sections covering Employee's Comments are to be completed by the employee. The appraiser may consider it would be helpful, if convenient, to give the forms to the employee and ask for these sections to be completed and returned in 24 hours.

The sections of the forms which cover Career Potential and Promotion/Succession Recommendations must not be completed until after the interview. The appraiser may wish to consider these in advance, in which case he should make rough notes for his own use.

Appraising Supervisors may find it helpful to give copies of the non-confidential sections of the completed forms to employees.

5. Appraiser's Assessment of Employee

The appraiser should give careful thought to all of the factors on the forms.

If in doubt, reference should be made to Section 'C' of this manual which gives guidelines for the completion of the forms.

The Objectives/Tasks set at the last main appraisal should be referred to, as should notes of any interim appraisals which may have taken place during the year. The extent to which success has been achieved and problems which arose together with action taken or still to be taken to solve them will be considered.

The appraiser will consider the new Objectives/Tasks to be set and how success is to be measured.

6. Interview Preparation

The environment in which the interview is carried out should be arranged so that the employee will feel at ease, and will be conducive to a free interchange of comment and ideas.

The interview must be conducted in private. If the appraiser's office is open to view, or conversation can be heard by people outside, an alternative private room should be used for the interview.

The desk at which the interview is to be conducted should be free of all extraneous matter, i.e. all files etc. should be put away.

Interruptions should not be allowed. Arrangements should be made for somebody else to take telephone calls.

Seating, lighting, etc. should be arranged to provide a comfortable atmosphere. Seating arrangements other than at each side of the desk should be considered.

(Continued)

(Continued)

If appropriate, e.g. with field personnel, the interview should be conducted at a neutral location remote from both parties' normal work place.

It is not generally intended that third parties would be present at the interview. Wherever possible, interviews should be conducted by the employee's Supervisor. The appraiser's Supervisor may, however, in certain circumstances, consider his own presence to be necessary

B. 7. The Appraisal Interview (First Stage)

The introduction to the interview should be as welcoming and friendly as possible, and should always commence with the normal social courtesies.

At the commencement, an effort should be made to find common ground, e.g. reference can be made to any projects successfully undertaken together during the previous year.

The employee's weaknesses should not be mentioned at the early stages of the interview, and favourable comment should be made on his strong points.

The appraiser should endeavour to let the employee appraise his own performance, by encouraging the employee to state his opinion about his performance for the period under review. Sufficient time should be allowed for this to develop. The appraiser must listen carefully to the views he expresses and to his replies to questions asked.

The object of the interview must be kept in mind at all times, and every effort should be made to avoid being sidetracked.

Careful notes to help when determining the employee's future training and development should be made by the appraiser.

When discussing the Tasks/Objectives to be set, the joint responsibility aspect should always be emphasised.

The appraiser should state his views on the employee's past performance and his achievement against the targets previously set. He should be prepared to justify such judgement with practical specific examples.

Action to be taken by both parties to improve performance should be agreed and recorded.

The progress made with the interview should be summarised at this stage.

(Continued)

(Second Stage)

The main tasks/objectives for the forthcoming period should be agreed. It is essential that these are not imposed by the appraiser or there will be no commitment for the employee to achieve them. They should be demanding, but achievable and measurable. Agreement must also be reached on how the performance will be measured.

The appraiser's judgement of the employee's relationship with colleagues should be discussed, and he should be prepared to use facts to justify his judgement.

Isolated examples should not be allowed to bias overall judgement. It is essential that the employee's strengths are recognised and that he is told of the intention to develop and use them.

The employee's ambitions and career desires should be discussed. The appraiser must be careful not to make any commitments. The employee's hopes must not be raised unless the appraiser is certain that he is in a position to implement the action to which he agrees.

The interview should be summarised again at this stage, with particular emphasis being placed on the action agreed to be taken to improve performance.

(Conclusion)

Before closing, the appraiser should check progress towards achievement of the objectives of the interview.

It may be helpful to establish dates for periodic review meetings.

So that up to date personnel records can be maintained, appraisers should check that there have been no changes in the employee's circumstances, i.e. change of address, number of children, next of kin, etc. If there have been any changes they should be notified to Employee Relations Department when the appraisal forms are returned to them.

B. 8. Follow Up of Performance Appraisal

Experience has shown that, immediately following a well conducted appraisal interview, there is a marked increase in performance which may just as quickly decline. Much of the value of the appraisal routine may, therefore, be lost, unless constant reviews are made.

A typical follow-up procedure would be:

A check by the Supervisor at least every three months on actions agreed with the employee at the appraisal interview.

Regular observation by the appraiser, with a comment to the employee on progress made.

Variation, should it be considered necessary, of the objectives and measures of achievement which were agreed.

Continued encouragement and advice given by the Supervisor to the employee.

Acknowledgment by the Supervisor that improvement in the performance of the employee is a shared responsibility.

B. 9. Return of Forms

Completed performance appraisal forms, together with Forms 27 (where applicable), will be returned to Employee Relations Department no later than the employee's anniversary date. In the case of new employees, or those transferred/promoted, the completed forms will be sent to Employee Relations Department no later than 30 days after the date when new objectives are set.

If Employee Relations Department do not receive the completed forms by the due date, they should contact the person to whom they were sent, to determine the reason why the forms have not been received.

C. GUIDELINES FOR THE COMPLETION OF EMPLOYEE PERFORMANCE APPRAISAL FORMS

PERFORMANCE APPRAISAL INTERVIEW PREPARATION SHEET - FORM 1011

See Section B.4.

Employee's Name____

Interview on________________________________at__________a.m./p.m.

PERFORMANCE APPRAISAL INTERVIEW PREPARATION SHEET

This form is given to you to help you to prepare for your performance appraisal. If you want to use it to note down any points you wish to raise, please do so. It is only for your personal use as a guide, and you do not have to show it to anyone or hand it in, but we hope that you will read it and think about the points raised in it before your interview.

1) Looking at your own work over the past year, what things do you think you have done particularly well?

2) Are there any aspects of your work which have not gone so well? If so, why was this?

3) What has given you the greatest personal satisfaction about your work here over the past year?

4) Is there any particular item in connection with your own job which has caused you dissatisfaction? If so, what can be done about it?

5) Do you feel you and the Company might benefit if you had additional training in any aspect of your work?

6) Is there any way in which you would want to change the duties or responsibilities of your job to improve the efficiency of your department?

7) Are there any other suggestions you would like to make to help improve efficiency or job satisfaction in your department or anywhere else in the Company?

Form 1011

EMPLOYEE PERFORMANCE APPRAISAL - FORMS 1011/C, 1011/M & 1011/O

FRONT PAGE

The front page which will show details of the employee and his present position in the Company is self-explanatory. Details will be entered by the appraiser and, after completion of the interview, the ratings will be transferred into the boxes in the lower section.

The 'Reviewed by' section at the bottom of the front page will be signed by the appraiser's Supervisor in conjunction with any comments he may enter in section 'J'.

SECTION 'A' PERFORMANCE ANALYSIS

The main tasks/objectives will be those set and agreed at the beginning of the appraisal period, i.e. at the last appraisal, or, in the case of new employees or those promoted or transferred, the objectives agreed at the time they commenced their present job.

The appraiser will enter his comments on the achievement of these main tasks/objectives.

SECTION 'B' PERFORMANCE RATING

The appraiser, using his remarks in Section 'A' to assist his judgement, will tick the box against the appropriate comment to establish a rating. This rating will be transferred to the first box on the front page.

SECTION 'C' ACTION TO BE TAKEN TO IMPROVE PERFORMANCE

The appraiser will enter clear and specific actions in the appropriate spaces, suggesting a time scale wherever this is practical. Any entry in space C.3. should be the subject of separate discussion by the appraiser with Employee Relations Department, to establish the nature of the counselling, guidance or training required.

SECTION 'D' WHAT IS TO BE ACCOMPLISHED IN THE COMING YEAR

The tasks/objectives agreed with the employee will be entered by the appraiser, as will the indicators/measures which should be in terms of Time, Cost, Quantity or Quality.

(Continued)

Amoco (UK) Limited Confidential

EMPLOYEE PERFORMANCE APPRAISAL

CLERICAL PERSONNEL

Employee's Name

Job Title

Department

Division

Location

Class.

Employment Date

Position Date

Class. Date

RATING:

Performance (From Section B)	☐	Personal Characteristics (From Section E)	☐	Career Potential (From Section H)	☐

Appraised by

– this employee's Supervisor for years months

Appraisal Date

Reviewed by

Form 1011/C

Amoco (UK) Limited | Confidential

EMPLOYEE PERFORMANCE APPRAISAL

MANAGEMENT/SALES PERSONNEL

Employee's Name

Job Title

Department

Division

Location

Class.

Employment Date

Position Date

Class. Date

RATING:

Performance (From Section B)	☐	Personal Characteristics (From Section E)	☐	Career Potential (From Section H)	☐

Appraised by

– this employee's Supervisor for years months

Appraisal Date

Reviewed by

Form 1011/M

Amoco (UK) Limited Confidential

EMPLOYEE PERFORMANCE APPRAISAL

OPERATING PERSONNEL

Employee's Name

Job Title

Department

Division

Location

Class.

Employment Date

Position Date

Class. Date

RATING:

Performance	☐	Personal Characteristics	☐	Career Potential	☐
(From Section B)		(From Section E)		(From Section H)	

Appraised by

– this employee's Supervisor for years months

Appraisal Date

Reviewed by

Form 1011/O

A. PERFORMANCE ANALYSIS

(a) Summarise the agreed main tasks/objectives for the period.

(b) Comment on achievements during the period, by reference to the agreed indicators/measures and mention any special circumstances that affected performance.

(a) MAIN TASKS/OBJECTIVES	(b) COMMENTS ON ACHIEVEMENTS
1.	
2.	
3.	
4.	

B. PERFORMANCE RATING

Indicate your opinion of overall performance by means of a tick in the box next to the appropriate comment. (Transfer rating ticked to front page)

☐	5	An exceptionally valuable member of staff; performance is consistently well above the required standards for the job.
☐	4	Displays good all round level of effectiveness; performance meets or exceeds requirements in all important tasks.
☐	3	A competent member of the staff; generally achieves the standards required.
☐	2	Performance does not always reach the required standards; room for improvement.
☐	1	Improvement mandatory; performance does not meet the required standards.

C. ACTION TO BE TAKEN TO IMPROVE PERFORMANCE

1. By the Supervisor:

2. By the Employee:

3. By Employee Relations Department: (Counselling, Guidance, Training, etc.)

D. WHAT IS TO BE ACCOMPLISHED IN THE COMING YEAR

(a) Summarise the main tasks/objectives agreed with the employee for the next period.

(b) List the indicators/measures that will be used in assessing achievements.
(Reference to the job description may be appropriate when listing the tasks/objectives)

(a) TASKS/OBJECTIVES	(b) INDICATORS/MEASURES OF ACHIEVEMENT
1.	
2.	
3.	
4.	

SECTION 'E' PERSONAL CHARACTERISTICS

This section is peculiar to one of the categories shown in Section B.4.

The headings are: Clerical
Operating
Management/Sales

A check should be made, prior to the interview, to ensure that the correct form is being used.

The appraiser will place a tick against each characteristic, in the most appropriate column, i.e. Less than Satisfactory, etc. A count of the ticks in each column should then be made and totals entered. These totals are then multiplied by the numbers pre-printed underneath them and the results entered where indicated. The total of these results will then be added and entered in the 'Grand Total' space. The Grand Total will be divided by the number of characteristics printed on the form, to find the Average Rating. This figure will be entered in the space provided and transferred to the centre box on the front page.

NOTE: The appraiser must enter a written comment against each characteristic to substantiate or explain each rating which has been ticked. EMPLOYEE RELATIONS DEPARTMENT WILL NOT ACCEPT APPRAISAL FORMS WHICH DO NOT CONTAIN THESE WRITTEN COMMENTS.

SECTION 'F' COMMENTS BY APPRAISER

The appraiser will use this space to make any written comments concerning the employee which he feels will back up the completed appraisal. The comments should be influenced by the employee's past performance, experience, strengths, potential and career desires.

The appraiser will sign and date this section.

SECTION 'G' - EMPLOYEE'S COMMENTS

The employee will be asked to complete this section, the headings of which are self-explanatory.

Employees will have been told by the appraiser that their comments should be frank and honest and may be made without fear of consequences.

The appraiser will guide the employee on the type of comments required in the 'career desires' space. General terms such as "To see more of the Company" and "To move into Management" are not acceptable. Brief details of the type of work and specialisation, and the action they believe is required to achieve these, should be quoted.

The employee will sign and date these sections at the bottom of the page.

(Continued)

E. PERSONAL CHARACTERISTICS – CLERICAL PERSONNEL

Tick the grade of satisfaction most applicable and ensure that written comment is made.

	Less than Satis-factory	Satis-factory	More than Satis-factory	APPRAISER'S WRITTEN COMMENTS	
KNOWLEDGE OF JOB: May vary with length of time in job. Is employee "not experienced", "experienced" or "very experienced". If present knowledge is lacking on or off the job, training must be considered.					
TECHNICAL ABILITY: Does employee have training and/or skill, not necessarily professional qualifications, associated with type of work whether for this Company or another.					
WORK ATTITUDE: Is employee's attitude to the work situation co-operative or not. This may change from time to time but what is overall impression given.					
ACCURACY: Can employee be relied upon to report or calculate correctly, or within fine tolerances.					
ABILITY TO LEARN: Can employee grasp and retain new ideas or techniques.					
ABILITY TO COMMUNICATE: How quickly and successfully is the employee able to put across ideas verbally or in writing.					
INITIATIVE: Having "judged" a situation, facts or figures, is employee willing to take risks and show initiative and resource when taking action.					
ATTITUDE/ADAPTABILITY: In the Appraiser's judgement is the employee's attitude negative or positive towards ideas from other people and work situations. Is a balance between "willingness to change" and "digging in his/her heels" shown.					
APPEARANCE: Is it suitable for the position.					
ATTENDANCE: Generally, is employee working when he/she should be.					
Count of ticks in each column				(Must total 10)	
Multiply by	2	3	4		
Result				**GRAND TOTAL**	
Divide Grand Total by 10				**AVERAGE RATING**	(Transfer to page 1)

E. PERSONAL CHARACTERISTICS – MANAGEMENT/SALES PERSONNEL

Tick the grade of satisfaction most applicable and ensure that written comment is made.

	Less than Satis-factory	Satis-factory	More than Satis-factory	APPRAISER'S WRITTEN COMMENTS	
ABILITY TO LEARN: Can employee grasp and retain new ideas or techniques.					
KNOWLEDGE OF JOB: May vary with length of time in job. Is employee 'not experienced", "experienced" or "very experienced". If present knowledge is lacking on or off the job, training must be considered.					
TECHNICAL ABILITY: Does employee have training and/or skill, not necessarily professional qualifications, associated with type of work whether for this company or another.					
ABILITY TO COMMUNICATE: How quickly and successfully is the employee able to put across ideas verbally or in writing.					
ANALYTICAL ABILITY: Has employee the ability to look at a situation, break open the components and define problems concisely.					
ORIGINALITY/CREATIVITY: Does employee make sound suggestions for improvements, and have any ability to develop/improve new ideas.					
INTERPRETATIVE JUDGEMENT: Coupled with Analytical Ability, is employee able to correctly interpret situations, facts, figures and opinions before taking action.					
RESOURCEFULNESS/INITIATIVE: Having "judged" a situation, facts or figures, is employee willing to take risks and show initiative and resource when taking action.					
ATTITUDE/ADAPTABILITY: In the Appraiser's judgement is the employee's attitude negative or positive towards ideas from other people and work situations. Is a balance between "willingness to change" and "digging in his/her heels" shown.					
APPEARANCE : Is it suitable for the position.					
ATTENDANCE: Generally, is employee working when he/she should be.					
Count of ticks in each column				(Must total 11)	
Multiply by	2	3	4		
Result				GRAND TOTAL	
Divide Grand Total by 11				AVERAGE RATING	(Transfer to page 1)

E. PERSONAL CHARACTERISTICS – OPERATING PERSONNEL

Tick the grade of satisfaction most applicable and ensure that written comment is made.

	Less than Satis-factory	Satis-factory	More than Satis-factory	APPRAISER'S WRITTEN COMMENTS	
OBSERVING SAFETY RULES: Does employee observe them, or not.					
WORK ATTITUDE: Is employee's attitude to the work situation co-operative or not. This may change from time to time but what is overall impression given.					
ADAPTABILITY: In the Appraiser's judgement is the employee's attitude negative or positive towards ideas from other people and work situations. Is a balance between "willingness to change" and "digging in his/her heels" shown.					
KNOWLEDGE OF JOB: May vary with length of time in job. Is employee "not experienced", "experienced" or "very experienced". If present knowledge is lacking on or off the job, training must be considered.					
TECHNICAL ABILITY: Does employee have training and/or skill, not necessarily professional qualifications, associated with type of work whether for this Company or another.					
ABILITY TO LEARN: Can employee grasp and retain new ideas or techniques.					
ABILITY TO COMMUNICATE: How quickly and successfully is the employee able to put across ideas verbally or in writing.					
INITIATIVE: Having "judged" a situation, facts or figures, is employee willing to take risks and show initiative and resource when taking action.					
APPEARANCE: Is it suitable for the position.					
ATTENDANCE: Generally, is employee working when he/she should be.					
Count of ticks in each column				(Must total 10)	
Multiply by	2	3	4		
Result				**GRAND TOTAL**	
Divide Grand Total by 10				**AVERAGE RATING**	(Transfer to page 1)

F. COMMENTS BY APPRAISER

Date

Appraiser's Signature

G. **EMPLOYEE'S COMMENTS**

1. On Appraisal:

2. On New Objectives:

3, On Career Desires:

Date Employee's Signature

SECTION 'H' CAREER POTENTIAL

This section is to be completed by the appraiser AFTER THE INTERVIEW and after the employee has completed Section 'G'.

The section is not to be discussed with the employee
If the appraiser considers that the employee is a candidate for promotion during the next two years, list in Section H (a) details of up to 3 positions he could possibly fill. Indicate when the promotion could take place by entering a tick in the appropriate column.

Alternatively, a transfer to another position at the same level may be suggested by entering a tick in the box and details of suitable positions in the space(s) in Section H (b); or, if it is considered most suitable to continue in the present position, a tick in the box in Section H (c).

If either H (b) or (c) are ticked, an explanation of the recommendation will be made, e.g. "Transfer as suggested would assist in this employee's career development".

Rating, which will be the highest area ticked, will be transferred to the right-hand box on the front page.

SECTION 'I' SUCCESSION RECOMMENDATION

The appraiser will enter the names of up to 3 Company employees who he considers could successfully fill the employee's position. Discussion on this point by the appraiser with his Supervisor may be necessary.

SECTION 'J' COMMENTS AND ACTION TO BE TAKEN BY APPRAISER'S SUPERVISOR

Prior to the completed appraisal forms being sent to Employee Relations Department, the reviewing Manager will enter any comments he wishes to make in this section.

His signature is required in the space provided on the front page.

(Continued)

H. CAREER POTENTIAL *(NOT TO BE DISCUSSED WITH THE EMPLOYEE)*

List below positions for which Employee should be considered.

(a) PROMOTION

POSITION	DEPARTMENT	Will be Ready		
		NOW Rates 5	1 YEAR Rates 4	2 YEARS Rates 3
1.				
2.				
3.				

(b) TRANSFER – Rates 2 ☐

1.
2.

(c) BEST SUITED TO PRESENT POSITION – Rates 1 ☐

If (b) or (c) ticked, explain

(Transfer highest rating ticked to front page)

I. SUCCESSION RECOMMENDATION FOR THIS EMPLOYEE'S POSITION

NAME	POSITION

J. COMMENTS AND ACTION TO BE TAKEN BY APPRAISER'S SUPERVISOR

REFINERY TECHNICIAN AND CLERICAL STAFF - PERFORMANCE REVIEW - FORM 1011/R

PAGE 1

The top half of the front page giving details of the employee and the appraisal interview is self-explanatory and should be completed by the appraiser. After completion of the interview the overall rating will be transferred to the appropriate space provided.

The 'Appraisal Reviewed by' section will be signed by the appraiser's Supervisor and the date on which this is done entered in the space below.

PERSONAL CHARACTERISTICS

The appraiser will enter appropriate comments in the spaces against each personal characteristic. Although these are not rated individually they may be considered in the final overall rating.

The appraiser must discuss his assessment of these characteristics with the employee.

PAGE 2

PERFORMANCE REVIEW

The spaces opposite the particular aspects of performance will be completed by the appraiser prior to the interview and a rating for each one entered following the instructions at the foot of the form. These ratings will later be used to arrive at an overall rating which will be entered both on Page 3 and on Page 1.

The appraiser must discuss his assessment of these particular aspects of performance with the employee.

Amoco (UK) Limited | Confidential

EMPLOYEE PERFORMANCE APPRAISAL

REFINERY TECHNICIAN AND CLERICAL STAFF

Name	
Position	
Department	
Service Date	
Period covered by Review	
Date of Appraisal Interview	
Interviewed by	
Overall Rating	
Appraisal reviewed by (Signature)	
Date	

PERSONAL CHARACTERISTICS	COMMENTS
ABILITY TO LEARN Can employee grasp and retain new ideas and techniques?	
ABILITY TO COMMUNICATE How quickly and successfully is the employee able to put across ideas verbally or in writing?	
RESOURCEFULNESS Does employee show individual initiative by taking action?	
ADAPTABILITY What is employee's attitude to, and ability to cope with, change?	

Instructions: 1. This page to be completed by appraiser before interview.

Form 1011/R

1

REFINERY TECHNICIAN AND CLERICAL STAFF

PERFORMANCE REVIEW

PERFORMANCE	COMMENTS	RATING
QUALITY OF WORK How good is employee's work? Consider specific examples.		
QUANTITY OF WORK How much does employee do? Consider specific examples.		
KNOWLEDGE OF JOB Consider employee's experience. How much does he/she know about the job?		
JUDGEMENT Is employee able to correctly interpret situations, facts, figures or opinions before taking action?		
ATTITUDE TO WORK Is employee's overall attitude to the work situation co-operative or not.		
ATTITUDE TO SAFETY Does employee observe safety regulations? Is employee generally safety conscious?		

Instructions: 1. Rate performance as follows – A Outstanding, B Very effective, C Satisfactory, D Barely satisfactory, E Unsatisfactory

2. This page to be completed by appraiser before interview.

2

(Continued)

PAGE 3

GENERAL STRENGTHS & WEAKNESSES OF EMPLOYEE

The appraiser will use this space to make any written comments concerning the employee which he feels back up the comments made on personal characteristics and individual performance. This will be completed and discussed at the interview.

REACTIONS OF EMPLOYEE TO: 1. CURRENT JOB 2. CAREER ASPIRATIONS 3. THIS PERFORMANCE REVIEW

This space will be used to record the reaction of the employee to what has been said during the interview about these three topics. The employee will be told that his comments will be recorded, should be frank and honest and may be made without fear of consequences.

The appraiser will guide the employee on the type of comments required in the Career Aspirations section so that general terms such as "to see more of the Company" are avoided.

ACTION TO BE TAKEN

This section will be completed by the appraiser at the interview giving details of action which should be taken by both the appraiser and the employee to both improve performance of the employee and to assist him/her in achieving the agreed career aspirations on both a long and short term basis.

POTENTIAL OF EMPLOYEE

The appraiser will complete this section at the interview and it will indicate the appraiser's opinion of the employee's career aspirations and substantiate the action to be taken which has been entered above.

OVERALL ASSESSMENT

The appraiser will tick the box opposite the appropriate rating which indicates his overall rating of the employee. This rating will then be transferred to the appropriate space on Page 1.

(Continued)

REFINERY TECHNICIAN AND CLERICAL STAFF

PERFORMANCE REVIEW

GENERAL STRENGTHS & WEAKNESSES OF EMPLOYEE:

REACTIONS OF EMPLOYEE TO: **(1) CURRENT JOB** **(2) CAREER ASPIRATIONS**
(3) THIS PERFORMANCE REVIEW

ACTION TO BE TAKEN including training requirements.

By Appraiser:

By Employee:

POTENTIAL OF EMPLOYEE

OVERALL ASSESSMENT

A Outstanding		B Very Effective		C Satisfactory		D Barely Satisfactory		E Unsatisfactory	

SIGNED: ____________________ ____________________

Appraiser Employee

Instructions: 1. This page to be completed and signed at interview.

3

Form 23 Salary/position recommendation

AMOCO (UK) LIMITED

Salary/Position Recommendation

Name ______________________ Effective Date of Change ______________

Date of Birth ______________ Date Employed ______________

	PRESENT	PROPOSED (Complete where changed)
SALARY STATUS	Base Salary ________ p.a. Last Increase (other than general) Type ________ Date ________ Amt. ________ % ______	Base Salary ________ p.a Proposed Increase Type ________ Amt. ______ % ______
POSITION STATUS		
Department		
Location		
Title Class		
	Date of Title ________ Class No. ______	Class No. ______
Salary Range	Min. ______ Mid ______ Max. ______	Min. ______ Mid ______ Max. ______

REASON FOR POSITION CHANGE

☐ Promotion ☐ Demotion ☐ Reclassif-ication ☐ Transfer

Supervisor's Comments (explain if new job, replacement, change in duties, etc.)

____
Supervisor

Authorised by ______________________ Date ______________

Termination of Employment Notice

Name ______________________ Date of Termination __________

Department ______________________ Mr/Mrs/Miss

Location ______________________

Job Title ______________________ Salary Classification __________

Salary/Wage __________ p.a./p.w.

	Discharge	Resignation	Redundancy	Deceased	Retirement
Termination	☐	☐	☐	☐	☐

If Discharged:- Reason ______________________

____

____

Dates of verbal and written Reprimands ______________________

If Resignation:- Employees reasons ______________________

____

____

Supervisors comments ______________________

____

____

Supervisors comments on employees work:- ______________________

____

____

____

Will employee be replaced? Yes ☐ No ☐

Income Tax Form P45 to be sent to:- ______________________

____

Money due from employee

Cash Advance ....

Other Advances .... ________ .

Total .... ________ .

Money due to employee

Salary/Wages ....

Less Income Tax and/or other deductions ... ________ .

Holiday Pay days ....

Less Income Tax and/or other deductions ... ________

Total ....

Less amount due from employee, as above ... ________ .

TOTAL DUE TO/FROM EMPLOYEE .... ________ .

Refund of Pension Contributions ....

Less Income Tax .... ________

TOTAL NET REFUND ________

Supervisor	Approved

No. ____________

AMOCO PENSION PLAN

Form of Application for Membership

PLEASE USE BLOCK CAPITALS

Name (in full) ____________ Mr/Mrs/Miss

Place of Birth ____________ Date of Birth ____________

Occupation ____________ Married/Single ____________

*Evidence of Age: Enclosed/To follow

FOR OFFICE USE ONLY

Birth Certificate	
Marriage Certificate	

Signature ____________

Date ____________ 19

* Evidence of Age: This is normally a Certificate of Birth, but in exceptional circumstances a baptismal certificate or other evidence may be accepted. For a married woman, a Certificate of Marriage is also required.

TO THE TRUSTEES:

AMOCO PENSION PLAN

1. I hereby apply for Membership of the Amoco Pension Plan and agree to be bound by the Trust Deed and Rules from time to time in force in relation thereto.
2. I hereby request and authorise the Company to retain out of my remuneration the amount of the contributions from time to time payable by me and to pay the same to you on my behalf.

Name (in full) ____________

FOR OFFICE USE ONLY

Company by which employed
Date of entry to service
Pensionable Salary

Signature ____________

Date ____________ 19

Form 26 Pension plan — form of declinature

AMOCO PENSION PLAN

Form of Declinature

I have read and understood the Booklet which describes the benefits to be provided under the Amoco Pension Plan and elect not to become a Member of it.

I understand that if I decline to join the Plan as at June 1st 1972 this means that I will not later be admitted to Membership without the specific consent of a Participating Company and the Trustees.

Name of Employee ______________________________

(BLOCK CAPITALS)

Signed ______________________________

Date ______________________________ 19 ____

TO THE TRUSTEES

AMOCO PENSION PLAN

Form of Nomination

I wish the following person to benefit, in accordance with the Trust Deed and Rules, in the event of my death and to cancel any previous wishes I may have expressed in this connection.

I understand that the Trustees are not bound to act in accordance with this wish in deciding to whom the sums set out in the Rules shall be paid.

Name of Beneficiary ______________________________
(IN FULL—BLOCK CAPITALS)

Address ______________________________

Relationship ______________________________

Nominee's Date of Birth: ______________

Name of Member ______________________________
(BLOCK CAPITALS)

Member's Signature ______________________________

Date ______________________________ 19

NOTE:
You may nominate more than one beneficiary. The name, address and relationship of any further beneficiaries should be written on the reverse side of this form together with your request as to the division between these beneficiaries.

Part Three

Johnson Matthey Group

Introduction

The Johnson Matthey Group consists of seven operating companies and the parent — Johnson Matthey & Co. Ltd. Each member of the group has its own forms, and the 39 that follow are in use by several of the operating companies, as well as by the parent company.

Form 1 Answer to applicant's letter

Dear

Thank you for your letter dated ...... in which you apply for the position of .... at our Royston Works.

In order that I may consider your application further would you please complete the enclosed Application and Medical History forms, returning them to me in the envelope provided.

On receipt of this information a mutually convenient date may be arranged for an informal interview.

Yours sincerely,
for Johnson Matthey Chemicals Ltd.,

M. Clarke
Personnel Manager

Enc

JMM Johnson Matthey Metals Limited

Application Form

Name..

FOR OFFICE USE ONLY

Department and code			Starting date		
Job title			Hours of work		
Clock no.			Rate of pay		
Handbook and other contractual information issued:			Birth Certificate	Received Returned	
References Requested Received	1	2	3	4	5
Car registration no.			Permit required		
Medical examination			Probationary period		
Comments Signature..					

(Continued)

(Continued)

Please answer the following questions in your own handwriting

A. PERSONAL DETAILS OF APPLICANT

Surname		Forenames		
Address Telephone no:				
Date of birth	Age	Maiden name (if applicable)		
Place and country of birth			Nationality	Married * Single Widowed Divorced
Date(s) of birth of children				
Next of kin: Name: Relationship: Address:				
Does your husband/wife work ?		If so, where ?		

B. EDUCATION

Secondary schools attended	Dates
Examinations passed	
Further education, including details of apprenticeships and additional training	

C. LEISURE INTERESTS

What are your hobbies, interests, sports ?

* *Delete where inappropriate*

(Continued)

(Continued)

D. PREVIOUS EMPLOYMENT

(Start with present or last employer and include any periods of unemployment)

	Dates of service	Name and address of company	Occupation and rate of pay	Reason for leaving
1				
2				
3				
4				
5				
6				
7				
8				

Have you ever worked for Johnson Matthey before ?	
If so, when ?	Job title
Have you ever applied for a job with Johnson Matthey before ?	
If so, when ?	
Do you have any friends or relatives working for Johnson Matthey ?	

PLEASE NOTE:

IT IS THE COMPANY'S INTENTION TO ASK FOR REFERENCES FROM ANY OF THE ABOVE PREVIOUS EMPLOYERS

(Continued)

(Continued)

E. HEALTH

Name and address of Doctor		National Insurance no.
Have you ever suffered from any chest complaint (eg asthma, bronchitis), back complaint or hernia, dermatitis or any serious illness, or undergone an operation ? If so, please give details		
Have you ever made a claim for industrial injury or disease ?		
Do you suffer from any physical defect or partial disability ?		
Registered disablement (if any)	Registered no.	Expiry date

F. SECURITY DECLARATION

Have you been convicted of a criminal offence (which is not a spent conviction within the meaning of the Rehabilitation of Offenders Act 1974) ?

G. TERMS AND CONDITIONS OF EMPLOYMENT

1. Terms and conditions relating to hours of work, holiday entitlement, sickness benefit, accident pay, participation in pension schemes, period of notice to terminate employment, and other information which the Company has a statutory duty to provide, are given in the handbook "Working with the JM Group of Companies". This handbook, together with other relevant information, will be given to you when you start employment and will form your Contract of Employment, and amendments will be posted on official notice boards.

2. All engagements depend on:

   (a) satisfactory references,

   (b) satisfactory medical examination. All new employees are required to undergo a medical examination by the Company's doctor to ensure that they are physically and medically suitable for the job offered, as soon after commencement as is practicable and thereafter as and when required by the Company.

   (c) satisfactory completion of an eight week probationary period.

3. Employees are required to join the Works Pension Fund on completion of one year's service or as soon thereafter as they have reached the age of 25 years (men) or 20 years (women), and are required to produce their birth certificate (and marriage certificate, if applicable) within seven days of engagement.

4. Employees are required to undertake shift or night work if directed by the Company so to do, and, in such circumstances, payment will be made according to the terms laid down in the handbook.

5. Service with a previous employer does not count towards service with the JM Group.

I confirm that to the best of my knowledge and belief, all the information recorded in Sections A,B,C,D,E and F of this application form is true, and I understand that if any such information is found to be incorrect my employment may be terminated forthwith.

I accept employment with Johnson Matthey Metals Limited on the above terms and conditions together with the general conditions prevailing within the Company,

as from...as a...

at a starting rate of...

Signed... date...

Form 3 Staff application form

Johnson, Matthey & Co., Limited

Staff Application Form

Full name of applicant ....

Position applied for ....

(Continued)

This form should be completed in the applicant's own handwriting.
The information submitted will be treated in strict confidence.

Surname	Forenames	
Address	Maiden name (if applicable)	
	Age	Date of Birth
	Telephone Number	
Name address and relationship of next of kin		
Town and Country of Birth	Nationality	
Marital Status	Children's Dates of Birth	
General Health *(Indicate, with dates, serious illnesses, operations, disabilities)* *(Engagement may depend upon the applicant successfully passing a medical examination)*		
Leisure Interests and Activities		

EDUCATION

SECONDARY EDUCATION Name(s) of School(s)	Dates	Examinations passed: *Results with grades (or awaiting results)*
FURTHER EDUCATION		
Membership of PROFESSIONAL INSTITUTIONS		
LANGUAGES indicating degree of fluency		
Where did you see this post advertised?		

(Continued)

(Continued)

PREVIOUS EMPLOYMENT *(please specify periods of unemployment)*						
	Full dates of Service (most recent first)		Name and Address of Employer	Position	Salary	Reasons for leaving
1.	From To					
2.	From To					
3.	From To					
4.	From To					
5.	From To					
6.	From To					
7.	From To					
8.	From To					

Application for a reference may be made to any previous employer. Please give below the names of TWO persons, NOT relatives, to whom we may also apply.

PERSONAL REFERENCES			
	Name	Address	Connection
9.			
10.			

I understand that if I accept an offer of employment and any of the above information is subsequently found to be incorrect, my employment may be terminated forthwith.

Date .... Signed ....

(Continued)

(Continued)

FOR OFFICE USE ONLY

Interviewed by .... Date ....

Job Title	Company and Site
	Dept. and Code
National Insurance Number	Starting date
Notice required by present employer	Starting salary
Holidays booked	Job grade

PRE-EMPLOYMENT MEDICAL QUESTIONNAIRE

NAME .... COMPANY ....

ADDRESS .... BRANCH ....

.... DEPT. ....

....

General Practitioner ....

....

....

Date of Birth .... Height .... Weight......................

Have you ever had or have you ever been treated for:-

	YES	NO		YES	NO
Asthma			Stomach Trouble or Ulcer		
Hay Fever			Back Strain		
Any other Allergy			Disc Trouble		
Diabetes			Heart Disease		
Jaundice			Fainting Spells		
Skin Rash			Shortness of Breath		
Dermatitis			High Blood Pressure		
Eczema			Psychiatric Treatment/ Nervous Breakdown		
Arthritis			Bronchitis		
Rheumatism			Chronic Cough		
Rupture			Rheumatic Fever		
Convulsions or Fits			Sinus Trouble		
Tuberculosis			Kidney Trouble		
Pneumonia			Varicose Veins		
Chest Pain			Eye Trouble		
Ear Trouble			Colour Blindness		

(Continued)

(Continued)

Do you have any physical defects or partial disability?

Have you worked in a dusty trade such as mining, pottery or foundry?

Have you ever made a claim for industrial injury or disease?

Have you ever had any other serious illness or surgical operation?

Do you smoke? Cigarettes Cigars Pipe Tobacco

Family History				
	Living		Dead	
	Present age	Present State of Health	Age at death	Cause of death
Father				
Mother				
Brothers				
,,				
,,				
Sisters				
,,				
,,				

Any family history of Asthma or Hay Fever?

I HEREBY CERTIFY that I have answered all questions to the best of my knowledge and that the answers are complete and true. I give permission for the Company Medical Officer to receive details of my illnesses from my Doctor if necessary.

Date: .... Signature: ....

Form 5 Request for reference plus questionnaire

PRIVATE & CONFIDENTIAL

Personnel Department

Telephone: 0279 6 24621
Telegrams: Matthey Harlow

Johnson Matthey Metals Limited

Edinburgh Way
Harlow Essex

Your ref.

Our ref.

Telephone Ext.

Date: ____________

Dear Sirs,

______________________ of ______________________

has applied to us for employment as a ______________________

stating that he/she was employed by you as a ______________________

from ______________________ to ______________________

We should be grateful if you would answer the questions below and return this form to us as soon as possible in the stamped addressed envelope enclosed.

Yours faithfully,

____

Personnel Officer

JM 38

1. When was he/she employed by you?	From:	To:
2. Was employment continuous?		
3. In what capacity was he/she employed?		
4. Why did he/she leave your employment?		
5. What was his/her rate of pay?		
6. Was the applicant satisfactory regarding:	a) ability?	b) honesty?
	c) sobriety?	d) timekeeping?
	e) industry?	f) health?
7. Did applicant receive any injury whilst in your employment?		
8. If so, state nature of injury and whether applicant is in receipt of Compensation and suffers from any disability.		
9. Do you know any reason why he/she should not be employed by us?		

Signature: ______________________ Date: ______________________

Further to your recent interview, we have pleasure in offering you an appointment, on behalf of *Johnson Matthey Chemicals Limited, as a .... in the .... Department, at Royston. Our offer is subject to satisfactory references and a probationary period of four weeks. On completion you will be required to sign a Statement of Contract of Employment. Your remuneration will be made up as follows:

Basic Salary (per hour) £... Phase I supplement £...
Phase II supplement of 5% on total gross earnings
subject to a minimum of £2.50 and a maximum of £4.00 per week

There will be a further entitlement in accordance with the Company's Self Financing Productivity Scheme as outlined to you at your interview. I would remind you that this scheme will be reviewed each year.

**Your contracted hours of work will be from .... to ...., Monday to Friday.

In addition for administrative purposes, our offer is subject to you producing your birth certificate and we would ask you to send this document together with your written acceptance. Failure to submit your birth certificate negates this offer of employment.

***On occasions, it may be necessary for you to work on process operator duties and it is part of your contract of employment that you will work on such duties, when so required. Where this means a higher hourly rate the increased rate will be paid.

We enclose a Works Handbook which sets out the main terms and conditions of employment in the Johnson Matthey Group of Companies. In due course you will be required to join the Works Pension Fund, details of which will be given to you at that time.

****We should be grateful if you would let us know whether this offer is acceptable to you and, if so, the date on which you will be able to commence your duties. If, however, you find yourself unable to accept this position would you please return the enclosures.

Yours faithfully,
for Johnson Matthey Chemicals Ltd.,

V. Treadwell (Mrs)
Assist. Personnel Officer c.c File

* Our Associated Company, Matthey Rustenburg Refiners(UK) Limited

** for Shift Workers in MRR (UK) Ltd. delete "your contracted hours of work ... Friday" and insert:
"As you will be working shifts, I am enclosing a copy of the Shift Working Agreement which sets out additional terms and conditions such as contacted hours of work, the premium paid for extended hours and the holiday and sickness payments."

*** Only insert when employing Mates or Employees in Groups II or III

**** Refer to alternative paragraphs

Form 7 Offer letter (weekly staff)

Dear

*Further to your recent interview, we have pleasure in offering you an appointment, on behalf of our **Parent Company, Johnson Matthey and Company Limited, as a .... in the ... Department ***of our Operating Company, ... at Royston. Our offer is subject to satisfactory references and a probationary period of six months. Your remuneration will be made up as follows:

Basic Salary £.... Phase I supplement £....
Phase II supplement of 5% on total gross earnings
subject to a minimum of £2.50 and a maximum of £4.00**** per week.
There will be a further entitlement in accordance with the Company's Self Financing Productivity Scheme as outlined to you at your interview. I would remind you that this scheme will be reviewed each year.
Please note that the salaries of Weekly Staff are paid a week in arrears and payment is made from Head Office (Southgate). Lunches are provided free of charge. Your hours of work will be from ... to .... Monday to Friday.
In addition, for administrative purposes, our offer is subject to you producing your birth certificate and we would ask you to send this document together with your written acceptance. Failure to submit your birth certificate negates this offer of employment.
We enclose a Weekly staff Rule Book together with a copy of the Royston Site House Rules and these documents set out the main terms and conditions of employment in the Johnson Matthey Group of Companies.

*****You will be required to join the Works Pension Fund, on completion of 6 months service, details of which will be given to you at the time.
******We should be grateful if you would let us know whether this offer is acceptable to you and, if so, the date on which you will be able to commence your duties. If, however, you find yourself unable to accept this position would you please return the enclosures.

Yours faithfully,
for Johnson Matthey & Company Ltd.,

M. Clarke
Personnel Manager
Johnson Matthey Chemicals Ltd.,

C.C Mr. R.S. Burgess
Manager of Department

*	Alternative
**	Associate Company, Matthey Rustenburg Refiners (UK) Limited
***	for MRR personnel omit 'of our Operating Company'
****	or pro rata
*****	Having attained the age of 20 (for female employees) Having attained the age of 25 (for male employees)
******	See alternative last paragraphs (page 10A)

Form 8 Offer letter (monthly staff — under 25)

Dear Sir/Madam,

*Further to your recent interview, we have pleasure in offering you an appointment on behalf of our **Parent Company, Johnson Matthey and Company Limited, as a ... in the ... Department ***of our Operating Company ...... at Royston. Our offer is subject to satisfactory references and a probationary period of six months. Your remuneration will be made up as follows:

Basic Salary £... Phase I supplement £...
Phase II supplement of 5% on total gross earnings,
subject to a minimum of £130 and a maximum of £208 per annum.

There will be a further entitlement in accordance with the Company's Self Financing Productivity Scheme as outlined to you at your interview. I would remind you that this scheme will be reviewed each year.

Lunches are provided free of charge, ****and your hours of work will be from .... to .... , Monday to Friday.

In addition for administrative purposes, our offer is subject to you producing your birth certificate and we would ask you to send this document together with your written acceptance. Failure to submit your birth certificate negates this offer of employment.

We enclose a Monthly Staff Rule Book together with a copy of the Royston Site House Rules and these documents set out the main terms and conditions of employment with the Johnson Matthey Group of Companies. On joining the Company you will be required to sign a Staff Agreement; a specimen copy of this Agreement together with some explanatory notes is enclosed. On completion of your six months probationary period and, on reaching the age of 25 years, you will be required to join the Staff Pension Scheme, paying contributions at the rate of ***** ... per annum of your salary in excess of ......
******We should be grateful if you would let us know whether this offer is acceptable to you and, if so, the date on which you will be able to commence your duties. If, however, you find yourself unable to accept this position would you please return the enclosures.

Yours faithfully,
for Johnson Matthey and Company Limited

M. Clarke
Personnel Manager
Johnson Matthey Chemicals Limited

Copies to: Manager of Department
Company Secretary
File

Form 9 Offer letter (monthly staff — over 25)

Dear Sir/Madam,

*Further to your recent interview, we have pleasure in offering you an appointment on behalf of our **Parent Company, Johnson Matthey and Company Limited, as a ... in the ... Department *** of our Operating Company .... at Royston. Our offer is subject to satisfactory references and a probationary period of six months. Your remuneration will be made up as follows:

Basic Salary £... Phase I supplement £...

Phase II supplement of 5% on total gross earnings, subject to a minimum of £130 and a maximum of £208 per annum.

There will be a further entitlement in accordance with the Company's Self Financing Productivity Scheme as outlined to you at your interview. I would remind you that this scheme will be reviewed each year.

Lunches are provided free of charge, ****and your hours of work will be from ... to ..., Monday to Friday.

In addition for administrative purposes, our offer is subject to you producing your birth certificate and we would ask you to send this document together with your written acceptance. Failure to submit your birth certificate negates this offer of employment.

We enclose a Monthly Staff Rule Book together with a copy of the Royston Site House Rules and these documents set out the main terms and conditions of employment with the Johnson Matthey Group of Companies. On joining the Company you will be required to sign a Staff Agreement; a specimen copy of this Agreement together with some explanatory notes is enclosed. On completion of your six months probationary period you will be required to join the Staff Pension Scheme, paying contributions at the rate of *****.. per annum of your salary in excess of .....

******We should be grateful if you would let us know whether this offer is acceptable to you and, if so, the date on which you will be able to commence your duties. If, however, you find yourself unable to accept this position would you please return the enclosures.

Yours faithfully,
for Johnson Matthey and Company Limited

M. Clarke
Personnel Manager
Johnson Matthey Chemicals Limited

NB

Copies to: Manager of Department
Company Secretary
File

(Continued)

(Continued)

* We have pleasure in confirming our offer of employment.....

** Associated Company, Matthey Rustenburg Refiners (UK) Limited

*** for MRR personnel omit 'of our Operating Company..'

**** for employees who will be working shifts in the Refinery omit " and your hours .... Friday" and substitute:
"As you are working shifts, I am enclosing a copy of the Shift Working Agreement which sets out the additional terms and conditions such as contracted hours of work, the premium paid for extended hours and the holiday and sickness payments.

***** MALE CONTRIBUTIONS 7% per annum of your salary in excess of £450
FEMALE CONTRIBUTIONS 6½% of your salary in excess of £350

****** <u>Alternative last paragraphs</u>

1) We understand that this offer is acceptable to you and that you will be able to commence your duties on ... However, we would be grateful if you would confirm this in writing as soon as possible.

2) We should be grateful if you would let us know whether this offer is acceptable to you and, if so, we understand that you will be able to commence your duties on .....

<u>RELOCATION EXPENSES</u>

In the offer letter insert the following paragraph where necessary. This would normally be inserted after the first paragraph in the offer letter.

It can be ascertained whether to include this paragraph by looking to see if there is any entry under R.E on the candidates application form. This will show the amount that the Company will pay.

The Company is also prepared to pay the sum of .... towards the cost of your relocation expenses.

Form 10 Offer letter (sandwich student)

Dear Sir/Madam

Further to your recent interview, we have pleasure in offering you employment as a Sandwich Student in our ... Department at Royston, commencing ... and terminating on .... During this period we shall consider you to be a member of our Weekly Staff and, as such, you will be bound by the terms and conditions described in the enclosed booklets.

Your salary will be £... plus a supplement of £... per week. In addition, you will also be entitled to a further supplement of 5% of your total gross earnings per week, subject to a minimum of £2.50 per week and a maximum of £4.00 per week. Please note that the salaries of Weekly Staff are paid a week in arrears and payment is made from Head Office (Southgate). Lunches are provided free of charge.

In addition, for administrative purposes, our offer is subject to your producing your birth certificate and we would ask you to send this document together with your written acceptance. Failure to submit your birth certificate negates this offer of employment.

Your hours of work will be from ... to ..., Monday to Friday, and the position is subject to a probationary period of one month.

*We would be grateful if you would let us know whether this offer is acceptable to you and, if so, the date on which you will be able to commence your duties.

If, however, you find yourself unable to accept the offer would you please return the enclosures.

Yours faithfully,
for JOHNSON MATTHEY CHEMICALS LTD,

M. Clarke
Personnel Manager

Copies to: Manager of Department
File

*Alternative paragraph.

Form 11 Standard acceptance letter (hourly — works)

Dear

Thank you for your letter of ..., accepting our offer of an appointment as a ... in the ... Department, *at Royston. **On your first morning, ..., will you please arrive at 8.00 a.m. and ask for me at the Security Post, bringing with you, if possible, your Income Tax form P45 and National Insurance number.

May I take this opportunity of welcoming you to the Johnson Matthey Group and wish you every success in your new appointment.

Yours sincerely,
for JOHNSON MATTHEY CHEMICALS LTD,

V. Treadwell (Mrs)
Assistant Personnel Officer

* For MRR personnel insert: 'of our Associated Company Matthey Rustenburg Refiners (UK) Ltd.'

** If in receipt of the birth certificate, add the following: 'We also confirm receipt of your Birth Certificate which will be returned as soon as possible.'

Form 12 Standard acceptance letter (weekly)

Dear

Thank you for your letter of ... accepting our offer of an appointment as a ... in the ... Department of our *Operating Company, ... , at Royston.**

On your first morning, ... , please delay your arrival until 8.45 a.m. and then ask for me at the Security Post, bringing with you, if possible, your Income Tax form P45 and National Insurance number or Form RD3.

***May I take this opportunity of welcoming you to the Johnson Matthey Group and wish you every success in your new appointment.

Yours sincerely,
for JOHNSON MATTHEY CHEMICALS LTD

V.Treadwell (Mrs)

Assistant Personnel Officer

* For MRR personnel: 'Associated Company Matthey Rustenburg Refiners (UK) Ltd.'

** If in receipt of Birth Certificate, add the following: 'We also confirm receipt of your birth certificate which will be returned to you as soon as possible.'

*** Insert a new paragraph for employee who is requiring accommodation:'We have booked bed and breakfast accommodation for you at ... from the night of .... This accommodation will be paid for by the Company for the first ... weeks. The landlady's name is ... and I would be glad if you could telephone her on ... nearer the time and let her know approximately the time you will be arriving. The location of ... is shown on the enclosed sketch map.'

Form 13 Standard acceptance letter (monthly)

Dear

Thank you for your letter of ....., accepting our offer of an appointment as a ..... in the ..... Department of our *Operating Company, ..., at **Royston.

On your first morning, ..., please delay your arrival until 8.45 a.m. and then ask for me at the Security Post bringing with you, if possible, your Income Tax Form P.45 and National Insurance Number or Form RD.3.

Please find enclosed an Authorisation of Salary form to be completed and returned in the envelope provided.

***

May I take this opportunity of welcoming you to the Johnson Matthey Group and wish you every success in your new appointment.

Yours sincerely,
for Johnson Matthey & Company Ltd.,

M. Clarke
Personnel Manager
Johnson Matthey Chemicals Ltd.,

Enc

* for MRR personnel: "Associated Company, Matthey Rustenburg Refiners (UK) Ltd

** If Birth Certificate received add "We also confirm receipt of your birth certificate which will be returned as soon as possible"

*** Insert new paragraph for employee requiring accomodation:

We have booked bed and breakfast accommodation for you at .... from the night of .... This accommodation will be paid for by the Company for the first .... weeks. The landlady's name is .... and I would be glad if you could let her know on ..... (tel. No.) approximately the time you will be arriving. The location of .... is shown on the enclosed sketch map.

NB Copies to: Manager of the Department
R.S. Burgess (HQ)
File

Form 14 Written statement of terms of employment referring to handbook

EMPLOYMENT PROTECTION (CONSOLIDATION) ACT 1978

JOHNSON MATTHEY CHEMICALS LIMITED, of Orchard Road, Royston, SG8 5HE

is employing you.

Name *Mr/Mrs./Miss*..of

Address ....

as a.................................... from.................................... (date)

Your hourly rate of pay is.................... and weekly wage £ ....

Your normal working hours are from....................to....................Monday to

Friday and your normal working week of....................hours' duration.

Details of your conditions of employment and employee benefits are set out in the handbook 'Working with the Johnson Matthey Group of Companies', a copy of which has been given to you. Information which the Company is required to give you: holidays, membership of trade unions, payment for accidents and sickness, pension fund membership, grievance procedure and termination of employment, is in green print in the handbook. Future changes to conditions of employment will be covered by amendments to the handbook.

EMPLOYMENT PROTECTION (CONSOLIDATION) ACT 1978

I acknowledge receipt of the handbook 'Working with the Johnson Matthey Group of Companies' and statement relating to my conditions of employment as required by the above Act.

Date.................... **Signed**....................

Form 15 Notice of change in terms of employment

EMPLOYMENT PROTECTION (CONSOLIDATION) ACT, 1978

Dear______________________________ Clock No: ________________________________

Please note the following change to your terms and conditions of employment:

With effect from ____

☐ Your new rate will be ________________ per hour (______________)
per________________hour week.

☐ Your new hours will be ____________________________ per week.

☐ Your new employing Company will be Johnson Matthey Chemicals Ltd/
Matthey Refiners Ltd.

____

For Johnson Matthey Chemicals Ltd
and Matthey Refiners Ltd

TERMS AND CONDITIONS OF EMPLOYMENT FOR MONTHLY STAFF WORKING FOR JOHNSON MATTHEY METALS LIMITED AND JOHNSON & SONS' SMELTING WORKS LIMITED AT BIRMINGHAM

1977

This booklet contains the more important conditions of employment applicable to monthly staff and, taken in conjunction with notices issued by the Company and correspondence between the Company and individual employees, fulfils the requirements of the Contracts of Employment Act 1972 (as amended by the Trade Union & Labour Relations Act 1974 and the Employment Protection Act 1975.) Changes to conditions and any regulations applying to this establishment are published from time to time as amendments to the booklet.

Full details of the main U.K. Companies in the Johnson Matthey Group are listed on the following pages. All members of the U.K. monthly staff are employed by the parent company — Johnson Matthey & Co., Limited. They will normally be working for one of the several Operating or Subsidiary Companies and eligible for transfer anywhere within the Group without interruption to their contracts of employment. Conditions of service are very similar throughout the Group but variations are necessary at each location to cater for local circumstances. This booklet applies to all those based at Birmingham, irrespective of which Company they work for.

INTERPRETATION

For the purpose of this booklet:

Company means the Company within the Johnson Matthey Group for which you are working

Directors means the Directors of the Company for which you are working

Company Secretary means the Company Secretary of the Company for which you are working

Local Director means the Senior Manager at Birmingham with full responsibility for administration and discipline

Manager means the person in charge of any department who reports direct to the Local Director

Premises means the Birmingham sites occupied by the Company

Security Officers include all personnel controlling access to or egress from the premises

National Insurance Benefits means State sickness or accident benefits and earnings related benefits which employees are entitled to claim for themselves and their dependants

JOHNSON, MATTHEY & CO., LIMITED
100 High Street, Southgate, London N14 6ET
01-882 6111

OPERATING COMPANIES

Blythe Colours Limited
Cresswell, Stoke-on-Trent, ST11 9RD
07818-5959

Albion Works, Liverpool Road East, Kidsgrove, Stoke-on-Trent, ST7 3AA
07818-5959

F. J. Dean Limited,
Albert Mill, Silverdale Road, Newcastle-under-Lyme, Staffordshire, ST5 2TA
0782-615251

Cowan Colours Limited,
Barbers Road, Stratford, London E15 2PH
01-534 3311

Johnson Matthey Bankers Limited
5 Lloyds Avenue, London EC3N 3DB
01-481 3181

43 Hatton Garden, London EC1N 8EE
01-405 6959

Johnson Matthey Commodities Limited
5 Lloyds Avenue, London, EC3N 3DB
01-481 3181

(Continued)

Johnson Matthey Chemicals Limited
Orchard Road, Royston, Hertfordshire SG8 5HE
0763-44161

Jeffreys Road, Brimsdown, Enfield, Middlesex, EN3 7PW
01-804 8111

Rare Earth Products Limited, Waterloo Road, Widnes, Cheshire, WA8 0QH
051-423 1166

Johnson Matthey Metals Limited
100 High Street, Southgate, London, N14 6ET
01-882 6111

Vittoria Street, Birmingham, B1 3NZ
021-236 9811

Edinburgh Way, Harlow, Essex CM20 2BL
0279-24621

173-175 Arundel Gate, Sheffield, S1 1JY
0742-23121

South Way, Exhibition Grounds, Wembley, Middlesex HA9 0HW
01-902 8864

43 Hatton Garden, London, EC1N 8EE
01-405 6959

Johnson & Sons' Smelting Works Limited, 104 Spencer Street, Birmingham, B18 6DB
021-554 5781

Johnson Matthey Services Limited
100 High Street, Southgate, London N14 6ET
01-882 6111

43 Hatton Garden, London EC1N 8EE
01-405 6959

Johnson Matthey Research Centre, Blount's Court, Sonning Common, Reading, Berkshire RG4 9NH
073-525 2811

Johnson Matthey Central Catering Service, 1 Merchant Drive, Mead Lane, Hertford, SG13 7BH
32-58393

Matthey Printed Products Limited
William Clowes Street, Burslem, Stoke-on-Trent, ST6 3AT
0782-85631

Matthey Rustenburg Refiners (U.K.) Limited
Orchard Road, Royston, Hertfordshire SG8 5HE
0763-44161

Jeffreys Road, Brimsdown, Enfield, Middlesex EN3 7PW
01-804 8111

And Overseas Companies in:
Australia, Austria, Belgium, Brazil, Canada, Eire, France, Holland, India, Italy, Japan, New Zealand, South Africa, Spain, Sweden, Switzerland, United States.

The registered office of the Parent Company and all Operating Companies except Blythe Colours Limited and F. J. Dean Limited is at 43 Hatton Garden, London EC1N 8EE.

CONTENTS

(Continued)

(Continued)

CONDITIONS OF EMPLOYMENT

Absence from Work
When members of the monthly staff are absent they are required to inform their Managers of the circumstances as soon as possible (preferably by telephone). Failure to do so may result in deduction from salary.

Absence due to Sickness
During the first year of service all absence must be covered by a medical certificate. From the second year of service employees are permitted to take up to two days of uncertified sick leave provided the Company is notified and the absence is not recurrent. If the absence extends beyond two days a certificate will be required to cover the whole period of the absence. This certificate may be either a private one or the National Insurance certificate.

Private certificates do not indicate an assumed period of incapacity and therefore further certificates must be submitted during each week of incapacity. A final clearance certificate is required before employees can restart work.

National Insurance certificates indicate an estimated period of incapacity and this will be accepted as the assumed period of absence and the employee will be expected to return to work on the date stated. Further certificates must be submitted to cover longer periods of absence and to indicate the date of return to work.

National Insurance certificates must be correctly completed and accompanied by an envelope addressed to the employee's local office of the Department of Health and Social Security. If this is not done the certificate will be returned to the employee and there may be delay in obtaining National Insurance benefit.

Payment during Absence due to Sickness
Provided your Manager has been notified and the necessary medical certificates submitted, the Company will make the following payments in any year from 1st April to 31st March to employees of three months' service or more. From all payments for sickness the appropriate National Insurance benefits will be deducted.

3 months — 2 years:
4 weeks at full pay 8 weeks at threequarters pay

2 years — 5 years:
8 weeks at full pay 8 weeks at threequarters pay

5 years — 10 years:
12 weeks at full pay 8 weeks at threequarters pay

10 years — 15 years:
16 weeks at full pay 13 weeks at threequarters pay

15 years — 20 years:
20 weeks at full pay 13 weeks at threequarters pay

Over 20 years:
26 weeks at full pay 13 weeks at threequarters pay

NOTE

1. So that errors do not occur in the amount of National Insurance benefits deducted from sick pay, employees must provide their Manager with forms BS12 and BF 168 which they receive from the Department of Health and Social Security as soon as possible.

2. Although a married woman or widow may have elected not to pay contributions under the Social Security Acts 1973-1975 there shall be deducted from the Company's sick pay the amount of National Insurance benefit she would have received had she been a contributor under the Acts.

3. Absence which continues from one benefit year into the next will be treated as one period of absence and eligible for the sick pay entitlement of the year in which the sickness commenced. Six consecutive weeks' work (excluding holidays in excess of 2 weeks and leave of absence) must be completed before the employee will be eligible for sick pay in the new benefit year.

4. No payment will be made for uncertified sickness during the first year of service. Thereafter up to two days' uncertified sick leave may be taken provided the Company is notified and the absence is not recurrent. All uncertified absence will be included in the annual sickness allowance.

Absence due to Other Causes
No payment will be made for other absences except at the discretion of the Company. When absence is due to jury service, court attendance as a witness or injury resulting from traffic accident, partial compensation for loss of earnings may be claimed from other sources.

The Company is willing to give sympathetic consideration to any hardship which might arise and the Company Secretary should be informed of the circumstances as soon as possible.

Accident Notification
Employees must report immediately every accident at work, however slight, to their Managers so that the appropriate treatment may be obtained and the necessary record made in the Accident Register. Not only is this to comply with current regulations but it is in the interests of the employees.

Payment during Absence due to Accident at Work
For a period of 13 weeks, employees will receive full pay, less National Insurance benefits, for certified absence resulting from an accident at work. If certified absence extends beyond this period, accident pay will be maintained at Management's discretion.

If the accident occurs as a result of the misuse

(Continued)

of equipment or materials, failure to use protective measures available or to comply with existing safety regulations, the Company reserves the right to withhold all or part of this payment.

Change of Address and Status
Employees must inform their immediate superior, in writing, immediately any change in their permanent address, marital status, birth of children or academic qualifications takes place.

Computation of Service
When an employee is re-engaged by the Company following a period of absence, whether the reason was compulsory service with the Armed Forces, redundancy or voluntary resignation, his past service may be taken into account when establishing his entitlement to Company benefits or facilities. Full details are available from the Local Director.

Expenses
When members of the staff are travelling on business their reasonable expenses will be reimbursed on production of accounts, countersigned by their Manager.

There is a standard form which must be completed when any expenses are claimed from the Company. This form is needed to facilitate the preparation of information required by the Inspector of Taxes and must be handed, together with any relevant receipts, to the person responsible for paying such expenses.

Grievance Procedure
Employees wishing to raise any matter with Management concerning their conditions of employment should proceed as follows. Every attempt will be made to settle the issue with a minimum of delay.

Employees who are members of a trade union or staff organisation recognised by the Company may be accompanied by a representative of that body at any stage in the procedure.

a) the employee should submit his problem, either verbally or in writihg, to his immediate superior, who will arrange a meeting between them.
b) if the employee is dissatisfied with the result of the meeting, he should inform his superior that he would like his problem to be considered by his Manager. His immediate superior will make the necessary appointment and will be present at the interview with the Manager.
c) failing satisfactory settlement of the problem by the Manager, the matter will be referred to the Local Director. The Manager will be present at the interview.
d) if the matter is still unresolved it will be referred to the Production Director in consultation with the Company Secretary. The Local Director will be present at the interview.
e) if the employee is still dissatisfied, the matter will be referred to the Managing Director. The Production Director and the Local Director will be present at the interview.
f) if the matter is still unresolved it will be referred to the Chairman of the Company. The Managing Director and the Local Director will be present at the meeting.

Holidays
Annual Holiday. All employees will receive the following entitlement in each calendar year according to service:—

Under 1 year	—1/12th of 20 days for each completed month of service
On completion of 1 year	—20 days

Those of long service with the Company qualify for long leave every fifth year. Details of this provision are shown on page 17.

Employees who join the Company on or before, or leave the Company on or after, the 15th day of any month will be credited with service for that month.

Payment for holidays will be at the basic rate for day work exclusive of any overtime, bonus or other premium or allowances, except for those employees regularly working shifts and receiving a shift work premium. In the case of such employees payment for holidays will be the basic rate plus shift work premium. Where the premium varies according to the particular shift, the basis will be the average of the premium for the full shift cycle.

Holidays are based on the calendar year, 1st January to 31st December, but Managers have discretion to permit a maximum of one week's holiday from one year to be carried over to the month of January in the following year.

Any entitlement to a proportion of a day in the year of joining will be paid for at the end of the following January. Apart from these provisions, holidays not taken in accordance with the Company's regulations will be forfeited.

THE TIMES AT WHICH HOLIDAYS ARE TAKEN MUST BE APPROVED IN ADVANCE BY THE MANAGER who will endeavour to suit the convenience of individuals as far as possible. Normally, staff of less than 15 years' service may not take more than two weeks' holiday between 1st June and 30th September.

The Company reserves the right to allocate one day of the holiday entitlement to any day between a statutory holiday and a weekend, provided three months' notice of the intention to do so is given.

Employees who leave the Company before taking holiday due to them will receive a pro rata payment with their final salary. Employees who leave after taking holidays will refund to the Company any unearned holiday pay.

(Continued)

Monthly staff with 25 or more years' service will be granted two extra weeks of holiday once every five years. The two extra weeks must be taken consecutively with at least two weeks of normal entitlement, making an absence of four to six weeks. Arrangements for long leave must be agreed with the Local Director and notified to the Company Secretary at least three months before it is due to commence.

Members of the Armed Services Reserves who are required to attend annual camp will use their annual holiday entitlement for this purpose. No additional time off will be allowed.

Statutory Holidays. 8 statutory holidays (normally New Year's Day, Good Friday (alternatively Easter Tuesday), Easter Monday, May Day, Spring and Summer Bank Holidays, Christmas Day and Boxing Day) are observed by the Company each year. Payment for these holidays will be at basic rate for contracted hours of work.

If a statutory holiday occurs during the period of annual holiday a further day may be added to that annual holiday period. This does not apply to any day on which Birmingham is closed but which is not a statutory holiday.

Staff required to work on a statutory holiday will receive the following additional payments:

Christmas Day Good Friday (alternatively Easter Tuesday)	double basic rate
Easter Monday Spring and Summer Bank Holidays Boxing Day New Year's Day *and May Day*	basic rate and a half

NOTE:

a) Good Friday will be treated as a normal working day when by local arrangement Easter Tuesday is being taken as a statutory holiday.

b) By arrangement with Management, a day off in lieu of the statutory holiday can be taken. In this case the additional payment for working on the holiday will be basic rate for Christmas Day and Good Friday (alternatively Easter Tuesday) and half basic rate for the other statutory holidays.

c) *Works Holidays.* Members of the staff required to work on days when Birmingham is closed but which are not statutory holidays, are not entitled to any special remuneration but will be given equivalent leave at a time convenient to themselves and the Company.

Hours of Work

The working hours will be those notified to employees at the time of their engagement. Monthly staff will normally work 37½ hours per week, from Monday to Friday, but a longer week is required for certain duties, particularly those concerned with factory supervision. Normal starting and finishing times for each member of the staff will be stated at the time of engagement and may be varied by local notices affecting the particular premises or by special instruction to an individual by his Manager. The working of extended hours on a permanent basis is recognised in basic salary.

Every employee must be ready to begin work at the proper starting time and must not cease work until the proper time for finishing, unless permission has first been obtained from his Manager.

Lateness

All late arrivals will be reported and any member of the monthly staff arriving late for work is required to give an explanation at once to his immediate superior. Persistent lateness is a ground for dismissal.

Lunch and Refreshments

Except where different local arrangements have been agreed, a period of one hour in the middle of the day is allowed for lunch which is provided free of charge. The times at which the break is taken vary according to Departments and are decided by the Manager concerned.

Refreshments are available in most departments. It should be noted that Health and Safety Regulations prohibit the serving of food and refreshments in some departments and local instructions will be issued where appropriate.

Maternity Leave

Maternity leave is provided for under the Employment Protection Act 1975 and details can be obtained from the Local Director on request.

Medical Examination

Engagement of new employees may depend upon their successfully passing a medical examination. Further examination may be required from time to time.

Membership of Trade Unions or Staff Organisations

Membership of a trade union or staff organisation is entirely a matter for employees to decide for themselves.

The Birmingham Staff Society is the organisation recognised by the Company for negotiations in respect of staff employed at Birmingham.

Overtime

Employees are expected to work overtime when the Company requires it. Overtime hours are those worked in excess of the standard hours per day, by prior arrangement with the Manager. Payment for overtime is detailed under the paragraph on salaries on page 24.

Pension Arrangements

On completion of six months' service and after they have attained the age of 25, new members

(Continued)

of the monthly staff will be required, as a condition of employment, to join the Staff Pension Scheme and to pay contributions in accordance with the rules set out in the explanatory booklet with which they will be provided.

Members of all this scheme are contracted-out of the State earnings-related pension scheme.

Redundancy
The Company recognises that security of employment is one of the prime needs of working life. In furtherance of this, the Directors will, as in the past, take all reasonable steps to prevent the occurrence of redundancy. Nevertheless, in a period of rapid changes in demand, economic depression or technological changes, the possibility of redundancy cannot be eliminated.

Provisions for employees who become redundant are as follows:

Redundancy pay:	payment according to the Company's scheme or the State scheme, whichever is the more favourable.
Pension Scheme:	Three options are available: 1. deferred pension 2. transfer of pension benefit to the new employer's scheme 3. return of employee's contributions but only in accordance with the Social Security Acts 1973-75 Full details of the options available can be obtained from the Local Director.
Holidays	for those who leave between 1st January and 31st March — 10 days for those who leave between 1st April and 30th June — 13 days for those who leave between 1st July and 30th September — 18 days for those who leave between 1st October and 31st December — 20 days
Service Allowance:	entitlement for the current year, to the date of leaving
Long Service Awards:	any award to which they may be entitled within 12 months of the date of termination.

All the provisions and requirements of the Redundancy Payments Acts 1965 and 1969 and the Employment Protection Act 1975 will apply.

Retirement
Employees will normally retire at the State age for retirement, i.e. 65 years for men and 60 years for women.

Right of Search
The Company reserves the right, as a condition of employment, to search or cause to be searched, whenever it sees fit, any employee of the Company and any property of employees which is on the premises. The search will be conducted in the presence of a Director or a person appointed for that purpose by the Directors. Search of a staff woman or examination of her handbag, will be conducted only by a woman.

The right of search extends to all parcels, suitcases, bags, vehicles etc. which are on the Company's premises; the search will be carried out in the presence of the owner.

Personal lockers or desks may be subject to general search in the presence of the owner, if on the premises, a Staff Society representative and a senior member of Management. Records will be kept of all such searches.

Safety Policy
It is the policy of the Company to ensure the health and safety at work of all employees. The safety precautions and provisions applicable to Birmingham are laid down in the Safety Handbook, a copy of which will be given to each new employee.

Salaries
Payment of Salaries. Payment is made by direct credit to employees' bank accounts on the last Friday of each month. A statement of payment and deductions is sent to each employee on the same day.

Salary Review. Salaries will be reviewed during the early part of each calendar year and any increase awarded will be effective from 1st April.

Additional Payments.
(i) Overtime. Authorised overtime will be paid for on the following basis:
Monday—Friday — first two hours per day at basic rate plus one-third. Thereafter per day at basic rate plus half.
Saturday (where this is not normally a working day) — All hours at basic rate plus half.
Sunday — All hours at double basic rate.
(basic rate is a flat hourly rate in direct proportion to annual salary)
Payment will not normally be made for overtime of less than one hour's duration.

Any member of staff called from home to deal with an emergency may claim for two hours' overtime as a minimum, irrespective of the time actually spent on the Company's premises. Payment for this overtime will be at the appropriate premium rate.

(*Continued*)

Periods of overtime worked during each calendar month will be totalled at the end of the month and paid for at the end of the following month. Managers and certain senior members of staff (who will be advised personally) will not be eligible for overtime payment.

(ii) Shift Work. Staff required to work on a shift system will be paid an appropriate shift premium.

Deductions from Salaries. The following deductions will be made from salaries:

(i) Income Tax, which has to be deducted from all payments by the Company to members of the staff for services rendered, whether these payments consist of salary, bonuses or overtime, or are made in respect of special services.

(ii) National Insurance Contributions. As provided for under the Social Security Acts 1973-1975, all employees will pay National Insurance contributions each month based on their total earnings within lower and upper limits. These contributions will be collected through the PAYE income tax arrangements.

(iii) Contributions to the appropriate Company Pension Fund, for those eligible for membership.

(iv) Subscriptions to the Sports and Social Club, to the Birmingham Hospital Saturday Fund the British United Provident Association, and to the Johnson Matthey Savings Scheme, if the employee so requests.

(v) Refund of loans from the Company for the purchase of annual season tickets, or for any other approved purpose, as authorised by the employee.

Service/Secrecy Agreement

All monthly staff whose work is of a technical or confidential nature may be required to enter into a formal service and/or secrecy agreement with the Parent Company.

Service Allowance

A service allowance is payable to employees of five or more years' service, at the end of June each year, as follows:

5- 9 years	—	£10
10-14 years	—	£25
15-19 years	—	£30
20th year	—	£35
21-24 years	—	NIL

When long leave is taken (normally on completion of 25 years' service and every fifth year thereafter) there will be a payment of £50 for each completed year since payment of the last service allowance. The total will be increased by a further £50, provided the full five years' entitlement has accumulated.

Employees leaving or retiring from the Company between the 21st and 25th years of service will be paid the sum of £50 for each completed year of service since they last received a service allowance. Employees leaving or retiring after having taken a first or subsequent long leave will be paid £50 for each completed year of service since their last long leave commenced.

For those employees who transfer from weekly to monthly staff after having completed 20 years' service, the payment associated with the first long leave will be £50 for each completed year of service since the date of their last service payment.

Those employees who, at the discretion of the Directors, are granted a long leave before completion of 20 years' service on grounds of status and responsibility will receive only the normal cash allowance associated with their service.

Those employees who, at the discretion of the Directors, are granted a long leave between their 21st and 24th years of service will receive £50 for each completed year of service since they last received a service allowance.

The allowance is based on the number of years actually completed by employees during the calendar year in which it is paid.

Part-time employees will receive a pro rata proportion of the full allowance according to their contracted hours of work.

Employees who leave the Company during the year will receive 1/12th of the full allowance for each completed month of service since the last anniversary of their starting date.

Employees who leave the Company before the anniversary of their starting date, after having received the full allowance for the year, will be required to refund the unearned portion of the allowance to the Company.

Termination of Employment

Notice of termination of employment (or payment in lieu of notice) given by the Company varies with the length of service of the employees, as follows:

Four calendar weeks' notice to employees of 4 or more weeks but less than 5 years' continuous service.

One week's notice for each year of service up to a maximum of 12 weeks, for employees of 5 or more years' continuous service.

These provisions shall not apply when an employee is dismissed for gross misconduct or breach of contract. The Company shall be entitled to terminate its contract with an employee who:—

a) refuses or fails to carry out efficiently the duties allocated

b) fails to observe and perform the employment conditions applicable

(Continued)

c) is guilty of gross or serious misconduct on the Company's premises or elsewhere which is likely to damage the reputation of the Company or its business, or to render it impossible to carry out satisfactorily the duties allocated.

Members of the monthly staff who wish to terminate their employment are required to give not less than one calendar month's notice, in writing, to the Company, except in those cases where a different period of notice is required to be given in accordance with the provisions of a formal agreement between the Company and the employee.

Before leaving the Company employees shall hand over all documents, books, records, correspondence and other papers relating to its business, together with any keys or other property of the Company which may be in their possession.

Working Late

It is important that the Security Officers on duty know exactly who is on the premises after the main doors are closed, both for the security of property and for the safety of the employees in the event of fire or accident. The following rules must therefore be observed:

(a) Staff are prohibited from working alone on the premises, except with the permission of their Manager.

(b) Staff who are likely to be working on the premises later than half an hour after the main entrance is closed must notify Security, if possible at least half an hour before their normal finishing time. Staff, who after giving in their names, do find it possible to leave earlier should ensure that their names are deleted from the list.

(c) In normal circumstances no staff, other than those on shift work, may remain on the premises after 20.00 hours. In exceptional cases, departments may arrange to work after 20.00 but such arrangements must be made in advance with Security by the Manager.

GENERAL DISCIPLINE

Admission outside Working Hours

Employees who need to enter the premises outside normal working hours for any purpose must first obtain permission to do so from their Manager who will give their names and intended time of arrival to Security beforehand.

An employee wishing to return to his department after having left the premises at the end of his normal working day can be permitted to do so only if escorted by a Security Officer.

Action in Case of Raids or Fire

Because valuable materials are stored at Birmingham it might be the target of organised raids. Raid alarms, in addition to the usual fire alarms, are located at suitable points on the premises and staff should ensure that they know exactly where to find the two types of alarm without delay.

In the case of raid, staff should:

i) sound the raid alarm

ii) call Control on telephone extension 222 stating where the emergency is and who is speaking.

In the case of fire:

i) during working hours —
anyone who discovers a fire should: —

a. sound the fire alarm

b. tell Control (Ext 222) where the fire is.

c. if possible, try to put out the fire, using available equipment.
Control will summon the Fire Crew and the City Fire Brigade.

ii) at other times —
the Security Personnel on duty will try to put the fire out, using available equipment
They will inform the City Fire Brigade.

Should it be necessary to evacuate the building, instructions will be given over the tannoy. Heads of Departments will ensure, as far as possible that precious metals are locked away before leaving. Supervisors will ensure that their areas are cleared.

A roll call by Departments will be held as soon as evacuation is complete, and reports made to Control.

At J.S.S.W. raid and fire alarms should be sounded as above. The senior staff member present will issue verbal instructions for summoning the City Fire Brigade or evacuating the premises.

Betting and Gambling

Employees may not practise or provide facilities for betting or gambling upon the Company's premises. Offenders are liable to disciplinary action which may include dismissal.

The organisers of any proposed sweepstake or raffle must apply to the Local Director for permission before proceeding and, if the activity is continuous or repeated annually, the application must be renewed every year.

Company Disciplinary Procedure

Should it be necessary for the Company to take disciplinary action against any employee, the normal procedure will be: —

recorded verbal warnings,
final warning in writing,
dismissal.

This procedure will not apply where an employee is guilty of breach of contract or gross misconduct.

(Continued)

Employees who are members of a trade union or staff organisation recognized by the Company may be accompanied by a representative of that body whenever a disciplinary interview is taking place.

At the request of the employee, the Company will provide a written statement of the reason for the dismissal.

Any dismissed employee who wishes to appeal against dismissal, may do so within two working days, by applying to the Local Director. The appeal will be considered by the Managing Director, unless he has been involved in the decision to dismiss. In this case the appeal will be considered by the Chairman of the Company.

Correspondence and Use of Telephone

(a) *Company's Business.* Any prestige which attaches to the name of the Company can be enhanced or damaged by the use of the telephone; a moment's apparent discourtesy can spoil the work of months of sales promotion and no circumstances whatever can justify it. The same considerations apply to the written communications sent to other firms on behalf of the Company. In particular, care should be taken that any references used by those dealing with the Company are quoted on out-going letters. Staff should also emphasise the importance of adequate references upon incoming correspondence.

(b) *Private Correspondence.* Staff should discourage the sending of private correspondence to them at the Company's address. The Company reserves the right to open mail addressed in this way, and in any case the quantity of mail arriving daily is such that private letters may be opened inadvertently. Holiday post cards should carry full addresses, including the names of the departments for which they are intended.

(c) *Private Telephone Calls.* The Directors are unwilling to prohibit entirely the use of the Company's telephone system for the private business of members of the staff, since they realize that sometimes such business can be transacted only during working hours. However, they ask the staff to remember that this privilege involves obligations and private business should be transacted on the Company's telephone system only when no other means are available.

The installation throughout the Johnson Matthey Group of the PABX Extension telephone system enables staff to call any number on the public system but as far as possible such calls should be made outside the peak hours of 09.00—13.00. Employees making private trunk or overseas calls direct through this system are required firstly to obtain permission from their Manager and, within 24 hours, to inform the telephone supervisor so that a charge for the call can be made.

Employees' Property

The Company takes every reasonable precaution to safeguard employees' property brought on to the premises, but cannot accept any responsibility for its loss or damage. Such loss or damage should be reported to your Manager as soon as it is discovered.

Intoxication

Members of the staff found on the Company's premises in a state of intoxication, or in possession of alcoholic drink without permission, will be liable to disciplinary action.

Money Collections

Employees may not collect money, whether for wedding presents, wreaths, or for any other purpose, outside their own departments without first obtaining permission from the Local Director.

Collections of money from employees for loan clubs or savings clubs even though they may be restricted to members of one department, are prohibited unless authorised in writing by the Local Director.

Notices

The passing of information and instructions to employees is normally effected by notices posted on the official notice boards.

Parking of Motor Vehicles and Bicycles

At Vittoria Street there is limited accommodation for parking of cars, motor cycles and bicycles. Parking facilities are governed by the space available at any given time and are controlled by the Local Director. The Company will not be responsible for damage or loss which may occur to privately owned vehicles on its premises or in car parks provided for the use of the Company's employees, although any such damage or loss should be reported. The Company reserves the right to search or cause to be searched (in the presence of the owner) any vehicles on the premises or car parks.

Passes for Goods Removed from the Premises

Before property or documents which have been borrowed or bought from the Company may be taken out of the premises, a pass must be obtained. Instructions for applying for the appropriate pass should be obtained from your Manager.

Protection of Company Property

It is a primary duty of all staff members to safeguard the Company's property. For example any theft or attempted theft should be reported to the Local Director or a Security Officer without delay. Suspicious circumstances or behaviour should always be reported. Information of this type is regarded as strictly confidential and will never be treated as trivial.

(Continued)

(Continued)

Relations with the Public, and Publicity
Apart from normal business communications, staff must not discuss the Company's business with people not employed in the organisation. This applies with particular force to such people as newspaper reporters, who should be referred to a Director or the Local Director, without further comment. Information on the nature of processes and operations will be published only as part of the considered policy of the Board of Directors of the Company, and under its direction.

Rewards
For the protection of the property of the Company and in the interests of its good name and that of its employees, the Directors will pay a reward of not less than £100 for information leading to conviction of any person concerned in the theft of precious metals belonging to the Company. A reward of not less than £200 will be paid for information which leads to the conviction of any person acting as an agent for the receiver. Subject to the minimum amount stated above, the amount of any reward will be at the Directors' discretion.

Smoking
Smoking by members of the staff during working hours is governed by the following considerations:

(a) Smoking is prohibited in the presence of the public at the counter, during the hours of admission of the public. It is also prohibited where 'No smoking' notices are displayed.

(b) Smoking is otherwise permitted at the discretion of Managers.

Use of the premises for Social Functions
Because of the strict controls imposed on persons entering and leaving the premises, the holding of social functions at Birmingham must, in general, be discouraged.

Visitors and Strangers
Business visitors must await escort before passing the Security Officers and must continue to be accompanied throughout their stay. They should be given access only to that part of the premises which business requires them to visit.

Private visitors will not be admitted to any offices without written permission from the Local Director.

Members of the staff should challenge any unaccompanied stranger whom they meet on the premises and if any employee has cause to believe that a stranger has no right to be on the premises he should report the matter to his Manager or the Security Officer on duty.

FACILITIES AND BENEFITS

The Birmingham Hospital Saturday Fund
Membership of this scheme is available through the Birmingham Branch and members may have their subscriptions deducted from salary.

Enquiries concerning this scheme and its benefits should be addressed to the Wages Office.

The British United Provident Association
This Association assists its members and their families to obtain medical treatment as private patients. Group membership rates are available to the staff and particulars can be provided by the BUPA Group Secretary, c/o the Pensions Department at Southgate.

Christmas Gifts
Christmas gifts of wine and/or poultry are distributed at the discretion of the Directors. Details of the arrangements are published each year.

Education and Training
Employees wishing to pursue courses of study may obtain advice and guidance from their Managers.

The Company will provide financial assistance towards fees, travel and books, for all courses of study which have been approved beforehand by their Managers. The continuance of such assistance is dependent upon satisfactory reports on attendance and progress, and upon the student having gained the desired qualifications within a reasonable time.

Life Assurance
Life assurance benefits are payable to the beneficiaries of employees who are members of the Staff Pension Scheme and who die whilst in the service of the Company. Details are given in the Pension Scheme explanatory booklet.

Beneficiaries of employees who were not members of the Staff Pension Scheme at the date of death will receive a life assurance benefit equivalent to twice the employee's basic salary at the date of death, less £900 or £700 for male or female employees respectively.

Long Service Awards
The Company recognizes long service with the following awards:

20 years service — the sum of £35, tax free, or a watch

30 years service — the sum of £50, tax free, or a watch

35 years service ladies }
40 years service men } — a gold watch

Presentations are made in November or December each year.

(Continued)

(Continued)

Medical Services
At Birmingham there is a well equipped first aid room on the ground floor and first aid boxes are located elsewhere on the premises. These facilities are controlled by qualified first aiders and any injury however trivial should receive proper attention.

Employees may see the Group Medical Officer when he is at Birmingham and should make the necessary arrangements through their Managers.

Membership of Institutes and Societies
The Directors wish to encourage employees' membership of the conferring and publishing societies connected with their work and in the case of more junior employees the Company will contribute towards the payment of fees and subscriptions. It will not subsidise membership of mutual assistance bodies or of qualifying bodies which confer upon the member a definite professional status which can be held to have a bearing on the remuneration he can command.

When the Directors invite senior employees to represent the Company on various bodies the dues will be paid in full by the Company.

Protective Clothing
Where appropriate certain articles of protective clothing and equipment are provided for the use of employees. They are required to take care of the protective clothing issued to them and may not take it away from the premises without permission.

Purchase of Annual Season Tickets
The Company is prepared to lend employees the money to purchase annual season tickets. Refund of the loans will be made from salaries. Details are available from the Local Director.

Saving Scheme
The Company operates a savings scheme in conjunction with the Abbey National Building Society and subscriptions will be deducted from salaries on request. Details are available from the Wages Department.

Sports and Social Club
The Birmingham Sports and Social Club provides certain sports and social activities. Subscriptions will be deducted from salary on request.

Transfer to other Branches or Companies
Members of the staff transferred at the request of the Company to another branch, or any other Company within the Johnson Matthey Group, in the U.K., as a result of which they have to move home or incur additional travelling expenses, will receive the following benefits:

Settling-in grant for new accommodation, as specified by the Company

Removal Expenses

Legal expenses and estate agents' expenses on selling and/or purchasing property

Excess travelling expenses for one year or until they have moved home, whichever is the shorter period

Details are available from the Company Secretary

The provisions for staff who transfer to overseas companies of the Johnson Matthey Group will be discussed with the persons concerned when the transfers are arranged, and included in the terms and conditions of their employment abroad.

Form 17 Acknowledgement of receipt of monthly staff handbook

TERMS AND CONDITIONS OF EMPLOYMENT FOR MONTHLY STAFF WORKING FOR JOHNSON MATTHEY METALS LIMITED AT BIRMINGHAM - 1977

This is to confirm that I have received a copy of the above booklet.

SIGNED

DATE

Please return to Miss Jill Deabill

Form 18 Authorisation of salary payment

Johnson Matthey Chemicals Limited
AUTHORISATION OF SALARY PAYMENT

Branch/Dept ______________________

I request that any salary due to me be credited on or before the last day of each month to my Bank Account as follows:

Bank ____

Full address of bank: ______________________________
____
____

Personal Account No: ______________________________

Signed: ____________________________

Date: ______________________________

Form 19 Authorisation for deduction of union subscription

Johnson Matthey Chemicals Limited
and
Matthey Rustenburg Refiners Limited
Royston

AUTHORISATION FOR DEDUCTION OF UNION SUBSCRIPTION

I hereby authorise you to deduct my Union Subscription of ________ per week or such amount as may later apply, from my wages with effect from __________ to be paid to the Iron and Steel Trades Confederation, Swinton House, Gray's Inn Road, London WC1, subject to my right to give in writing one week's notice of cancellation.

Signature ____________________________

Full name: ____________________________ Date: ______________

Clock or roll no: _______________ Department: ________________________

Dept. code: ____________________ Member's Branch no: __________________

Form 20 Overtime and absences record (monthly staff)

NOTES.

This form should be prepared in manuscript by Branch Secretaries. No copy should be kept and the form should reach Secretary's Dept. H. Gdn. not later than the 7th. of each month.

No name should appear more than once. When necessary, details of overtime and absence of the same employee MUST be shown on the same line.

Please write only in the shaded columns.

DO NOT USE THIS SPACE

JM 940

MONTHLY STAFF - OVERTIME and ABSENCES for the MONTH of

BRANCH

OVERTIME						ABSENCES											
NUMBER	SURNAME ONLY	O'TIME HOURS	RATE			INCLUSIVE DATES OF ABSENCE	DAYS	RATE	S.B. DEDUCTED		SICK PAY DEDUCTED				SUBTRACT		
				£	p				£	p	RATE	£	p	BALANCE	E E	E R	S E T

Form 21 Notification of engagement

To: SALARIES CONTROL
SOUTHGATE

NOTIFICATION OF ENGAGEMENT

WEEKLY/MONTHLY STAFF

DATE OF START ....

DEPARTMENT ....

FULL NAME ....

ADDRESS ....

DATE OF BIRTH ....

MARITAL STATUS ....

CHILDREN UNDER 18 ....

NATIONAL INSURANCE NO. ....

SALARY ....

GRADE ....

HOURS PER WEEK ....

P.45. SIGNATURE ....

DATE ....

MONTHLY STAFF ONLY

NAME OF EMPLOYEE ....

BRANCH/DEPT ....

BANK SORTING CODE ....

ACCOUNT NO. ....

BANK NAME ....

BANK ADDRESS ....

Form 22 Notification of transfer

NOTIFICATION OF TRANSFER

To: From:

Full name: Address:

Present Dept: New Dept:

Present code: New code:

Present position: New position:

Present salary: New salary:

Date of transfer: Transferred:

Signature: ______________________

Date: ______________________

Form 23 Departmental transfers — hourly paid employees

JOHNSON MATTHEY CHEMICALS LTD and MATTHEY REFINERS LTD

HOURLY PAID EMPLOYEES - DEPARTMENTAL TRANSFERS

Clock no: NAME	
Present Dept. code	
New Dept. code	
Date of transfer	
Employee classification	Direct Indirect (Please delete part not applicable)

Dear ......

I have pleasure in confirming your transfer from the Weekly Staff to the Monthly Staff with effect from ......, at a salary of £..... per annum. The terms and conditions of the Monthly Staff are given in the enclosed booklet.

* You will now be required to join the Company's Staff Pension Scheme paying contributions at the rate of ** ...... per annum of your salary in excess of .... If you are already a member of the Works Pension Fund you will cease to pay into it.

You will also be asked to sign a Staff Agreement, and a specimen copy of this, together with some explanatory notes is enclosed. When you have read the Agreement, will you please return it to me, and I will have copies prepared for signature by yourself and the Company.

The Salaries Department will now require the name and address of your bank, together with the number of your account. I should be grateful therefore, if you would complete and return the enclosed form as soon as possible.

Please accept my congratulations on your transfer.

Yours sincerely,

S.M.S. Gray (Miss)
STAFF OFFICER

Encs.

---

* If applicant is under the age of 25 paragraph 2 should read:

When you reach the age of 25 years you will be required to join the Staff Pension Scheme, details of which will be given to you at that time. If you are already a member of the Works Pension Fund you will continue to pay into it for the time being.

** Male contributions:	7%	£450
* Female contributions:	6½%	£350

N.B. The letter should be addressed to the person at his/her place of work and sealed with the enclosures BUT sent to their Manager together with a copy for the Manager in a large envelope marked 'Private & Confidential' to be openedonly by ....

A separate copy to be sent to Miss S. Read, Salaries Department.

Form 25 Employee assessment form

Johnson Matthey Metals Limited - Harlow

CONFIDENTIAL TO ________

EMPLOYEE ASSESSMENT FORM
PROBATION PERIOD

PERSONAL DETAILS

Name: ____________________ Clock No: __________

Department: ____________________ Date of start: __________

ATTENDANCE RECORD

Number of times late during first four weeks service: __________

Number of days uncertified sickness during first four weeks service: ___

Number of days certified sickness during first four weeks service: ____

Number of days domestic absence during first four weeks service: _____

ASSESSMENT

Are you satisfied with the employee's Conduct? YES/NO*

Are you satisfied with the employee's Ability? YES/NO*

Are you satisfied with the employee's Attendance? YES/NO*

Do you wish this individual's employment to be continued after the probation period? YES/NO*

If NO, please state reasons:

Signed: ____________________ Date: ____________________

*Delete as applicable

PLEASE RETURN TO THE PERSONNEL OFFICER BY: ____________

(Continued)

(Continued)

Johnson Matthey Metals Limited - Harlow

CONFIDENTIAL TO PERSONNEL DEPARTMENT ONLY

EMPLOYEE ASSESSMENT FORM - Part B

PROBATION PERIOD

PERSONAL DETAILS

Name: ______________________ Clock No: __________

Department: __________________ Date of start: ______

REFERENCES

* (1) Not yet received/Suspect/Unsatisfactory/Satisfactory

* (2) Not yet received/Suspect/Unsatisfactory/Satisfactory

* (3) Not yet received/Suspect/Unsatisfactory/Satisfactory

MEDICAL REPORT

* Satisfactory/Restricted/Unsatisfactory

Details if unsatisfactory:

DEPARTMENTAL ASSESSMENT

Satisfactory/Unsatisfactory

DECISION

*Employment confirmed/Employment to be terminated on: __________

Reason for termination:

Signed: ____________________ Date: ______________

*Delete as applicable

Johnson Matthey & Co., Limited

CONFIDENTIAL STAFF APPRAISAL FORM

....19 ....

Name:

Department:

Qualifications:
Date of Birth:
Date of Start:

Job Title

Have there been any major changes in the job since the last assessment?
If so, have the principal accountabilities been appropriately revised?

Current Effectiveness

Consider the employee's performance over the year and the extent to which the objectives, as indicated in the accountabilities above, have been met.

	Inadequate	Incomplete	Standard	Superior	Outstanding
Knowledge of work					
Effectiveness in meeting objectives					
Initiative and self-reliance					
Overall performance					

Comments

(Continued)

(Continued)

Recommendations

Are there any specific training recommendations to enable the employee to fulfil better his accountabilities, or foreseeable future responsibilities?

Manager's Summary of Appraisal Interview

Include action agreed upon between Manager and employee as well as those points regarded by the Manager as being the most significant parts of the interview. Managers should bear in mind aspects performed particularly well/areas failing to meet standards. Identify strengths/weaknesses.

Employee's Comments

Signed . . . . Manager

Seen . . . . Employee

Date . . . .

The three forms that follow concern Maternity Rights. These rights are now contained in Sections 45-48 of The Employment Protection (Consolidation) Act, 1978. *The first form outlines the rights of mothers and mothers-to-be, the second is filled in by the employee's supervisor and the third by the employee herself. Note: under paragraph 4 of this latter form the current maximum claimable is £110 per week.*

THE JOHNSON MATTHEY GROUP OF COMPANIES

Employment Protection Act 1975

Interpretation of the Rights for the Expectant Mother

The Employment Protection Act gives three important rights to a woman who is expecting a baby:

From 1.6.76 — the right not to lose her job — pregnancy itself will not be a valid reason for dismissal;

— the right to return to her job after the baby is born; and

From 1.4.77 — the right to maternity pay.

These rights apply to all women, married or unmarried, and whether employed full-time or part-time, so long as they work at least *21 hours* a week for their employer.

The right not to lose her job through pregnancy depends on a woman having worked for her employer *for at least six months.* To obtain the other two rights she must have been employed by her employer *for at least two years.*

The Right to Return to Work
A woman is entitled to return to her job any time up to *29 weeks* after the birth of her baby with the rate of pay, holidays and other conditions of work which would be applicable had she not stopped work. Pension and seniority rights, however, will carry on from what they had been when she stopped work — the period of absence will not count towards them. Should the actual job no longer be available she should be prepared to accept another of the same kind, provided that the terms, conditions and location are the same.

Conditions
The right to return to work is subject to the following conditions:

The employee must have continued her employment with her employer up to the *eleventh week* before the baby is due, as certified by a midwife or doctor in a Certificate of Expected Confinement. She may, and it is entirely her decision, continue to work after the eleventh week.

At that time — *the eleventh week* — she must have been employed by her employer for at least *two years.*

She must tell her employer that she intends to stop work because of her condition, at least *three weeks* before she stops work, at the *same time* saying that she intends to *return to work* after the baby is born. The employer is entitled to ask for these notices in writing, and may ask to see the Certificate of Expected Confinement.

Date of Return
The date on which an employee returns to work is for her to decide provided it is no later than 29 weeks after the birth of the baby. But she must notify her employer at least one week before the intended date of return.

An employer may put off an employee's return for up to four weeks from the date she notifies if reasons are given and she is told when she can resume work. An employee may put off her return for up to four weeks from the date she notifies or, if she has not notified a date, for up to four weeks from the end of the 29-week period, if she is ill and produces a medical certificate. If she has not told her employer when she intends to start work again she should do so and she must start work no later than *14 days* after the interruption is over.

The Right to Maternity Pay
After 5th April 1977, a woman who stops work to have a baby is entitled to claim maternity pay from her employer.

Entitlement will be subject to these conditions:

She must have continued her employment with her employer up to the *eleventh week* before the baby is due.

At that time — the eleventh week — she must have been employed by her employer for at least *two years.*

She must tell her employer that she intends to stop work because of her condition at least *three weeks* before she stops work.

Maternity pay covers the first *six weeks* the employee is away. For each of the *six weeks* her employer should pay *nine tenths of her normal weekly pay less the amount of the standard social security maternity allowance: this deduction is made even if she does not receive the allowance.*

Interpretation for the Johnson Matthey Group employees who intend to return to work

The period of absence a woman takes for maternity suspension does not break her continuity of employment for the following Company benefits, although the period of absence itself does not count as a period of employment for calculating entitlement to these benefits.

Holidays,
Payment for sickness,
Service Allowance,
Redundancy Pay,
Notice to terminate employment,
Christmas Distribution.

The period of absence will not count towards the woman's pension rights on retirement, for the Company's long service awards or for seniority of position.

(Continued)

(Continued)

Holidays
At the start of maternity suspension, the employee will be entitled to the holiday for the current year to the date of leaving. No payment will be made for holidays whilst she is absent and on returning to work her entitlement will start from that date, for the remainder of that current year.

Example 1
An employee starts maternity suspension on 1st March and returns on 6th December after an absence of 40 weeks (11 weeks pre-natal and 29 weeks post-natal absence). Holiday entitlement for that year will be:
28th February — on leaving — 2/12ths of 20 days
6th December — on returning — 1/12th of 20 days
In the following year she will be eligible for the full holiday entitlement as if the break had not occurred.

Example 2
An employee starts maternity suspension on 15th October and returns 40 weeks later on 26th July of the following year. Holiday entitlement for both years will be:
15 October — on leaving — 10/12ths of 20 days
26th July — on returning — 5/12ths of 20 days

i.e. she does not receive payment for holidays whilst she is not at work but there will be no break in service for calculation of holiday entitlement in the future.

Note An employee may have taken the full holiday entitlement for the current year before advising the Company that she will be absent for maternity suspension. In such cases the Company will be entitled to obtain a refund of unearned holiday pay, as laid down in the employees' handbooks.

Service Allowance
At the start of maternity suspension an employee who is eligible for service allowance will receive 1/12th of the full allowance for each complete month of service since the last anniversary of her starting date, to the date of leaving.

On returning to the Company and at the time of the next payment of service allowance, the employee will receive the full allowance due from the commencement of maternity suspension.

Christmas Distribution
The employee will not be entitled to Christmas distribution during her period of maternity suspension. On her return she will be eligible for the next Christmas distribution.

Payment for Sickness, Redundancy and Notice to Terminate Employment
On her return to work the employee will be eligible for calculation of these conditions of employment as if there had been no break in service.

Pensions
The Company will make the statutory payment of wages or salary for the first six weeks of maternity suspension (from 1.4.77) and from this payment will be deducted contributions to the appropriate pension fund. During the period of absence the employee's contributions will remain in the fund and on returning to work she will resume payment of contributions.

If during maternity suspension the employee decides not to return to work her contributions will be dealt with in accordance with the provisions of the Social Security Acts 1973-1975 and details will be forwarded to her by the Manager of the Pensions Department.

Calculation of her period of service in the appropriate pension fund for the purpose of pension at retirement age will exclude any period of absence for maternity suspension.

Income Tax Form P45
This document will only be issued by the Company when the employee states positively that she will not be returning to work. Any income tax rebate due will be dealt with at the same time.

Statement of Intention to return to work
At the time of notification of impending maternity suspension, the employee will sign a statement of her intention to return to work. She will be given a copy of the statement.

Certificate of Estimated Confinement and Birth Certificate of child
The Company will ask the employee to produce both of these documents at the appropriate time.

Long Service Award
Calculation of her period of service for the Company's long service award will exclude any period of absence for maternity suspension.

Maternity Pay
From 1.4.77 the Company will be liable to make maternity payments for the first six weeks of maternity suspension. This payment will be 9/10ths of the woman's basic weekly wage or salary (up to a maximum of £80 per week) from which will be deducted the amount of the standard Social Security maternity allowance. This deduction will be made even if the woman does not receive the allowance.

Dates of Start and Finish of Maternity Suspension
Maternity Suspension will start from the first day of absence and finish on the last day of absence.

MATERNITY: Termination/Suspension of Employment

Name of Employee .... Department ....

D.O.S. .... Section ....

Contracted Hours ....

Section 1

Does the employee intend to return to work? No/Yes*

If 'No', date of termination of employment ....

If 'Yes' estimated date of confinement...
Certificate of estimated confinement seen No/Yes*

Date maternity leave to start ....
(not more than 11 weeks before confinement)

Provisional date of return to work...
(not later than 29 weeks after birth of baby)

Confirmation of date of return to work...
(minimum — 1 week's notice) *(to be completed at the appropriate time)*

Has the situation regarding contributions to Pension Fund, reimbursement**, income tax form P45 and any tax rebate due been explained? No/Yes*

Has the situation regarding the job to which she will return been explained? No/Yes*

Indicate what has been established, if possible:

....

....

....

Section 2 *(to be completed at the appropriate time)*

Date of birth of baby...
Birth certificate seen No/Yes*

Date of return to work ....
(minimum — 1 week's notice)

* delete as appropriate
** not applicable until 6.4.77

INTENT TO RETURN TO WORK

Name ....

I intend to return to work after the birth of my baby and I understand that:

1. The date of my return must be not later than 29 weeks after the birth, unless:
   a) the Company wishes to delay my return by up to 4 weeks,
   b) I am certified medically unfit to return for up to 4 weeks.

2. At least 1 week before I intend to return to work I must notify the Company of my intention, in writing, and forward for registration and return a copy of the baby's birth certificate.

3. If my present job is not available on my return to work, I will accept another job at .... provided the terms and conditions are the same.

**4. I will be entitled to reimbursement from the Company for the first six weeks of absence on the basis of 9/10ths of my present salary (up to a maximum of £80 per week) less Social Security Maternity Allowance, whether or not I receive this allowance.

**5. My contributions to the Johnson Matthey Pension/Superannuation Fund will be deducted by the Company from any payments made to me during my period of maternity suspension.

6. My total reckonable service for calculation of pension at retirement will be reduced by the period during which I have not contributed to the Fund.

7. My contributions to the Johnson Matthey Pension/Superannuation Fund will remain in the Fund during my period of maternity suspension and I will resume payment of contributions on my return to work.

8. Income Tax form P45 will not be issued at the start of my period of maternity suspension.

9. My period of absence for maternity suspension WILL COUNT towards establishing my entitlement to the following conditions of employment:

   holidays, payment for sickness, service allowance, redundancy pay, notice to terminate employment and Christmas distribution,

   but WILL NOT COUNT towards my total service for the Company's Long Service Award, or for seniority of position.

10. If during my absence I decide not to return to work I will notify the Company, in writing. In this case I understand that my Income Tax form P45 and any income tax due will be forwarded to me. My Pension/Superannuation contributions will be dealt with in accordance with the provisions of the Social Security Acts 1973-1975 and details will be forwarded to me by the Manager of the Pensions Department.

11. If I do not take up my right to return to work within the time and under the conditions specified by the Employment Protection Act 1975, I cannot do so at a later date.

Signed ....

Date ....

** After 6.4.77

Copy to be retained by the employee.

JOHNSON, MATTHEY & CO., LIMITED

Sick Certificates

1. Doctors' certificates no longer state that an individual is unfit for work. They merely advise that he should refrain from work.

2. Doctors are very reluctant to provide certificates for one or two days' absence. They point out that often the patient asks for a retrospective certificate on the grounds that he has not been well enough to attend surgery earlier. Also many complaints such as backache, headache etc. cannot be confirmed or refuted by a doctor's examination. In short - doctors' certificates may show only that the patient has visited the surgery, which he would not have done but for the need to obtain a certificate. Such visits are looked upon by many doctors as an unjustified waste of their time.

3. In view of the circumstances described above it is proposed to experiment at Southgate, Hatton Garden and Hertford with a system of Company medical certificates to be signed by the patient.

4. A supply of certificates and draft regulations are enclosed.

5. The proposals were put to the Staff Society on 23rd March and accepted by them for a 12 month trial period.

If the experiment proves successful, this will not imply that the same practice will necessarily be adopted elsewhere. Regulations on terms and conditions of employment have been de-centralised for the reason that procedures which are suitable at one location may not be appropriate at other sites where local circumstances are different.

If you have any comments or questions, please let Mr. C.J. Taylor know as soon as possible.

24th March 1977 K.A. Venus

JOHNSON, MATTHEY & CO., LIMITED

(Southgate, Hatton Garden and Hertford)

Sickness Certificates

The following arrangements for monthly and weekly staff will be introduced on 1st April 1977 for an experimental period of one year.

1. A Company form of Sickness Certificate will be available from Departmental Managers.

2. Employees of more than one year's service may sign declarations on these certificates that they were prevented from attending work by illness which confined them to their homes except for time spent attending hospital, clinic or surgery. After completion the certificates will be handed to the Departmental Manager or his deputy, who will make any further enquiries he thinks necessary about the nature of the disability before counter-signing the certificate and passing it to Staff Department.

3. Company certificates may only be used for absences of two days or less.

4. Absence on a Friday and the following Monday will imply an illness lasting four days which will necessitate a doctor's certificate.

5. As indicated in (2) above, the Company certificates will not cover absence where the patient is not confined to home. Such absences must be contained within the three-day limit for absence without a certificate or else must be covered by a doctor's certificate.

The Staff Society and the Management believe that these arrangements will have the support and co-operation of the majority of employees and have agreed to take all practical steps to ensure that the system is not abused by a minority.

25th March 1977

K.A. Venus
Secretary

Form 32 Sickness certificate (sample form)

JOHNSON MATTHEY & CO. LTD
Southgate, Hatton Garden and Hertford

SICKNESS CERTIFICATE

I certify that on ____________(day) a.m./p.m. __________________(date)
and on _________________ a.m./p.m. ________________________
because of illness/injury, I was confined to my home apart from time spent attending Hospital/Clinic/Surgery.

The nature of my disability was:

Signed: ______________________

Name: ________________________
(Block capitals)

Department: __________________ Manager: ____________________

Form 33 Notification of termination of employment (staff)

Johnson Matthey Group

NOTIFICATION OF TERMINATION OF EMPLOYMENT (STAFF)

To: From:

Name:	Address:
Department:	Position:
Date of leaving:	Code:
Date of start:	Date of birth:
Holidays taken:	

Signature: _________________________
Date: ______________________________

Form 34 Acknowledgement of receipt of termination letter

Dear

I acknowledge receipt of your letter dated .... giving notice that you wish to resign from the Company, with effect from .... I will arrange for your final payment* and Income Tax papers to be sent to you on that date.

I would like to thank you for your services to the Company and send my best wishes for the future.

Yours sincerely,

V. Treadwell or K.J.B. Durbridge
Assist. Personnel Officer

* for married female employee, insert "National Insurance Exemption Certificate.

Form 35 Termination receipt

Johnson Matthey Chemicals Ltd and
Matthey Refiners Ltd, Royston

TERMINATION RECEIPT

I acknowledge receipt of____ packet(s) containing final payment of__________ and of my National Insurance card and Income Tax form P45, plus Works Pension Fund contributions of________ and Company Savings of________ , these being due to me on terminating my employment with the Company. I also certify that:

1 I have handed in my locker key.

2 I have returned all the protective clothing and equipment issued to me.

3 I have returned my Emergency 50p coach money issued to me.

4 I have not unlawfully retained any other Company property in my possession.

Signed: ______________________________ Date: ______________________________

Clock number: ________________________ Name: ______________________________

Handbook on

Safety

and

Occupational Health

for the employees of

Matthey Printed Products Limited

at

Burslem

1976

The purpose of this booklet is to state, in accordance with the Health and Safety at Work, etc. Act, 1974:

(a) The Company's statutory general duties and its policy in respect of the health and safety at work of all of its employees,

and

(b) The general duties of employees at work.

The General Duties of Employers to their Employees: *(Part 1, Section 2-(1) of the Act).*

It shall be the duty of every employer to ensure, so far as is reasonably practicable, the health, safety and welfare at work of all his employees.

The General Duties of Employees at Work: *(Part 1, Section 7 of the Act)*

It shall be the duty of every employee while at work–

(a) to take reasonable care for the health and safety of himself and of other persons who may be affected by his acts or omissions at work;

and

(b) as regards any duty or requirement imposed on his employer or any other person by or under any of the relevant statutory provisions, to co-operate with him so far as is necessary to enable that duty or requirement to be performed or complied with.

Throughout this booklet the word "Safety" is intended to apply to "Health and Safety".

POLICY ON HEALTH AND SAFETY AT WORK

It is the policy of Johnson, Matthey & Company Limited, through its Operating Companies, to ensure the health and safety at work of all employees. To implement this policy the Company requires that accident prevention is just as much an aspect of efficient operation as is any other major management function. But accident prevention must not only be a function of management; it requires the co-operation of all employees who must accept a responsibility for health and safety at work, to prevent injury to themselves and others.

The co-ordination and monitoring of the safety at work policy and effective safety communication within the Johnson Matthey Group of Companies is the responsibility of the Group Safety Adviser. Occupational health is the responsibility of the Group Medical Officer. They are required to report to the Boards of the Operating Companies and Johnson, Matthey & Company Limited, matters which they consider need their attention.

Signed: P. D. F. VARRALL, *Director*

Johnson Matthey & Co. Limited,

43 Hatton Garden,

London EC1N 8EE

(Continued)

1. COMPANY SAFETY ORGANISATION

The Production Director is responsible to his Board of Directors for safety. He makes a monthly safety report to the Board.

The Safety Officer is responsible for the safety at the branch and he has the responsibility of assisting management at all levels and employees in every respect of safety at work. He is part-time and is directly responsible to the Production Director on safety matters. He is authorised to take steps to stop dangerous or illegal practices and, where necessary, to require the stoppage of plant if in his opinion danger to personnel is critical. Where such ultimate action is taken he will immediately inform the Production Director in person.

He gives a monthly report on all accidents to the Production Director. Near accidents and unsafe practices which can lead to accidents are brought forward by him for discussion by the Safety Steering Committee whenever necessary.

He is aided in the performance of his safety function by a part-time Assistant Safety Officer who assumes the Safety Officer's responsibility in the event of his absence.

He will:–

(i) Carry out from time to time, safety inspections with the head of department and prepare reports on findings and action taken for the Safety Steering Committee.

(ii) Develop the quarterly theme into appropriate action and report results to Safety Steering Committee.

(iii) Receive and review all communications regarding safety practices from the shop floor.

(iv) Transmit all information obtained regarding safety from authorised sources to shop floor personnel.

(v) He will advise on the safety aspects of new products and their application both inside and outside the Company.

The Environmental Adviser has the part-time responsibility of advising management at all levels in every aspect of environmental matters, toxic fume, wastes, etc., and he is directly responsible to the Safety Officer in its execution. He will carry out regular environmental checks and keep appropriate records. He will associate closely with the Group Medical Officer on these matters.

The Environmental Adviser is authorised to take steps to stop any dangerous or illegal practices and, where necessary, to require the stoppage of processes which in his judgement present a hazard for personnel. Where such ultimate action is taken he will immediately report to the Production Director in person.

Departmental Management, at all levels, is responsible within each department for safety.

Managers and Departmental Heads concerned with new projects, equipment or products, are to ensure that the Safety Officer is kept informed about proposed installations so that proper advice can be given on safety matters.

Safety Committees

(a) **The Safety Steering Committee**

Constitution:

Chairman – Production Director

Secretary – Assistant Safety Officer

Members: Safety Officer
Production Manager – Electronics
Production Manager – Printing
Works Engineer

By invitation – Environmental Adviser

Terms of Reference:

(i) The Committee will meet at least once every three months.

(ii) The Committee will provide a forum for the discussion and examination of any aspect of the company's operations which could conceivably affect the safety of its employees, and will take all possible steps to publicise the value of constant attention to operating safety.

(iii) It will receive from, and pass to employees, information of general interest concerning operating standards and procedures, new legislation and regulations.

(iv) It will review safety records and accident statistics as well as the achievement of exceptional safety performances.

(v) It will provide guide lines for action in dealing with safety problems and initiate enquiries and suggest studies into specific topics of safety.

(vi) It will review the results of safety inspections; review accident reports and confirm or recommend action to be taken.

(vii) Minutes of the meeting of the Steering Safety Committee will be posted on all Notice Boards and copies sent to the members of the Committee, the Directors, all members of the General Safety Committee, F.O.Cs and Shop Stewards, the Group Safety Adviser and the Group Medical Officer.

(b) **The General Safety Committee**

The General Safety Committee consists of twenty-two members representing each of the Trade Unions on the site, together with members of the Safety Steering Committee and the Nursing Sister.

Terms of Reference:

(i) The Committee is to use all members as "Safety Ambassadors" so that there is a ready means of communications of information on all safety matters from management to the shop floor and vice versa.

(ii) The Committee will meet every three months and receive reports on any occurrences in the safety field which have taken place on the site and, at the same time, the opportunity is taken to invite a visiting speaker to talk on some safety matter or to present a film with a safety flavour.

(iii) Each member is responsible for conducting frequent safety inspections in his area and will report any dangers to his supervisor and the Safety Officer.

(Continued)

(Continued)

2. SAFETY PROCEDURES

Departmental Safety Inspections. Departmental supervision will carry out frequent safety inspections of the working areas under their control.

Departmental Safety Rules and Regulations. Each department has its own safety rules and regulations, copies of which are posted in each department. Those which apply to particularly hazardous machinery or operations are also posted immediately beside it or them.

The Safety Officer has copies of all departmental safety rules and regulations.

Any employee who contravenes these regulations will be liable to disciplinary action.

Accident Investigation. A thorough investigation of all significant accidents, dangerous occurrences and near misses is a clear responsibility of management. The investigation will be carried out by the Safety Officer and the appropriate Safety representative and a report will be sent to the Safety Steering Committee.

3. HAZARD CONTROL

Toxic or noxious processes. The Environmental Adviser will ensure that programmes established by management for monitoring working atmospheres are implemented.

Protective clothing or equipment. There are areas of risk at the branch where the provision and use of safety clothing is a statutory requirement. In addition, the Company encourages its employees to wear or use any items which will protect them from injury. Full details of all the protective clothing and equipment which is available for use in each department is available from departmental supervision. Some of this equipment is issued free of charge, some of it is available at a nominal charge.

Major Disaster Plan. A major disaster plan has been drawn up by management to enable the branch to deal with a large scale emergency such as extensive fire, explosion or any other serious occurrence. Details have been issued to all Directors, Managers and Departmental Heads, and Safety Representatives.

4. FIRE PREVENTION AND CONTROL

It is of major importance that no person is at risk due to fire. The Company also has substantial investment in stock, equipment and buildings and all available steps must be taken to eliminate fire risk.

The Company provides adequate protection against fire hazard; from time to time fire drills are carried out and the building is evacuated.

All employees have a duty to obey instructions for fire prevention and control.

Fire Prevention Measures. The most important aspect of the Company's fire policy is fire prevention. To this end it is necessary for all levels of management to become thoroughly familiar with the minimum requirements of fire prevention and fire fighting and to have an understanding of the cause and nature of fire.

Works Fire Brigade. The Works Fire Brigade is composed of voluntary firemen who undertake fire drills on a regular basis.

5. HEALTH AND HYGIENE

Potentially harmful substances. The Company is aware that certain known hazards exist in the manufacture and processing of some of its materials and is constantly vigilant in order to ensure that reasonable precautions are taken to prevent injury to health.

Health Services

The Group Medical Officer will give assistance to the Safety Officer and the Environmental Adviser on all aspects of Industrial Hygiene and Health.

The Company Nursing Sister is responsible for all pre-engagement and routine medical tests and examinations and will provide any advice and assistance to the Safety Officer as required.

The First Aid Centre on the plant – administered by the Personnel Department – is open daily between 8.15 a.m. and 4.40 p.m. Employees who are trained in first aid and in the use of first aid equipment are also available in most departments in cases of emergency. First aid treatment may be obtained, outside these hours, at the Security Office; in addition access to the First Aid Centre is available upon application to the Security Office.

Managerial Training. It is fundamental to the success of the Company's safety policy that all sectors of management should have received the training necessary to control effectively the areas for which they are responsible.

7. CONTRACTORS

Advance notice of the proposed use of contractors must be given to the Safety Officer by the persons responsible for issuing the contracts.

Before the Company allows any contracting firm to carry out work on its premises the contractor or sub-contractor must understand their duties under statutory regulations applicable to the work they will be carrying out.

The Company also expects the contractor to know his duties under common law, both to his own employees and to ourselves, and to conduct his business and methods of work to conform to the best practices.

The Company has established departmental safety rules which it expects all personnel to obey in the interest of safety, and will insist that the contractor's employees or any sub-contractor commissioned by them obey these rules.

To assure ourselves that the contractor understands his obligations whilst on our premises we make available copies of the relevant departmental safety rules which we ask him to read before he starts work.

8. VISITORS

It is the Company's duty to ensure the safety of all visitors to its premises. If visitors have to enter areas where hazards exist they must be made aware of these and, if necessary, be provided with protective clothing or equipment.

HEALTH AND SAFETY AT WORK ACT 1974

Operative from 1st April 1975.

JOHNSON, MATTHEY & CO. LIMITED

POLICY ON HEALTH AND SAFETY AT WORK

It is the policy of the Parent Company, through its Operating Companies, to ensure the health and safety at work of all employees. To implement this policy the Company requires that accident prevention is just as much an aspect of efficient operation as is any other major management function. But accident prevention must not only be a function of management; it requires the co-operation of all employees who must accept a responsibility for health and safety at work, to prevent injury to themselves and others.

The co-ordination and monitoring of the safety at work policy and effective safety communication within the Johnson Matthey Group of Companies is the responsibility of the Group Safety Adviser. Occupational Health is the responsibility of the Group Medical Officer. They are required to report to the Boards of the Operating Companies and Johnson, Matthey & Co. Limited matters which they consider need their attention.

MATTHEY PRINTED PRODUCTS LIMITED

POLICY STATEMENT TO ALL EMPLOYEES

It is the policy of Johnson, Matthey & Co. Limited (the Parent Company), through its Operating Companies, to take all reasonably practicable steps to ensure the health and safety at work of employees and members of the general public.

The Management will ensure that every effort is made to meet statutory requirements and codes of practice relating to the Company's activities and any relevant recommendations from bodies dealing with industrial health and safety.

To achieve this, the Company will -

(i) provide safety training;

(ii) establish and consult with the site Safety Committee;

(iii) give information about specific hazards to anyone concerned;

(iv) issue personal protective equipment where necessary;

(v) check and continually improve safety arrangements.

Since employees are now under a legal obligation to co-operate in matters of health, safety and welfare, all must accept personal responsibility for the prevention of accidents.

As and when the law requires, employees will be informed of any revision to this policy statement.

SAFETY ORGANISATION

JOHNSON, MATTHEY & CO. LIMITED (the Parent Company)

		Function
Group Safety Adviser	Mr. D.A. Chappell	Group Safety Co-ordination
Group Medical Officer	Dr. E.G. Hughes	Group Occupational Health

MATTHEY PRINTED PRODUCTS LIMITED

Production Director	Mr. D.M. Lloyd	Responsible to the Board for all aspects of health, safety and welfare.
Safety Officer	Mr. C.J. Henshall	Responsible for the implementation of all aspects of safety and welfare. Maintain statutory documents and conduct safety inspection.
Works Engineer	Mr. K.G. Aldridge	Responsible for the safe design, construction and maintenance of all plant and machinery.
Training Officer	Mr. B.R. Kirton	Responsible for all safety and operational training.
Occupational Health	Sister E.P.H. Cope	Responsible for all pre-engagement and routine medical tests and examinations.
Environmental Assessor	Mr. W.G. Sanderson	Responsible for pollution monitoring.

W. F. EMMERTON
Managing Director.

1 April 1975.

NOTIFICATION OF ACCIDENT
(All questions must be answered)

To; Personnel (or other appropriate) Department Date ....

From: .... Dept. ....

1. Name of injured person .... Initials .... C/No ....
2. Section/Department .... Job Title/Occupation ....
3. Date of accident .... Time of accident .... hours
4. Date accident reported .... Time accident reported .... hours
5. Time injured person actually stopped work on day of accident .... hours
6. Time injured person re-commenced work on day of accident, if he did .... hours
7. Time injured person should have stopped work on day of accident .... hours
8. Nature and extent of injuries where known (state Left or Right where applicable)

   ....

   ....

9. How did accident happen? (Full description of incident)

   ....

   ....

   ....

   ....

10. Where did the accident occur? (Precise Location)

    ....

11. Was accident due to lifting by hand? (Yes or No) ....

If so, state:

a) total weight of load lifted ....

b) How many other persons assisted with the lifting ....

12. Was accident due to hot, molten or corrosive material? (Yes or No) ....

If so, state:

a) What material ....

b) Where material came from ....

(Continued)

(Continued)

13. Was accident caused by machinery? (Yes or No) ....

If so, state:

a) The name and type of machine ....

b) Part causing injury ....

c) Whether in motion by mechanical power at the time (Yes or No) ....

d) If caused by crane or other lifting machine, specify type ....

e) Was a guard fitted where necessary (Yes or No) ....

If not, why not? ....

f) Was it in good working order/good condition? (Yes or No) ....

g) Had any complaints been made? (Yes or No) .... If so, when ....

by whom? ....

14. If accident due to ejection of material/machine part, state:

a) Weight of material/part ....

b) Method of ejection ....

15. Was accident relative to a fall of persons, material, plant, etc? (Yes or No) ....

If so, state approximate height of fall ....

16. Was the accident caused during movement of material? (Yes or No) ....

If so, state:

a) What material ....

b) From where to where material should be moved ....

c) From where to where material was moved ....

17. Was accident caused by faulty plant/equipment? (Yes or No) ....

If so, state:

a) What plant/equipment..

b) How plant/equipment failed ....

18. Was accident caused by fault of any person? (Yes or No) ....

If so, state:

a) Name, if known ....

b) Nature of fault ....

19. What exactly was the employee doing at the time of the accident? ....

....

20. Was he/she authorised or permitted to do what he/she was doing at the time of the accident? (Yes or No) .....

(Continued)

21. Was this a written down procedure? (Yes or No) .... If not, was this custom and practice? (Yes or No) ....

22. Were any general or specific instructions given prior to commencement of work? (Yes or No) ....

If so, state what instructions and by whom given ....

....

23. Was protective clothing or equipment necessary for the work being done at the time of the accident?

(Yes or No) .... If so,

a) Give description of such protection

....

b) Was it provided? (Yes or No) .... If so, when, signature? ....

c) Was it being used at the time of the accident? (Yes or No) ....

If not, why not? ....

24. Has the accident been entered in the Departmental Accident Book? (Yes or No) ....

25. Did injured person report to the First Aid Post/Surgery? (Yes or No) ....

If so, state;

a) At what time .... (b) Accompanied by anyone? (Yes or No) ....

If so, by whom? ....

26. State name(s) of witness(s) ....

....

27. Have you:

a) Obtained a statement from each witness? (Yes or No) ....

b) Drawn a sketch or taken a photograph showing location of accident and relevant people? (Yes or No) ....

c) Kept the offending tool/implement? (Yes or No) ....

If so, what has been kept and where is it? ....

....

Signature ....

(Please do not delay completing and sending this form to the Personnel (or other appropriate) department, and follow up with photographs, sketches and statements as necessary).

(Continued)

(Continued)

TO BE COMPLETED BY PERSONNEL (OR OTHER APPROPRIATE DEPARTMENT)

1. Is accident reportable to Factory Inspector? ....

   (i.e. has employee been prevented from earning full wages at normal place of work for at least three consecutive days?)

2. Date entered in General Register ....

3. Date Form 43/ Form OSR 2 completed ....

4. Date Eagle Star form completed ....

5. Date B.I. 76 completed ....

6. Date Accident Investigation Report completed ....

7. Date of return to work ....

8. Number of hours lost ....

9. Any disablement on return? ....

Form 39 Accident — relevant documents

To: Miss J. Townsend
Group Personnel Relations Department
Southgate

From: Date:

Re: ______________________ Clock No. (Works) ____________

Accident Date: ____________

Please find enclosed documents, as ticked, relevant to the above accident:

1.	Eagle Star Injury Form	2 copies (original + 1)	___
2.	First Aid/Surgery Report	2 copies	___
3.	Notification of Accident	2 copies	___
4.	Form F.43 (Works) Form O.S.T.2 (Staff)	2 copies	___
5.	Form B.I.76	2 copies	___
6.	Medical Certificates	2 copies	___
7.	General Register, F.33	2 copies	___
8.	Industrial Injury Register Form B.I.510 (Accident Book)	2 copies	___
9.	Wages Return	2 copies	___
10.	Witnesses Statements	2 copies (original + 1)	___
11.	Treatment Book (if required)	2 copies	___
12.	Photographs, sketches, or any other relevant documents	2 copies	___

Date of return to work: __________ Same/different job* ______________

Date of recurring absence: __________ Date of return to work: __________

* Delete as appropriate

Part Four

A procedural agreement

PROCEDURAL AGREEMENT

BETWEEN

UNIGATE FOODS LIMITED

AND

THE TRANSPORT & GENERAL WORKERS' UNION

AND

THE UNION OF SHOP, DISTRIBUTIVE & ALLIED WORKERS'

COVERING

THE FACILITIES TO BE AFFORDED TO SAFETY REPRESENTATIVES

SAFETY REPRESENTATIVE

A safety representative is a person appointed by a recognised trade union to represent a group or groups of employees in consultations with the employer in matters concerning health, safety and welfare at work.

CONTENTS

1. PERFORMING THE FUNCTIONS OF A SAFETY REPRESENTATIVE

1.1. It is accepted that each safety representative will need some time away from his normal work as an employee to carry out his safety function. Permission to leave his job should, under normal circumstances, be obtained in advance from his immediate superior who will not unreasonably refuse this.

1.2. Should a safety representative wish to leave the Company premises in connection with his safety functions, permission must be obtained in advance from the Factory or Depot Manager or their deputy.

2. ELECTIONS

2.1. Should a Union wish its membership to elect their safety representatives, the Company, where requested may provide locally the following facilities:-

(a) Elections for safety representatives to take place in Company time.

(b) Provide ballot boxes, notice board space and duplicating facilities.

(c) Provide polling stations throughout the factory or depot.

3. APPOINTMENT OF SAFETY REPRESENTATIVES

3.1. Each Union will inform local management through the local full time officer, in writing, of the appointment of each safety representative.

3.2. Where it is agreed between Unions that a safety representative is to represent the membership of more than one Union, each Union will inform local management in writing of such an agreement.

3.3. Wherever possible, the safety representative should have been employed by the Company for at least two years.

3.4. The termination of any appointment of a safety representative will be notified, in writing, to local management by the Union.

4. CREDENTIALS - AREAS OF OPERATION

4.1. Management and Unions should agree locally on the number and boundaries of work place constituencies and the number of safety representatives to be appointed to represent them.

4.2. It is accepted that, particularly at larger sites, the Union may appoint a senior safety representative who will normally be involved in such areas as:-

4.2. cont.

(a) Issues which affect the whole factory or depot.

(b) Issues which an individual safety representative has been unable to settle.

(c) To receive information from and consult with Inspectors.

4.3. Management and Unions should issue credentials to safety representatives.

4.4. Each safety representative will normally act on issues applicable to their own constituency, except in special circumstances, with Factory or Depot Managers or their deputy's agreement, to cover for sickness or holiday absence or where he/she has particular knowledge or experience, etc.

5. <u>FUNCTIONS OF SAFETY REPRESENTATIVES</u>

5.1. The Company will encourage safety representatives to carry out inspections of the work place and investigate accidents, dangerous occurances, notifiable diseases and complaints in conjunction with the factory or depot safety officer.

5.2. Where safety representatives elect to carry out independant perioric inspections of the work place, these shall

5.2. cont.

be carried out at frequencies agreed between local management and the Unions, which shall not be in excess of 90 days, and be subject to the following conditions:-

(a) Local management shall be informed of the intention to carry out an inspection at least 24 hours prior to such an inspection.

(b) Local management will receive a written report of the results of any inspection, but this should not preclude a verbal report of any serious observations made.

(c) Formats for requirements for (a) and (b) will be agreed with local management and provided by the Company.

5.3. Where safety representatives elect to carry out independant investigations into accidents, dangerous occurances and notifiable diseases, they shall communicate the results of their investigation to local management in writing.

6. <u>SITE FACILITIES</u>

6.1. Facilities on site may be provided according to particular needs. These can include:-

6.1. cont.

(a) Reasonable access to external telephones with regard to the need for privacy.

(b) Space on notice boards.

(c) Occasional typing or duplicating facilities.

(d) Some secure record storage facility.

7. PROVISION OF INFORMATION

7.1. Various sources of information in respect of health and safety advice and legislation will be kept on site in the charge of the safety officer; safety representatives shall have access to these sources at all reasonable times by request to the Safety Officer.

7.2. The Company will provide such other information relating to health and safety of its employees, as from time to time is applicable particularly in respect of:-

(a) Proposed changes in the working environment.

(b) Accidents, dangerous occurrences and notifiable diseases.

(c) Articles and substances used, or contemplated for use at work.

(d) Results of surveys, etc, carried out.

7.3. The Company, nowever, reserves the right to with-hold such information where, in its own opinion, disclosure:-

(a) Would be contrary to any other regulations or enactments.

(b) Would be damaging to the Company's position in the field of commerce.

(c) Would result in breaking confidence with an individual, except with the individual's written consent.

(d) Would be to the detriment of the Company interests in respect of legal proceedings, having obtained it for this purpose.

8. CONSULTATION

8.1. There shall be at every Unit a means of consultation in respect of Health and Safety, these shall be through Joint Consultative and/or Safety Committees, the method being agreed with local management.

8.2. The Company will encourage safety representatives support of and involvement in such committees.

8.3. Minutes of all such meetings shall be produced and circulated to all appropriate persons by the Company.

9. COMMUNICATION

9.1. Where agreement cannot be reached with local management on courses of action, acceptance of proposals etc.,

9.1. cont.

the involvement of the Company Safety Adviser, or in his absence the Personnel Director, will be sought prior to taking the matter to enforcement authorities.

9.2. Contact with the Company Safety Adviser shall be with the prior knowledge of local management.

9.3. From time to time, there may be a need for Safety Representatives/Union Officer Meetings where management may not be involved or present. Matters in respect of:-

(a) The use of Company premises,

(b) Payment for those attending,

should be agreed with local management in advance of every meeting.

10. TRAINING

10.1. Management and Unions will jointly review the type of training appropriate to the business and the individual safety representatives.

10.2. Newly appointed safety representatives should be given formal off the job training at the earliest opportunity, preferably on joint Company/Trade Union organised courses. When this is not practicable, external facilities may be used.

11. LOSS OF EARNINGS

The principle that safety representatives will suffer no loss of earnings resulting from his functions or undergoing acceptable training as a safety representative shall apply.

SIGNED ON BEHALF OF THE TRANSPORT AND GENERAL WORKERS' UNION

....
P.W. ADAMS,
COMMERCIAL TRADE GROUP SECRETARY

SIGNED ON BEHALF OF THE UNION OF SHOP, DISTRIBUTIVE AND ALLIED WORKERS

....
G. KIELY,
NATIONAL OFFICER

SIGNED ON BEHALF OF UNIGATE FOODS LIMITED

....
J.C.J. CATT,
SAFETY ADVISER

....
G.T.K. ROBINSON,
EMPLOYEE RELATIONS MANAGER

DATE: ....20th July, 1978....

APPENDIX A

LETTER ACKNOWLEDGING THE APPOINTMENT OF A UNION SAFETY REPRESENTATIVE

Dear

The Company has been informed that you have been appointed as Safety Representative for the .... Department on the .... A Safety Representative's job is an important one and this letter is written with the object of helping you to do the job well.

With this letter is enclosed a copy of the Procedural Agreement covering facilities to be afforded to Safety Representatives, between the Company and the Union, and your statement of credentials. These will be explained to you, but if you are in any doubt about the interpretation of these agreements please consult your Union Officer or myself.

You are expected both by the Company and the Union to see that the steps laid down are carried out correctly, and by your example to see that the members you represent also adhere to the safety regulations and procedures.

The Procedural Agreement lays down that you should not, under normal circumstances, leave your work without the permission of your Superior. Under normal circumstances you will only act for the Section or Department for which you have been appointed, except in special cases by agreement with the Factory or Depot Manager or their deputy. The Agreement also states that you will be assured of the maintenance of your average earnings for the time spent in carrying out your functions as a Safety Representative, providing any time spent away from your normal work is approved in advance by Management, and that action taken by you in good faith as a Safety Representative will in no way affect your employment with the Company.

(Signed)
Factory Manager

APPENDIX B

UNION SAFETY REPRESENTATIVES' CREDENTIALS

The Company and Trade Union jointly agree on the following credentials for M....................... who has been elected to represent the Union members of the .... Department on ....(Date).

1. He will be the Accredited Safety Representative from the date of appointment for a minimum of two years. If he ceases to be an employee of the Company or a member of the Union his appointment as Representative automatically terminates.

2. When acting in his Union capacity he shall be subject to the Rules and Regulations of the Union.

3. He accepts the functions laid down within the Procedural Agreements in respect of the employees in the above Department.

4. He agrees to abide, and to use his best endeavours to see that the members abide by all Agreements (of which he will receive copies) between the Company and the Union in respect of Health and Safety, whether present or future, in particular the Consultative Procedure for settling issues.

5. He will continue to be a working member of his Department but may leave his work to conduct Union safety business, normally with the Supervisor's agreement, which will not be unreasonably withheld.

6. He will not act outside the Department which he was elected to represent, except in special circumstances, with the Factory or Depot Manager's, or their deputy's agreement, to cover for sickness or holiday absence etc.

7. He is assured that his average earnings will be maintained for the time he spends in carrying out his functions as defined by the Agreements and his credentials.

8. Action taken by him in good faith in pursuance of his functions shall in no way affect his employment with the Company.

9. In all other respects he shall conform to the same working conditions as other employees.

....
(Signed on behalf of the Company)

....
(Signed on behalf of the Union)

....
(Signed by the Representative)

Book Three

OFFICIAL FORMS

Introduction

This final book contains a selection of the most vital forms supplied for use by industry and commerce. These are provided by the Department of Employment, the Industrial Tribunals, the Health and Safety Commission and the Advisory, Conciliation and Arbitration Service — my thanks to them all.

Form 1 Application to employ an overseas worker (OW1)

Department of Employment – Immigration Act 1971

APPLICATION TO EMPLOY AN OVERSEAS WORKER

NOTE: Work permits are generally issued only for skilled or highly experienced workers. You are strongly advised to read leaflet OW5 (*OW6 for hotel and catering workers*) before submitting an application, acceptance of which does not mean that the proposed employment will be approved.

FOR OFFICIAL USE
Case No. ....
Length .... Months
MLH ....
CODOT ....

Part 1 PARTICULARS OF OVERSEAS WORKER

1 Surname (*block letters*) ....

2 Other names (*block letters*) ....

3 Date of birth .... 4 Sex ....

5 Country of birth .... 6 Nationality ....

7 Number of passport (*if known*) ....

8 Issuing government ....

Part 2 PARTICULARS OF EMPLOYMENT OFFERED

9 Full name of employer/company (*block letters*) ....

....

10 Address ....

11 Telephone STD code and No. .... Extn ....

12 Full address of factory, office or site at which the worker will be employed (*if different from above*) ....

....

13 Occupation ....

Part 3 FURTHER PARTICULARS OF OVERSEAS WORKER

14 Where is he/she living at present? (*Give full address including country*)

....

....

15 Has he/she been here before? ....

16 If he/she is a qualified nurse state:–

(a) date of registration with the General Nursing Council ....

(b) registration number ....

17 If he/she is a member of one of the professions supplementary to medicine state:–

(a) date of registration with the council ....

(b) registration number ....

18 *To be completed for all resident domestic workers and nursing auxiliaries/nursing assistants:–*

(a) Is he/she married or single? ....

(b) Married couples – have they children under age of 16? ....

(c) Single man or single woman – has he/she dependants? ....

19 Give details of employment during the last seven years and attach documentary evidence of qualifications and experience:–

Occupation	Name and address of employer	Dates employed from	Dates employed to

SPECIMEN

(Continued)

(Continued)

20 Details of special qualifications etc which make him/her suitable for the employment in question:–

21 Are you satisfied that he/she has sufficient command of the English language to undertake the employment offered? ....

22 How was the offer of his/her services obtained? *(If through an employment agency please state name and address)*

Part 4 FURTHER PARTICULARS OF EMPLOYMENT

23 Nature of business/type of establishment:–

24 Precise nature of job offered:–

25 Salary offered £ .... per ....

26 Give details of any additional payments (*tips, bonuses, commission etc*):–

27 (a) Are full board and lodging provided for the worker at the place of work? ....

(b) If 'yes,' what deduction if any is made from salary? ....

28 Hours of work ....per week

29 Date from which the worker is required ....

30 Proposed length of employment ....

31 Is the employment seasonal? ....

32 *To be completed for all work in the hotel and catering industry*

(a) Are the premises licensed? ....

(b) Is overnight accommodation for guests provided?

Part 5

State in full the reasons for wishing to employ an overseas worker and the steps taken to find suitable candidates from among the resident labour force. *(This should include details of any advertising*)*

*PARTICULARS OF ADVERTISING		
Newspaper/Journal etc	Date(s)	Results

UNDERTAKING

I declare that the particulars given in this application are true to the best of my knowledge and belief and I hereby apply to the Department of Employment for permission to employ the overseas worker named on this application.

I GUARANTEE THAT NO PERSON WHO IS ORDINARILY RESIDENT IN THE UNITED KINGDOM WILL BE DISPLACED OR EXCLUDED IN CONSEQUENCE OF THE ENGAGEMENT OF THE OVERSEAS WORKER IN QUESTION.

Company stamp

Signature of Employer .... Mr/Ms

Position held ....

Date ....

ADDRESS TO WHICH THE COMPLETED FORM SHOULD BE SENT:–

(1) If the worker is already here and his passport is endorsed to prohibit his taking employment in this country, to Home Office, Lunar House, Wellesley Road, Croydon, CR9 2BY

(2) In other cases, to the Jobcentre/Employment Office at

NOTE: If the worker is already in Great Britain and holds a work permit/employment certificate (*in the case of a commonwealth citizen*) or a police certificate of registration (*in the case of a foreign national*) it should be submitted with this form.

Form 2 Application for permission to provide a Commonwealth citizen with training for a limited period (OW8)

Department of Employment – Immigration Act 1971

APPLICATION FOR PERMISSION TO PROVIDE A COMMONWEALTH CITIZEN WITH TRAINING FOR A LIMITED PERIOD

Note:- Please read leaflet OW7 before completing this form

FOR OFFICIAL USE
Case no. ....
Duration .... months

Part 1 PARTICULARS OF COMMONWEALTH CITIZEN

1 Surname (in block letters) ....

2 Other names (in block letters) ....

3 Date of birth .... 4 Sex ....

5 Number of passport (if known) ....

6 Issuing government ....

Part 2 PARTICULARS OF EMPLOYER

1 Full name (in block letters) ....

....

2 Address ....

....

....

3 Telephone Number ....

4 Address at which the trainee will be employed (if different from above)

....

....

5 Occupation in which training will be offered ....

Part 3 FURTHER PARTICULARS OF COMMONWEALTH CITIZEN

1 Country of birth .... 2 Nationality ....

3 Is he/she at present in the United Kingdom? ....

4 Present address including country:–

5 How long have you known him/her? ....

6 How were you introduced?

7 Details of his/her recent employment:–

8 What qualifications has he/she already obtained which show him/her to be suitable for and likely to benefit from the training offered:–

9 Is the application supported by any overseas government firm or organisation? ....

If 'yes' please name:–

10 Are you satisfied that he/she has a sufficient command of the English language to undertake the training offered? ....

11 What arrangements have been made with him/her for

(a) remuneration? (please state salary)

(b) accommodation during period of training?

12 Have travel arrangements been made? ....

If 'yes' when is he/she expected to leave for this country?

(Continued)

(Continued)

Part 4 PARTICULARS OF TRAINING OFFERED

1 Nature of Employer's business/type of establishment:–

2 Details of training offered:–

3 Period of training: from .... to ....

4 If the training on the job is accompanied by instruction at school, technical college etc please give details:–

5 If the trainee will gain any recognised qualifications please give details:–

Part 5 UNDERTAKING

I declare that the particulars given in this application are true to the best of my knowledge and belief and I offer the training specified to the Commonwealth citizen named in this application on the understanding that at the end of the period he/she will return to his/her home country. I undertake to notify the Department of Employment if the Commonwealth citizen leaves the arranged training.

Signature of Employer .... Mr/Mrs/Miss

Position held .... date ....

Company stamp

This form when completed should be sent to the Department of Employment at the following address:–

Form 3 Application for permission to engage a foreign national as a student employee (OW10)

Department of Employment – Immigration Act 1971

APPLICATION FOR PERMISSION TO ENGAGE

A FOREIGN NATIONAL AS A STUDENT EMPLOYEE

FOR OFFICIAL USE
Case no ....
Duration .... months
Student Employee/O ....

Note:– *Please read leaflet OW9 before completing this form.*

Part 1 PARTICULARS OF FOREIGN NATIONAL

1 Surname *(in block letters)* ....

2 Other names *(in block letters)* ....

3 Date of birth .... 4 Sex ....

5 Number of passport *(if known)* ....

6 Issuing government ....

Part 2 PARTICULARS OF EMPLOYER

1 Full name *(in block letters)* ....

....

2 Address ....

....

....

3 Telephone number ....

4 Address at which foreign national will be employed *(if different from above)*

....

....

Part 3 FURTHER PARTICULARS OF FOREIGN NATIONAL

1 Country of birth .... 2 Nationality ....

3 Present address including country:–

Part 4 PARTICULARS OF STUDENT EMPLOYMENT

1 Nature of Employer's business:–

2 Details of training offered:–

SPECIMEN

3 How was the offer of training obtained?

4 Will the foreigner be surplus to your normal staffing requirements? ....

5 Maintenance allowance proposed £ .... per week

6 Date from which required ....

7 Proposed length of student employment ....

(Continued)

(Continued)

Part 5 UNDERTAKING

I declare that the particulars given in this application are true to the best of my knowledge and belief, and I hereby apply to the Department of Employment for permission to employ the foreign national named in this application as a student employee.
I certify that I understand and accept the conditions governing the granting of permission for the employment of foreign nationals as student employees, as set out in leaflet OW 9.

Signature of Employer .... Mr/Mrs/Miss

Position held .... date ....

Company stamp

This form when completed should be sent to the:—

Department of Employment
Overseas Labour Section
Ebury Bridge House
Ebury Bridge Road
London SW1W 8PY

Note *If the foreign national is already in Great Britain his/her police certificate of registration should be submitted with this form.*

Form 4 Notice of taking into employment or transference of a young person

Department of Employment

FACTORIES ACT 1961, EMPLOYMENT MEDICAL ADVISORY SERVICE ACT 1972

NOTICE OF TAKING INTO EMPLOYMENT OR TRANSFERENCE OF A YOUNG PERSON

Section 119A of the Factories Act 1961 requires an employer not later than seven days after taking a young person under the age of 18 into employment to work in premises or on a process or operation subject to the Factories Act 1961 or transferring a young person to such work from work not subject to that Act, to send written notice to the local Careers Office.

NAME OF OCCUPIER ________________________________

ADDRESS OF FACTORY OR PLACE OF WORK (If construction industry and the young person has been taken into employment, or transferred, to work on a particular site, the address of the SITE should be given).

____

____

____

DATE OF TAKING INTO EMPLOYMENT/TRANSFERENCE ________________
(Delete appropriate item)

NATURE OF WORK TO BE DONE BY YOUNG PERSON

____

____

Please give the following information so far as it is known:

SURNAME OF YOUNG PERSON (Capitals) ________________

CHRISTIAN NAME (or FORENAME) ________________

ADDRESS ________________________________

____

DATE OF BIRTH ________________________________

NAME AND ADDRESS OF LAST SCHOOL ATTENDED

____

____

____

Signature: ____________________ Date: ____________

Position in firm: ____________________

Form 5 Settlement reached as a result of conciliation action (COT2)

ADVISORY CONCILIATION AND ARBITRATION SERVICE

* Equal Pay Act 1970
* Sex Discrimination Act 1975
* Race Relations Act 1976
* Employment Protection Act 1975
* Employment Protection (Consolidation) Act 1978

Tribunal case number
....

* AGREEMENT IN RESPECT OF AN APPLICATION MADE TO THE INDUSTRIAL TRIBUNALS

* AGREEMENT IN RESPECT OF A REQUEST FOR CONCILIATION MADE TO THE ADVISORY CONCILIATION & ARBITRATION SERVICE (NO APPLICATION MADE TO TRIBUNAL AT TIME OF AGREEMENT)

Applicant	Respondent
Name	Name ....
Address	Address ....
....	....

Settlement reached as a result of conciliation action.

We the undersigned have agreed:

* 1 that the applicant shall be *engaged/re-engaged/reinstated in employment by

.... with effect from ....(date):

(a) on the terms and conditions under which he/she was employed prior to dismissal

(b) on the following terms and conditions

* 2 that the applicant shall be paid £.................. by the respondent.

Applicant .... date ....

Respondent .... date ....

* Delete or complete as appropriate

Complete (a) and/or (b) as appropriate

Form 6 Alternative form for recording settlement reached as a result of conciliation action (COT3)

ADVISORY CONCILIATION AND ARBITRATION SERVICE

Tribunal case number
....

* Equal Pay Act 1970

* Sex Discrimination Act 1975

* Race Relations Act 1976

* Employment Protection Act 1975

* Employment Protection (Consolidation) Act 1978

* AGREEMENT IN RESPECT OF AN APPLICATION MADE TO THE INDUSTRIAL TRIBUNALS

* AGREEMENT IN RESPECT OF A REQUEST FOR CONCILIATION MADE TO THE ADVISORY CONCILIATION & ARBITRATION SERVICE (NO APPLICATION MADE TO TRIBUNAL AT TIME OF AGREEMENT)

Applicant	Respondent
Name .... Address	Name .... Address ....

Settlement reached as a result of conciliation action.

We the undersigned have agreed:

Applicant .... date ....

Respondent .... date ....

* Delete inappropriate item

Form 7 Withdrawal of an application made to the Industrial Tribunals (COT4)

ADVISORY CONCILIATION AND ARBITRATION SERVICE

Tribunal Case number

....

WITHDRAWAL OF AN APPLICATION MADE TO THE INDUSTRIAL TRIBUNALS UNDER ONE OR MORE OF THE FOLLOWING ACTS:

* Equal Pay Act 1970
* Sex Discrimination Act 1975
* Race Relations Act 1976
* Employment Protection Act 1975
* Employment Protection (Consolidation) Act 1978

Name of applicant ....

Address ....

....

SPECIMEN

I wish to withdraw the application I have made to the industrial tribunal.

Signed.. Date..................................

* Delete whichever is not appropriate

COT4

Originating Application to an Industrial Tribunal

NOTES FOR GUIDANCE

Before completing the application form please read –

THESE NOTES for guidance

LEAFLET ITL 1 which you were given along with this form

THE APPROPRIATE BOOKLET referred to under the relevant Act of Parliament – see paragraph 2 below.

1 QUALIFYING PERIODS AND TIME LIMITS

IN ORDER TO MAKE A VALID APPLICATION YOU MUST SATISFY ANY APPROPRIATE QUALIFYING PERIOD OF CONTINUOUS EMPLOYMENT AND YOUR APPLICATION MUST BE RECEIVED WITHIN THE APPROPRIATE TIME LIMIT. Information on both of these requirements is given in the booklets mentioned in paragraph 2 below. For example, to be able to complain of unfair dismissal you must normally have been employed by the same employer for 26 weeks, and the time limit for the receipt of such an application is normally 3 months from and including the effective date of dismissal. There is no qualifying period of employment for certain jurisdictions eg Equal Pay, Sex Discrimination or Race Relations complaints or where dismissal is for trade union activities, but time limits for making an application apply.

2 RELEVANT ACTS OF PARLIAMENT

You can ask the Tribunal to decide various questions as provided for in relevant Acts of Parliament. Details of these questions, the relevant Acts of Parliament and the titles of booklets explaining in simple terms the provision of these Acts and what the Tribunal can decide are given in leaflet ITL 1 which should be issued to you with this form. These booklets are obtainable FREE from any employment office, jobcentre or unemployment benefit office. This form may be used for any of the matters referred to in leaflet ITL 1.

3 PREPARATION OF APPLICATION FORM

When completing the application form you should fill in items 1, 2, 4 and 12 and any other items which are relevant to your case. You should keep a copy of entries on the form. If in doubt about the respondent to name in item 4 you may seek advice from any employment office, jobcentre or unemployment benefit office. A Citizens' Advice Bureau or Trade Union may be able to help you complete the form or advise you as to whether you have a complaint which an Industrial Tribunal could consider.

4 PREPARATION OF YOUR CASE AND REPRESENTATION AT THE HEARING

At the hearing you may state your own case or be represented by anyone who has agreed to act for you. If you intend to have a representative it is advisable that he or she should be consulted at the earliest possible stage – preferably before the application form is completed (but see note above regarding time limits).
In cases under the Equal Pay and Sex Discrimination Acts the Equal Opportunities Commission, and in cases under the Race Relations Act the Commission for Racial Equality, may provide assistance or representation – see appropriate booklet. **IF YOU NAME A REPRESENTATIVE ALL FURTHER COMMUNICATIONS WILL BE SENT TO HIM OR HER AND NOT TO YOU; YOU SHOULD ARRANGE WITH YOUR REPRESENTATIVE TO BE KEPT INFORMED OF THE PROGRESS OF YOUR CASE AND OF THE HEARING DATE.**

Do not forget to sign the form.

PLEASE DETACH THESE NOTES before sending the application form to the Central Office of the Industrial Tribunals. **KEEP THE NOTES FOR FUTURE REFERENCE.**

(Continued)

(Continued)

ORIGINATING APPLICATION TO AN INDUSTRIAL TRIBUNAL

For Official Use	
Case Number	

IMPORTANT: DO NOT FILL IN THIS FORM UNTIL YOU HAVE READ THE NOTES FOR GUIDANCE. THEN COMPLETE ITEMS 1, 2,4 AND 12 AND ALL OTHER ITEMS RELEVANT TO YOUR CASE, AND SEND THE FORM TO THE FOLLOWING ADDRESS

To: THE SECRETARY OF THE TRIBUNALS
CENTRAL OFFICE OF THE INDUSTRIAL TRIBUNALS (ENGLAND AND WALES)
93 EBURY BRIDGE ROAD, LONDON SW1W 8RE Telephone: 01 730 9161

1 I hereby apply for a decision of a Tribunal on the following question. **(STATE HERE THE QUESTION TO BE DECIDED BY A TRIBUNAL. EXPLAIN THE GROUNDS OVERLEAF).**

....

2 My name is (Mr/Mrs/Miss Surname in block capitals first):–

....

My address is:– ....

....

.... Telephone No. ....

My date of birth is ....

3 If a representative has agreed to act for you in this case please give his or her name and address below and note that further communications will be sent to your representative and not to you *(See Note 4)*

Name of Representative:– ....

Address:– ....

.... Telephone No. ....

4 **(a)** Name of respondent(s) (in block capitals) ie the employer, person or body against whom a decision is sought *(See Note 3)*

....

Address(es) ....

.... Telephone No. ....

(b) Respondent's relationship to you for the purpose of the application (eg employer, trade union, employment agency, employer recognising the union making application, etc). ....

....

5 Place of employment to which this application relates, or place where act complained about took place.

....

6 My occupation or position held/applied for, or other relationship to the respondent named above (eg user of a service supplied in relation to employment).

....

7 Dates employment began .... and *(if appropriate)* ended ....

8 **(a)** Basic wages/salary ....

(b) Average take home pay ....

9 Other remuneration or benefits ....

10 Normal basic weekly hours of work ....

11 (In an application under the Sex Discrimination Act or the Race Relations Act)
Date on which action complained of took place or first came to my knowledge ....

(Continued)

(Continued)

12 Please explain the grounds for your application below. It will be helpful to the Tribunal if you can give details of the reasons for the application; you will be able to amplify them at the hearing.

13 If you wish to state what in your opinion was the reason for your dismissal, please do so here.

14 If the Tribunal decides that you were unfairly dismissed, please state which of the following you would prefer: reinstatement, re-engagement or compensation. (Before answering this question please consult the leaflet "Dismissal – Employees Rights").

....

Signature .... Date ....

FOR OFFICIAL USE

Received at COIT	Code	ROIT	Inits

Form 9 Notice of originating application (IT2)

INDUSTRIAL TRIBUNALS (LABOUR RELATIONS) REGULATIONS 1974

NOTICE OF ORIGINATING APPLICATION

Case No.

1. I enclose a copy of an originating application for a decision of a tribunal in which you are named as respondent. Under the rules of procedure you are required to enter an appearance within 14 days of receiving the copy of the originating application. You can do this either by completing and sending to me the enclosed form of notice of appearance or by sending a letter giving the information called for on the form. This form and any other communications addressed to me may be sent by post or delivered to me at the above address.

2. The proceedings on this application will be regulated by the rules of procedure contained in the above Regulations and these are explained in the enclosed leaflet. The case number of the application is indicated above and should be quoted in any communications with regard to these proceedings.

3. If you name a representative at item 3 of the form, further communications regarding the case will be sent to him and not to you, and you should arrange to be kept informed by him of the progress of the case and of the hearing date. When the application is heard by the tribunal the parties (other than a respondent who has not entered an appearance) may appear and be heard in person or be represented by anyone they choose.

4. If you do not send me the completed form (or other notice of appearance) you will not be entitled to take any part in the proceedings (except to apply for an extension of time to enter an appearance). If you do not take part in the proceedings a decision which may be enforceable in the county court may be given against you in your absence. Whether or not you enter an appearance you will be notified of the date of hearing and sent a copy of the tribunal's decision.

5. In all cases where the Act under which the application is made provides for conciliation the services of a conciliation officer are available to the parties. In such cases a copy of the application is sent to the Advisory Conciliation and Arbitration Service accordingly, (see leaflet ITL1 paragraph 21)

Signed .... Dated ....

for Secretary of the Tribunals

To the Respondent(s)

Form 10 Notice of appearance by respondent (IT3)

Industrial Tribunals — Case Number ....

NOTICE OF APPEARANCE BY RESPONDENT

To the Secretary of the Tribunals

FOR OFFICIAL USE	
Date of receipt	Initials

1. I *do/do not intend to resist the claim made by
2. *My/Our Name is *Mr/Mrs/Miss/title (if company or organisation)

   address

   telephone number
3. If you have arranged to have a representative to act for you, please give his name and address below and note that further communications will be sent to him and not to you.

   name

   address

   telephone number
4. a Was the applicant dismissed *YES/NO

   b If YES, what was the reason for the dismissal?

   c Are the dates given by the applicant as to his period of employment correct? *YES/NO

   d If NO, give dates of commencement .... and termination ....

   e Are details of remuneration stated by the applicant correct? *YES/NO

   f If not, or if the applicant has not stated such details please given the correct remuneration here:-

   Basic wages/salary .... other pay or remuneration ....
5. If the claim is resisted, please give below sufficient particulars to show the grounds on which you intend to resist the application. It will be helpful to the tribunal if you give details of your reasons for resisting it; you will be able to add to them at the tribunal hearing (continue on reverse if there is insufficient space below):-

SIGNATURE.. DATE.....................

*Delete inappropriate items.

Form 11 Notice of hearing (IT4)

THE INDUSTRIAL TRIBUNALS

NOTICE OF HEARING

Case No ....

NOTICE IS HEREBY GIVEN THAT THE application of

has been listed for hearing by an Industrial Tribunal at

on day, 19 at am/pm

1. Attendance should be at the above time and place. The parties (other than a respondent who has not entered an appearance) are entitled to appear at the hearing and to state their case in person or be represented by anyone they wish. A party can choose not to appear and can rely on written representations (which if additional to any already submitted must be sent to the Tribunal and copied to the other party not less than 7 days before the hearing). However, experience shows that it is normally in his own interests for each party and his witnesses (if any) to attend in person even if they have made statements or representations in writing.

2. It is very important that he should bring with him any documents that may be relevant, e g a letter of appointment, contract of employment, Working Rule Agreement, pay slips, income tax forms, evidence of unemployment and other social security benefits, wages book, details of benefits and contributions under any pension or superannuation scheme, etc.

3. If the complaint is one of unfair dismissal or refusal of permission for a woman employee to return to work after a pregnancy the tribunal may wish to consider whether to make an order for reinstatement or re-engagement. In these cases the respondent should be prepared to give evidence at the hearing as to the availability of the job from which the applicant was dismissed, or held before absence due to pregnancy, or of comparable or suitable employment and generally as to the practicability of reinstatement or re-engagement of the applicant by the respondent.

4. If for any reason a party (other than a respondent who has not entered an appearance) does not propose to appear at the hearing, either personally or by representative, he should inform me immediately, in writing, giving the reason and the case number. He should also state whether he wishes the hearing to proceed in his absence, relying on any written representations he may have made.

5. The hearing of this case will take place at the time stated above or as soon thereafter as the tribunal can hear it.

SPECIMEN

To the Applicant(s) (Ref)

Signed ....
for Assistant Secretary of the Tribunals

Date ....

NOTE Representatives who receive this notice must inform the party they represent of the date, time and place of the hearing. The party will not be notified direct.

and the Respondent(s) (Ref)

and the Secretary of State for Employment
and the Conciliation Officer, Advisory Conciliation and Arbitration Service

Preparation of documents for the hearing

At an Industrial Tribunal hearing parties frequently wish to refer to certain letters or documents in support of their case.

It will be helpful, and may simplify and shorten the hearing, if each party sends to the other, well in advance of the hearing date, a list of documents which he or she intends to produce at the hearing.

It will then be open to either party to ask to see, or to receive a copy of, particular documents before the hearing. Experience has shown that compliance with such a request may be to the advantage of both parties in avoiding delays or adjournments of hearings to permit documents to be studied.

Would you please send to this office a copy of any list of documents which you send to the other party. The documents themselves or copies of them should not be sent to this office.

Note for professional advisers

Professional advisers should prepare a bundle containing all correspondence and other documents on which they intend to rely at the hearing arranged in correct sequence and numbered consecutively. It is desirable, whenever it is practicable, that there should be an agreed bundle.

Three sets of documents should be made available for the use of the tribunal.

Form 13 Notice of Industrial Tribunal application (IT5)

Your reference

Case No

Date

INDUSTRIAL TRIBUNALS (LABOUR RELATIONS) REGULATIONS 1974

NOTICE

1. The application for a decision of a tribunal under the above Regulations has been received. It has been entered in the Register and allotted the case number shown above. This number should be quoted in any further communications which should be sent to the address at the head of this notice.

2. A copy of the application has been sent to the respondent and a copy of any reply will be sent to you.

3. A notice of hearing will be sent to you not less than 14 days before the date fixed for the hearing of the application.

4. In all cases where the Act under which the application is made provides for conciliation the services of a conciliation officer are available to the parties. In such cases a copy of the application is sent to the Advisory Conciliation and Arbitration Service accordingly.

Signed .... Dated ....
for Assistant Secretary of the Tribunals

Form 14 Notice of appeal from decision of an Industrial Tribunal (EAT 1)

EMPLOYMENT PROTECTION ACT 1975

NOTICE OF APPEAL FROM DECISION OF INDUSTRIAL TRIBUNAL

1. The appellant is [name and address of appellant]:-

2. Any communication relating to this appeal may be sent to the appellant at [appellant's address for service, including telephone number, if any]:-

3. The appellant appeals from
[here give particulars of the decision of the industrial tribunal from which the appeal is brought]:-

on the following questions of law:-
[here set out the question of law on which the appeal is brought].

4. The parties to the proceedings before the industrial tribunal, other than the appellant, were [names and addresses of other parties - and of their representatives if applicable - to the proceedings resulting in decision appealed from]:-

5. The appellant's grounds of appeal are:-
[here state the grounds of appeal].

6. A copy of the industrial tribunal's decision is attached to this notice.

Date: ______________________________ Signed: ______________________________

Form 15 Claim for rebate of maternity pay (MP 1)

BEFORE COMPLETING THIS FORM PLEASE READ CAREFULLY THE LEAFLET "EMPLOYMENT RIGHTS FOR THE EXPECTANT MOTHER", *AVAILABLE FROM JOBCENTRES, EMPLOYMENT OFFICES AND UNEMPLOYMENT BENEFIT OFFICES*

DEPARTMENT OF EMPLOYMENT

EMPLOYMENT PROTECTION ACT 1975

CLAIM FOR REBATE OF MATERNITY PAY

Redundancy Payments Office
DEPARTMENT OF EMPLOYMENT REDUNDANCY PAYMENTS OFFICE 1 BARNSBURY ROAD LONDON, N1 0EX.

Full name of firm ....

Address ....

....

Name, position and telephone number of person to be contacted in case of query

....

A Details of employee in respect of whom rebate is claimed

1 Name ....

2 Address ....

....

3 Nature and place of employment ....

....

4 National Insurance number ....

5 Income Tax reference number ....

6 Date when current period of continuous employment with present employer began ....

7 Expected date of confinement ....
(as notified to employer)

8 Date maternity pay period commenced ....
NOTE: *This date must not be before the beginning of the 11th week before the expected week of confinement*

9 * If employment ceased before maternity pay period commenced:

a give date on which it ceased ....

b state reasons for employment ceasing

* *Under Section 35(3) an employee who is dismissed before the 11th week before expected confinement is still entitled to maternity pay if the reason for dismissal is that she is not capable because of her condition of continuing to work, or she would be in breach of a statutory restriction by continuing to work, and if she would have had 104 weeks continuous employment at the 11th week had she not been dismissed.*

(Continued)

(Continued)

B Calculation of Maternity Pay

NOTE: If maternity pay has been paid following an award of an Industrial Tribunal paragraphs 1 and 6 only should be completed

1 * Gross amount of normal week's pay £ ....

2 Deduct:

$\frac{1}{10}$th of week's pay £ ....

† Flat rate weekly national insurance maternity allowance £ ....

Total weekly deductions £ ....

3 Gross weekly amount of Maternity Pay payable by employer (item 1 minus item 2) £ ....

4 Number of weeks for which payment made (maximum 6) ....

5 Total gross amount of Maternity Pay payable by employer (item 3 x item 4) £ ....

6 Amount awarded by industrial tribunal (if appropriate) £ ....

– please attach copy of award if available (this will be returned) or state reference number of case and date and place of hearing

....

7 Date on which payment or, if paid in instalments, final payment of maternity pay was made

....

* *For difficult cases see booklet "Continuous Employment and 'a Week's Pay'", available from Jobcentres, Employment Offices and Unemployment Benefit Offices.*

†NATIONAL INSURANCE MATERNITY ALLOWANCE

This is deducted whether it is due to the employee or not. As the amount is always liable to change, the current amount should be ascertained from your local Social Security office. No deduction should be made in respect of earnings related supplements.

NOTE: Claims for rebate should not be submitted until the full payment period is complete (item 4) and the employee has received the full amount due

(Continued)

(Continued)

C Calculation of Amount of Rebate Claimed

1 Total gross amount paid by employer **(amount at item B5 or amount of tribunal award, as appropriate)** £ ....

2 Total secondary (**employers**) national insurance contributions paid by employer on amount at C1 £ ....

3 Amount claimed as rebate (1 + 2) £ ....

D Claim

NOTE: This part of the form must be signed and dated AFTER the end of the maternity pay period.

The above named employee was absent during the period of the claim (item B4). She appears to be entitled to maternity pay in accordance with the Employment Protection Act 1975 and I have paid to her the sum of

£ .... being the gross amount shown at item C1 above. The appropriate tax and national insurance deductions have been paid over to the appropriate authorities.
† Receipt(s) for this payment is / are attached. No previous claim has been made for the same weeks for the same person.

I claim rebate of £ .... being the amount calculated at C3 above.

Signature .... Date ....

Position in firm ....
(eg Director, Secretary, Personnel Manager)

† *Evidence of receipt of payment is required. If it is not possible to obtain a receipt on form MP1 (R) please contact the office indicated below.*

This form is to be sent to:
(Address of Local Redundancy Payments Office)

DEPARTMENT OF EMPLOYMENT
REDUNDANCY PAYMENTS OFFICE
1 BARNSBURY ROAD
LONDON. N1 0EX.

NOT LATER THAN 6 MONTHS AFTER DATE AT B7.

(Continued)

(Continued)

FOR OFFICIAL USE

To the RFO ....

I certify that Form MPI has been checked. No previous claim has been received in respect of the employee named.

Claim is approved for the payment of £ ....

Signature .... Office ....
(Approving Officer)

Date ....

FOR USE IN REGIONAL FINANCE OFFICE

Cashier please pay £ .... and make the following accounting entries:–

Authorising Officer .... Date ....

Paid by Payable Order No. .... Dated ....

Form 16 Employee's receipt for maternity pay (MP 1(R))

DEPARTMENT OF EMPLOYMENT

EMPLOYEE'S RECEIPT FOR MATERNITY PAY

Name and address of Employee ....

....

....

....

Name and address of Employer ....

....

....

....

I acknowledge that maternity pay amounting to £ .... gross

(from which deductions of tax and national insurance have been made)

for the period / / to / / was paid to me on / / *

Signature ....

Date ....

* If payment was made in instalments give date of final payment. Do not sign this form until you have received your full entitlement of pay.

SEX DISCRIMINATION ACT 1975

THE QUESTIONS PROCEDURE

CONTENTS

A complainant should obtain TWO copies of this booklet, one to send to the respondent and the other to keep.
Before completing the questionnaire or the reply form (as appropriate), the complainant and the respondent should read Part I of the guidance and (again as appropriate) Part II or III.

Issued by The Home Office and
The Department of Employment

(Continued)

(Continued)

SEX DISCRIMINATION ACT 1975 – GUIDANCE ON THE QUESTIONS PROCEDURE

PART I – INTRODUCTION

1 The purpose of this guidance is to explain the questions procedure under section 74 of the Sex Discrimination Act 1975*. The procedure is intended to help a person (referred to in this guidance as the **complainant**) who thinks she (or he) has been discriminated against by another (the **respondent**) to obtain information from that person about the treatment in question in order to –

(a) decide whether or not to bring legal proceedings, and

(b) if proceedings are brought, to present her complaint in the most effective way.

A questionnaire has been devised which the complainant can send to the respondent and there is also a matching reply form for use by the respondent (both are included in this booklet). The questionnaire and the reply form have been designed to assist the complainant and respondent to identify information which is relevant to the complaint. It is not, however, obligatory for the questionnaire or the reply form to be used: the exchange of questions and replies may be conducted, for example, by letter.

2 This guidance is intended to assist both the complainant and the respondent. Guidance for the complainant on the preparation of the questionnaire is set out in Part II; and guidance for the respondent on the use of the reply form is set out in Part III. The main provisions of the Sex Discrimination Act are referred to in the appendix to this guidance. Further information about the Act will be found in the various leaflets published by the Equal Opportunities Commission and also in the detailed **Guide to the Sex Discrimination Act 1975.** The leaflets and the **Guide** may be obtained, free of charge, from the Equal Opportunities Commission at –

Overseas House
Quay Street
Manchester M3 3HN
Telephone: 061 – 833 9244

The **Guide** and the EOC's leaflets on the employment provisions of the Act may also be obtained, free of charge, from any employment office or jobcentre of the Employment Service Agency or from any unemployment benefit office of the Department of Employment. The EOC's leaflets may also be obtained from Citizens Advice Bureaux.

How the questions procedure can benefit both parties

3 The procedure can benefit both the complainant and the respondent in the following ways:–

(1) If the respondent's answers satisfy the complainant that the treatment was not unlawful discrimination, there will be no need for legal proceedings.

(2) Even if the respondent's answers do not satisfy the complainant, they should help to identify what is agreed and what is in dispute between the parties. For example, the answers should reveal whether the parties disagree on the facts of the case, or, if they agree on the facts, whether they disagree on how the Act applies. In some cases, this may lead to a settlement of the grievance, again making legal proceedings unnecessary.

(3) If it turns out that the complainant institutes proceedings against the respondent, the proceedings should be that much simpler because the matters in dispute will have been identified in advance.

What happens if the respondent does not reply or replies evasively

4 The respondent cannot be compelled to reply to the complainant's questions. However, if the respondent deliberately, and without reasonable excuse, does not reply within a reasonable period, or replies in an evasive or **ambiguous** way, his position may be adversely affected should the complainant bring proceedings against him. The respondent's attention is drawn to these possible consequences in the note at the end of the questionnaire.

Period within which questionnaire must be served on the respondent

5 There are different time limits within which a questionaire must be served in order to be admissible under the questions procedure in any ensuing legal proceedings. Which time limit applies depends on whether the complaint would be under the employment, training and related provisions of the Act (in which case the proceedings would be before an industrial tribunal) or whether it would be under the education, goods, facilities and services or premises provisions (in which case proceedings would be before a county court or, in Scotland, a sheriff court).

Industrial tribunal cases

6 In order to be admissible under the questions procedure in any ensuing industrial tribunal proceedings, the complainant's questionnaire must be served on the respondent either:

(a) before a complaint about the treatment concerned is made to an industrial tribunal, but not more than 3 months after the treatment in question; or

(b) if a complaint has already been made to a tribunal within 21 days beginning when the complaint was received by the tribunal.

However, where the complainant has made a complaint to a tribunal and the period of 21 days has expired, a questionnaire may still be served provided the leave of the tribunal is obtained. This may be done by sending to the Secretary of the Tribunals a written application, which must state the names of the complainant and the respondent and set out the grounds of the application. However every effort should be made to serve the questionnaire within the period of 21 days as the leave of the tribunal to serve the questionnaire after the expiry of that period will not necessarily be obtained.

Court cases

7 In order to be admissible under the questions procedure in any ensuing county or sheriff court proceedings, the complainant's questionnaire must be served on the respondent before proceedings in respect of the treatment concerne

** The prescribed forms, time limits for serving questions and manner of service of questions and replies under section 74 are specified in The Sex Discrimination (Questions and Replies) Order 1975 (SI 1975 No. 2048).*

are brought, but not more than 6 months after the treatment*. However, where proceedings have been brought, a questionnaire may still be served provided the leave of the court has been obtained. In the case of county court proceedings, this may be done by obtaining form Ex 23 from the county court office, and completing it and sending it to the Registrar and the respondent, or by applying to the Registrar at the pre-trial review. In the case of sheriff court proceedings, this may be done by making an application to a sheriff.

PART II–GUIDANCE FOR THE COMPLAINANT

NOTES ON PREPARING THE QUESTIONNAIRE

8 Before filling in the questionnaire, you are advised to prepare what you want to say on a separate piece of paper. If you have insufficient room on the questionnaire for what you want to say, you should continue on an additional piece of paper, which should be sent with the questionnaire to the respondent.

Paragraph 2

9 You should give, in the space provided in paragraph 2, as much relevant factual information as you can about the treatment you think may have been unlawful discrimination, and about the circumstances leading up to that treatment. You should also give the date, and if possible and if relevant, the place and approximate time of the treatment. You should bear in mind that in paragraph 4 of the questionnaire you will be asking the respondent whether he agrees with what you say in paragraph 2.

Paragraph 3

10 In paragraph 3 you are telling the respondent that you think the treatment you have described in paragraph 2 may have been unlawful discrimination by him against you. It will help to identify whether there are any legal issues between you and the respondent if you explain in the space provided **why** you think the treatment may have been unlawful discrimination. However, you **do not have** to complete paragraph 3; if you do not wish or are unable to do so, you should delete the word "because". If you wish to complete the paragraph, but feel you need more information about the Sex Discrimination Act before doing so, you should look to the appendix to this guidance.

11 If you decide to complete paragraph 3, you may find it useful to indicate-

(a) what **kind** of discrimination you think the treatment may have been ie whether it was
direct sex discrimination,
indirect sex discrimination,
direct discrimination against a married person,
indirect discrimination against a married person, or
victimisation.

(For further information about the different kinds of discrimination see paragraph 1 of the appendix)

(b) which provision of the Act you think may make unlawful the kind of discrimination you think you may have suffered. (For an indication of the provisions of the Act which make the various kinds of discrimination unlawful, see paragraph 2 of the appendix.)

Paragraph 6

12 You should insert here any other question which you think may help you to obtain relevant information. (For example, if you think you have been discriminated against by having been refused a job, you may want to know what were the qualifications of the person who did get the job and why that person got the job.)

13 Paragraph 5 contains questions which are especially important if you think you may have suffered direct sex discrimination, or direct discrimination against a married person, because they ask the respondent whether your sex or marital status had anything to do with your treatment. Paragraph 5 does not, however, ask specific questions relating to indirect sex discrimination, indirect discrimination against a married person or victimisation. If you think you may have suffered indirect sex discrimination (or indirect discrimination against a married person) you may find it helpful to include the following question in the space provided in paragraph 6:

"Was the reason for my treatment the fact that I could not comply with a condition or requirement which is applied equally to men and women (married and unmarried persons)?
If so –
(a) what was the condition or requirement?
(b) why was it applied?"

14 If you think you may have been victimised you may find it helpful to include the following question in the space provided in paragraph 6:

"Was the reason for my treatment the fact that I had done, or intended to do, or that you suspected I had done or intended to do, any of the following:
(a) brought proceedings under the Sex Discrimination Act or the Equal Pay Act; or
(b) gave evidence or information in connection with proceedings under either Act; or
(c) did something else under or by reference to either Act; or
(d) made an allegation that someone acted unlawfully under either Act?"

Signature

15 The questionnaire must be signed and dated. If it is to be signed on behalf of (rather than by) the complainant, **the person signing** should –

(a) describe himself (eg "solicitor acting for *(name of complainant)*)", *and*
(b) give his business (or home, if appropriate) address.

WHAT PAPERS TO SERVE ON THE PERSON TO BE QUESTIONED

16 You should send the person to be questioned the whole of this document (ie the guidance, the questionnaire and the reply forms), with the questionnaire completed by you. **You are strongly advised to retain, and keep in a safe place, a copy of the completed questionnaire** (and you might also find it useful to retain a copy of the guidance and the uncompleted reply form).

(Continued)

**Where the respondent is a body in charge of a public sector educational establishment, the six month period begins when the complaint has been referred to the appropriate Education Minister and 2 months have elapsed or, if this is earlier, the Minister has informed the complainant that he requires no more time to consider the matter.*

(Continued)

HOW TO SERVE THE PAPERS

17 You can either deliver the papers in person or send them by post. If you decide to send them by post you are advised to use the recorded delivery service, so that, if necessary, you can produce evidence that they were delivered.

WHERE TO SEND THE PAPERS

18 You can send the papers to the person to be questioned at his usual or last known residence or place of business. If you know he is acting through a solicitor you should send them to him at his solicitor's address. If you wish to question a limited company or other corporate body or a trade union or employers' association, you should send the papers to the secretary or clerk at the registered or principal office of the company, etc. You should be able to find out where its registered or principal office is by enquiring at a public library. If you are unable to do so, however, you will have to send the papers to the place where you think it is most likely they will reach the secretary or clerk (eg at, or c/o, the company's local office). It is your responsibility, however, to see that the secretary or clerk receives the papers.

USE OF THE QUESTIONS AND REPLIES IN INDUSTRIAL TRIBUNAL PROCEEDINGS

19 If you decide to make (or already have made) a complaint to an industrial tribunal about the treatment concerned and if you intend to use your questions and the reply (if any) as evidence in the proceedings, you are advised to send copies of your questions and any reply to the Secretary of the Tribunals before the date of the hearing. This should be done as soon as the documents are available; if they are available at the time you submit your complaint to a tribunal, you should send the copies with your complaint to the Secretary of the Tribunals.

PART III – GUIDANCE FOR THE RESPONDENT

NOTES ON COMPLETING THE REPLY FORM

20 Before completing the reply form, you are advised to prepare what you want to say on a separate piece of paper. If you have insufficient room on the reply form for what you want to say, you should continue on an additional piece of paper, which should be attached to the reply form sent to the complainant.

Paragraph 2

21 Here you are answering the question in paragraph 4 of the questionnaire. If you **agree** that the complainant's statement in paragraph 2 of the questionnaire is an accurate **description** of what happened, you should delete the second sentence.

22 If you **disagree** in any way that the statement is an accurate description of what happened, you should explain in the space provided in what respects you disagree, or your version of what happened, or both.

Paragraph 3

23 Here you are answering the question in paragraph 5 of the questionnaire. If, in answer to paragraph 4 of the questionnaire, you have agreed with the complainant's description of her treatment, you will be answering paragraph 5 on the basis of the facts in her description. If, however, you have disagreed with that description, you should answer paragraph 5 on the basis of **your** version of the facts. To answer paragraph 5, you are advised to look at the appendix to this guidance and also the relevant parts of the **Guide to the Sex Discrimination Act 1975.** You need to know:–

(a) how the Act defines discrimination – see paragraph 1 of the appendix;

(b) in what situations the Act makes discrimination unlawful – see paragraph 2 of the appendix; and

(c) what exceptions the Act provides – see paragraph 3 of the appendix.

24 If you think that an exception (eg the exception for employment where a person's sex is a genuine occupational qualification) applies to the treatment described in paragraph 2 of the complainant's questionnaire, you should mention this in paragraph 3a of the reply form and explain why you think the exception applies.

Signature

25 The reply form should be signed and dated. If it is to be signed on behalf of (rather than by) the respondent, the person signing should –

(a) describe himself (eg "solicitor acting for (*name of respondent*)" or "personnel manager of (*name of firm*)"), and

(b) give his business (or home, if appropriate) address.

SERVING THE REPLY FORM ON THE COMPLAINANT

26 If you wish to reply to the questionnaire you are strongly advised to do so without delay. **You should retain, and keep in a safe place, the questionnaire sent to you and a copy of your reply.**

27 You can serve the reply either by delivering it in person to the complainant or by sending it by post. If you decide to send it by post you are advised to use the recorded delivery service, so that, if necessary, you can produce evidence that it was delivered.

28 You should send the reply form to the address indicated in paragraph 7 of the complainant's questionnaire.

THE SEX DISCRIMINATION ACT 1975 SECTION 74 (1)(a)

QUESTIONNAIRE OF PERSON AGGRIEVED (THE COMPLAINANT)

Name of person to be questioned (the respondent)	To ....
Address	of ....
	....
Name of complainant	1. I ....
Address	of ....
	.... consider that you may have discriminated against me contrary to the Sex Discrimination Act 1975.
Give date, approximate time, place and factual description of the treatment received and of the circumstances leading up to the treatment (see paragraph 9 of the guidance)	2. On
Complete if you wish to give reasons, otherwise delete the word "because" (see paragraphs 10 and 11 of the guidance)	3. I consider that this treatment may have been unlawful because

(Continued)

(Continued)

This is the first of your questions to the respondent. You are advised not to alter it

4. Do you agree that the statement in paragraph 2 is an accurate description of what happened? If not in what respect do you disagree or what is your version of what happened?

This is the second of your questions to the respondent. You are advised not to alter it

5. Do you accept that your treatment of me was unlawful discrimination by you against me?
If not
 a why not?
 b for what reason did I receive the treatment accorded to me?
 c how far did my sex or marital status affect your treatment of me?

Enter here any other questions you wish to ask (see paragraphs 12–14 of the guidance)

6.

*** Delete as appropriate If you delete the first alternative, insert the address to which you want the reply to be sent**

7. My address for any reply you may wish to give to the questions raised above is
* that set out in paragraph 1 above/the following address

See paragraph 15 of the guidance

Signature of complainant ....

Date ....

NB *By virtue of section 74 of the Act, this questionnaire and any reply are (subject to the provisions of the section) admissible in proceedings under the Act and a court or tribunal may draw any such inference as is just and equitable from a failure without reasonable excuse to reply within a reasonable period, or from an evasive or equivocal reply, including an inference that the person questioned has discriminated unlawfully.*

THE SEX DISCRIMINATION ACT 1975 SECTION 74 (1)(b)

REPLY BY RESPONDENT

Name of complainant	To ....
Address	of ....
	....
Name of respondent	1. I ....
Address	of ....
	....
Complete as appropriate	hereby acknowledge receipt of the questionnaire signed by you and dated
	.... which was served on me on (date) ....
*** Delete as appropriate**	2. I ***agree/disagree** that the statement in paragraph 2 of the questionnaire is an accurate description of what happened.
If you agree that the statement in paragraph 2 of the questionnaire is accurate, delete this sentence. If you disagree complete this sentence (see paragraphs 21 and 22 of the guidance)	I disagree with the statement in paragraph 2 of the questionnaire in that
*** Delete as appropriate**	3. I *** accept/dispute** that my treatment of you was unlawful discrimination by me against you.
If you accept the complainant's assertion of unlawful discrimination in paragraph 3 of the questionnaire delete the sentences at a, b and c. Unless completed a sentence should be deleted (see paragraphs 23 and 24 of the guidance)	a My reasons for so disputing are

(Continued)

(Continued)

b The reason why you received the treatment accorded to you is

c Your sex or marital status affected my treatment of you to the following extent:–

Replies to questions in paragraph 6 of the questionnaire should be entered here	4.
Delete the whole of this sentence if you have answered all the questions in the questionnaire. If you have not answered all the questions, delete "unable" or "unwilling" as appropriate and give your reasons for not answering.	5. I have deleted (in whole or in part) the paragraph(s) numbered .... above, since I am **unable/unwilling** to reply to the relevant questions of the questionnaire for the following reasons:–
See paragraph 25 of the guidance	Signature of respondent .... Date ....

THE SEX DISCRIMINATION ACT 1975 SECTION 74 (1)(b)

REPLY BY RESPONDENT

Name of complainant	To ....
Address	of ....
	....
Name of respondent	1. I ....
Address	of ....
	....
Complete as appropriate	hereby acknowledge receipt of the questionnaire signed by you and dated .... which was served on me on (date) ....
***Delete as appropriate**	2. I ***agree/disagree** that the statement in paragraph 2 of the questionnaire is an accurate description of what happened.
If you agree that the statement in paragraph 2 of the questionnaire is accurate, delete this sentence. If you disagree complete this sentence (see paragraphs 21 and 22 of the guidance)	I disagree with the statement in paragraph 2 of the questionnaire in that
***Delete as appropriate**	3. I ***accept/dispute** that my treatment of you was unlawful discrimination by me against you.
If you accept the complainant's assertion of unlawful discrimination in paragraph 3 of the questionnaire delete the sentences at a, b and c. Unless completed a sentence should be deleted (see paragraphs 23 and 24 of the guidance)	a My reasons for so disputing are

(Continued)

(Continued)

b The reason why you received the treatment accorded to you is

c Your sex or marital status affected my treatment of you to the following extent:–

Replies to questions in paragraph 6 of the questionnaire should be entered here

4.

Delete the whole of this sentence if you have answered all the questions in the questionnaire. If you have not answered all the questions, delete "unable" or "unwilling" as appropriate and give your reasons for not answering.

5. I have deleted (in whole or in part) the paragraph(s) numbered .... above, since I am **unable/unwilling** to reply to the relevant questions of the questionnaire for the following reasons:–

See paragraph 25 of the guidance

Signature of respondent ....

Date ....

APPENDIX

NOTES ON THE SCOPE OF THE SEX DISCRIMINATION ACT 1975

Definitions of discrimination

1 The different kinds of discrimination covered by the Act are summarised below (the references in the margin are to the relevant paragraphs in the **Guide to the Sex Discrimination Act 1975**). Some of the explanations have been written in terms of discrimination against a woman, but the Act applies equally to discrimination against men.

2.4 to 2.8 **Direct sex discrimination** arises where a woman is treated less favourably than a man is (or would be) treated **because of her sex.**

Indirect sex discrimination arises where a woman is treated unfavourably because she cannot comply with a condition or requirement which

(a) is (or would be) applied to men and women equally, **and**

(b) is such that the proportion of women who can comply with it is considerably smaller than the proportion of men who can comply with it, **and**

(c) is to the detriment of the woman in question because she cannot comply with it, **and**

(d) is such that the person applying it cannot show that it is justifiable regardless of the sex of the person to whom it is applied.

2.9 to 2.12 **Direct discrimination against married persons in the employment field** arises where a married person is treated, in a situation covered by the employment provisions of the Act (ie those summarised under Group A in the table on the next page), less favourably than an unmarried person of the same sex is (or would be) treated **because she or he is married.**

Indirect discrimination against married persons in the employment field arises where a married person is treated, in a situation covered by the employment provisions of the Act, unfavourably because she or he cannot comply with a condition or requirement which

(a) is (or would be) applied to married and unmarried persons equally, **and**

(b) is such that the proportion of married persons who can comply with it is considerably smaller than the proportion of unmarried persons of the same sex who can comply with it, **and**

(c) is to the detriment of the unmarried person in question because she or he cannot comply with it, **and**

(d) is such that the person applying it cannot show it to be justifiable irrespective of the marital status of the person to whom it is applied.

2.13 and 2.14 **Victimisation** arises where a person is treated less favourably than other persons (of either sex) are (or would be) treated because that person has done (or intends to do or is suspected of having done or intending to do) any of the following:—

(a) brought proceedings under the Act or the Equal Pay Act; or

(b) given evidence or information in connection with proceedings brought under either Act; or

(c) done anything else by reference to either Act (eg given information to the Equal Opportunities Commission); or

(d) made an allegation that someone acted unlawfully under either Act.

Victimisation does **not**, however, occur where the reason for the less favourable treatment is an allegation which was false and not made in good faith.

Unlawful discrimination

2 The provisions of the Act which make discrimination unlawful are indicated in the table on the next page. Those in Group A are the employment provisions, for the purposes of which discrimination means direct sex discrimination, indirect sex discrimination, direct discrimination against married persons, indirect discrimination against married persons, and victimisation. Complaints about discrimination which is unlawful under these provisions must be made to an industrial tribunal. For detailed information about these provisions see chapter 3 of the **Guide.** For the purposes of the provisions in Group B, discrimination means direct sex discrimination, indirect sex discrimination and victimisation, but not direct or indirect discrimination against married persons. Complaints about discrimination which is unlawful under these provisions must be made to a county court or, in Scotland, a sheriff court. For detailed information about these provisions see chapters 4 and 5 of the **Guide.**

Exceptions

3 Details of exceptions to the requirements of the Act not to discriminate may be found in the **Guide.** The exceptions applying only to the employment field are described in chapter 3; those applying only to the educational field, in chapter 4; and those applying only to the provision of goods, facilities and services and premises, in chapter 5. General exceptions are described in chapter 7.

(Continued)

(Continued)

PROVISIONS OF THE SEX DISCRIMINATION ACT WHICH MAKE DISCRIMINATION UNLAWFUL

	Section of Act	Paragraphs of Guide
GROUP A		
Discrimination by employers of six or more employees in recruitment and treatment of employees	6	3.3–3.18
Discrimination against contract workers	9	3.19
Discrimination against partners	11	3.20
Discrimination by trade unions, employers' associations etc	12	3.21, 3.22
Discrimination by bodies which confer qualifications or authorisations needed for particular kinds of jobs	13	3.23–3.25
Discrimination in the provision of training by industrial training boards, the Manpower Services Commission, the Employment Service Agency, the Training Services Agency and certain other vocational training bodies	14	3.27, 3.28
Discrimination by employment agencies	15	3.29–3.31
Discrimination by the Manpower Services Commission, the Employment Service Agency and the Training Services Agency other than in vocational training or employment agency services	16	3.32
GROUP B		
Discrimination by bodies in charge of educational establishments	22	4.2–4.6, 4.11–4.15
Discrimination (other than that covered by section 22) by local education authorities	23	4.7, 4.8, 4.14, 4.15
Discrimination in the provision of goods, facilities or services to the public or a section of the public	29	5.2–5.9, 5.13–5.16
Discrimination in the disposal of premises	30	5.10–5.16
Discrimination by landlords against prospective assignees or sublessees	31	5.17

RACE RELATIONS ACT 1976

THE QUESTIONS PROCEDURE

CONTENTS

A complainant should obtain TWO copies of this booklet, one to send to the respondent and the other to keep.
Before completing the questionnaire or the reply form (as appropriate), the complainant and the respondent should read Part I of the guidance and (again as appropriate) Part II or III.

Issued by The Home Office and
The Department of Employment

(Continued)

(Continued)

RACE RELATIONS ACT 1976

GUIDANCE ON THE QUESTIONS PROCEDURE

PART I – INTRODUCTION

1 The purpose of this guidance is to explain the questions procedure under section 65 of the Race Relations Act 1976*. The procedure is intended to help a person (referred to in this guidance as the **complainant**) who thinks he has been discriminated against by another (the **respondent**) to obtain information from that person about the treatment in question in order to –

(a) decide whether or not to bring legal proceedings, and

(b) if proceedings are brought, to present his complaint in the most effective way.

A questionnaire has been devised which the complainant can send to the respondent and there is also a matching reply form for use by the respondent (both are included in this booklet). The questionnaire and the reply form have been designed to assist the complainant and respondent to identify information which is relevant to the complaint. It is not, however, obligatory for the questionnaire or the reply form to be used: the exchange of questions and replies may be conducted, for example, by letter.

2 This guidance is intended to assist both the complainant and the respondent. Guidance for the complainant on the preparation of the questionnaire is set out in Part II; and guidance for the respondent on the use of the reply form is set out in Part III. The main provisions of the Race Relations Act are referred to in the appendix to this guidance. Further information about the Act will be found in the various leaflets published by the Commission for Racial Equality and also in the detailed **Guide to the Race Relations Act 1976.** The leaflets and the **Guide** may be obtained, free of charge, from the Commission for Racial Equality at –

Elliot House
10/12 Allington Street
London SW1E 5EH

The **Guide** and the CRE's leaflets on the employment provisions of the Act may also be obtained, free of charge, from any employment office or jobcentre of the Employment Service Agency or from any unemployment benefit office of the Department of Employment. The CRE's leaflets may also be obtained from local community relations councils

How the questions procedure can benefit both parties

3 The procedure can benefit both the complainant and the respondent in the following ways:–

(1) If the respondent's answers satisfy the complainant that the treatment was not unlawful discrimination, there will be no need for legal proceedings.

(2) Even if the respondent's answers do not satisfy the complainant, they should help to identify what is agreed and what is in dispute between the parties. For example, the answers should reveal whether the parties disagree on the facts of the case, or, if they agree on the facts, whether they disagree on how the Act applies. In some cases, this may lead to a settlement of the grievance, again making legal proceedings unnecessary.

(3) If it turns out that the complainant institutes proceedings against the respondent, the proceedings should be that much simpler because the matters in dispute will have been identified in advance.

What happens if the respondent does not reply or replies evasively

4 The respondent cannot be compelled to reply to the complainant's questions. However, if the respondent deliberately, and without reasonable excuse, does not reply within a reasonable period, or replies in an evasive or **ambiguous** way, his position may be adversely affected should the complainant bring proceedings against him. The respondent's attention is drawn to these possible consequences in the note at the end of the questionnaire.

Period within which questionnaire must be served on the respondent

5 There are different time limits within which a questionnaire must be served in order to be admissible under the questions procedure in any ensuing legal proceedings. Which time limit applies depends on whether the complaint would be under the employment, training and related provisions of the Act (in which case the proceedings would be before an industrial tribunal) or whether it would be under the education, goods, facilities and services or premises provisions (in which case proceedings would be before a designated county court or, in Scotland, a sheriff court).

Industrial tribunal cases

6 In order to be admissible under the questions procedure in any ensuing industrial tribunal proceedings, the complainant's questionnaire must be served on the respondent either:

(a) before a complaint about the treatment concerned is made to an industrial tribunal, but not more than 3 months after the treatment in question; or

(b) if a complaint has already been made to a tribunal, within 21 days beginning when the complaint was received by the tribunal.

However, where the complainant has made a complaint to a tribunal and the period of 21 days has expired, a questionnaire may still be served provided the leave of the tribunal is obtained. This may be done by sending to the Secretary of the Tribunals a written application, which must state the names of the complainant and the respondent and set out the grounds of the application. However every effort should be made to serve the questionnaire within the period of 21 days as the leave of the tribunal to serve the questionnaire after the expiry of that period will not necessarily be obtained.

Court cases

7 In order to be admissible under the questions procedure in any ensuing county or sheriff court proceedings, the complainant's questionnaire must be served on the respondent before proceedings in respect of the treatment concerned are

**The prescribed forms, time limits for serving questions and manner of service of questions and replies under section 65 are specified in The Race Relations (Questions and Replies) Order 1975 (SI 1977 No. 842).*

brought, but not more than 6 months after the treatment*. However, where proceedings have been brought, a questionnaire may still be served provided the leave of the court has been obtained. In the case of county court proceedings, this may be done by obtaining form Ex 23 from the county court office, and completing it and sending it to the Registrar and the respondent, or by applying to the Registrar at the pre-trial review. In the case of sheriff court proceedings, this may be done by making an application to a sheriff.

PART II – GUIDANCE FOR THE COMPLAINANT

NOTES ON PREPARING THE QUESTIONNAIRE

8 Before filling in the questionnaire, you are advised to prepare what you want to say on a separate piece of paper. If you have insufficient room on the questionnaire for what you want to say, you should continue on an additional piece of paper, which should be sent with the questionnaire to the respondent.

Paragraph 2

9 You should give, in the space provided in paragraph 2, as much relevant factual information as you can about the treatment you think may have been unlawful discrimination, and about the circumstances leading up to that treatment. You should also give the date, and if possible and if relevant, the place and approximate time of the treatment. You should bear in mind that in paragraph 4 of the questionnaire you will be asking the respondent whether he agrees with what you say in paragraph 2.

Paragraph 3

10 In paragraph 3 you are telling the respondent that you think the treatment you have described in paragraph 2 may have been unlawful discrimination by him against you. It will help to identify whether there are any legal issues between you and the respondent if you explain in the space provided **why** you think the treatment may have been unlawful discrimination. However, you **do not have** to complete paragraph 3; if you do not wish or are unable to do so, you should delete the word "because". If you wish to complete the paragraph, but feel you need more information about the Race Relations Act before doing so, you should look to the appendix to this guidance.

11 If you decide to complete paragraph 3, you may find it useful to indicate –

(a) what **kind** of discrimination you think the treatment may have been ie whether it was
 direct discrimination,
 indirect discrimination, or
 victimisation

(b) which provision of the Act you think may make unlawful the kind of discrimination you think you may have suffered. (For an indication of the provisions of the Act which make the various kinds of discrimination unlawful, see paragraph 2 of the appendix.)

(For further information about the different kinds of discrimination see paragraph I of the appendix)

Paragraph 6

12 You should insert here any other question which you think may help you to obtain relevant information. (For example, if you think you have been discriminated against by having been refused a job, you may want to know what were the qualifications of the person who did get the job and why that person got the job.)

13 Paragraph 5 contains questions which are especially important if you think you may have suffered direct discrimination because they ask the respondent whether racial considerations had anything to do with your treatment. Paragraph 5 does not, however, ask specific questions relating to indirect discrimination or victimisation. If you think you may have suffered indirect discrimination you may find it helpful to include the following question in the space provided in paragraph 6:

paragraph 6:

"Was the reason for my treatment the fact that I could not comply with a condition or requirement which is applied equally to people regardless of their racial group?

If so –

(a) what was the condition or requirement?
(b) why was it applied?"

14 If you think you may have been victimised you may find it helpful to include the following question in the space provided in paragraph 6:

"Was the reason for my treatment the fact that I had done, or intended to do, or that you suspected I had done or intended to do, any of the following:

(a) brought proceedings under the Race Relations Act; or
(b) gave evidence or information in connection with proceedings under the Act; or
(c) did something else under or by reference to the Act; or
(d) made an allegation that someone acted unlawfully under the Act?"

Signature

15 The questionnaire must be signed and dated. If it is to be signed on behalf of (rather than by) the complainant, the person signing should –

(a) describe himself (eg "solicitor acting for *(name of complainant)*"), and
(b) give his business (or home, if appropriate) address.

WHAT PAPERS TO SERVE ON THE PERSON TO BE QUESTIONED

16 You should send the person to be questioned the whole of this document (ie the guidance, the questionnaire and the reply forms), with the questionnaire completed by you. **You are strongly advised to retain, and keep in a safe place, a copy of the completed questionnaire** (and you might also find it useful to retain a copy of the guidance and the uncompleted reply form).

**Where a person has applied in writing to the CRE for assistance in respect of his case, the time limit of 6 months (or 8 months in respect of public sector education complaints) is extended by 2 months. It is open to the CRE to extend the period by a further month.*

(Continued)

(Continued)

HOW TO SERVE THE PAPERS

17 You can either deliver the papers in person or send them by post. If you decide to send them by post you are advised to use the recorded delivery service, so that, if necessary, you can produce evidence that they were delivered.

WHERE TO SEND THE PAPERS

18 You can send the papers to the person to be questioned at his usual or last known residence or place of business. If you know he is acting through a solicitor you should send them to him at his solicitor's address. If you wish to question a limited company or other corporate body or a trade union or employers' association, you should send the papers to the secretary or clerk at the registered or principal office of the company, etc. You should be able to find out where its registered or principal office is by enquiring at a public library. If you are unable to do so, however, you will have to send the papers to the place where you think it is most likely they will reach the secretary or clerk (eg at, or c/o, the company's local office). It is your responsibility, however, to see that the secretary or clerk receives the papers.

USE OF THE QUESTIONS AND REPLIES IN INDUSTRIAL TRIBUNAL PROCEEDINGS

19 If you decide to make (or already have made) a complaint to an industrial tribunal about the treatment concerned and if you intend to use your questions and the reply (if any) as evidence in the proceedings, you are advised to send copies of your questions and any reply to the Secretary of the Tribunals before the date of the hearing. This should be done as soon as the documents are available; if they are available at the time you submit your complaint to a tribunal, you should send the copies with your complaint to the Secretary of the Tribunals.

PART III – GUIDANCE FOR THE RESPONDENT

NOTES ON COMPLETING THE REPLY FORM

20 Before completing the reply form, you are advised to prepare what you want to say on a separate piece of paper. If you have insufficient room on the reply form for what you want to say, you should continue on an additional piece of paper, which should be attached to the reply form sent to the complainant.

Paragraph 2

21 Here you are answering the question in paragraph 4 of the questionnaire. If you **agree** that the complainant's statement in paragraph 2 of the questionnaire is an accurate **description** of what happened, you should delete the second sentence.

22 If you **disagree** in any way that the statement is an accurate description of what happened, you should explain in the space provided in what respects you disagree, or your version of what happened, or both.

Paragraph 3

23 Here you are answering the question in paragraph 5 of the questionnaire. If, in answer to paragraph 4 of the questionnaire, you have agreed with the complainant's description of his treatment, you will be answering paragraph 5 on the basis of the facts in his description. If, however, you have disagreed with that description, you should answer paragraph 5 on the basis of **your** version of the facts. To answer paragraph 5, you are advised to look at the appendix to this guidance and also the relevant parts of the **Guide to the Race Relations Act 1976.** You need to know:–

(a) how the Act defines discrimination – see paragraph I of the appendix;

(b) in what situations the Act makes discrimination unlawful – see paragraph 2 of the appendix; and

(c) what exceptions the Act provides – see paragraph 3 of the appendix.

24 If you think that an exception (eg the exception for employment where being of a particular racial group is a genuine occupational qualification) applies to the treatment described in paragraph 2 of the complainant's questionnaire, you should mention this in paragraph 3a of the reply form and explain why you think the exception applies.

Signature

25 The reply form should be signed and dated. If it is to be signed on behalf of (rather than by) the respondent, the person signing should –

(a) describe himself (eg "solicitor acting for *(name of respondent)*" or "personnel manager of *(name of firm)*"), and

(b) give his business (or home, if appropriate) address.

SERVING THE REPLY FORM ON THE COMPLAINANT

26 If you wish to reply to the questionnaire you are strongly advised to do so without delay. **You should retain, and keep in a safe place, the questionnaire sent to you and a copy of your reply.**

27 You can serve the reply either by delivering it in person to the complainant or by sending it by post. If you decide to send it by post you are advised to use the recorded delivery service, so that, if necessary, you can produce evidence that it was delivered.

28 You should send the reply form to the address indicated in paragraph 7 of the complainant's questionnaire.

THE RACE RELATIONS ACT 1976 SECTION 65(I)(a)

QUESTIONNAIRE OF PERSON AGGRIEVED (THE COMPLAINANT)

Name of person to be questioned (the respondent)	To ....
Address	of ....
	....
Name of complainant	1. I ....
Address	of ....
	....
	consider that you may have discriminated against me contrary to the Race Relations Act 1976.
Give date, approximate time, place and factual description of the treatment received and of the circumstances leading up to the treatment (see paragraph 9 of the guidance)	2. On
Complete if you wish to give reasons, otherwise delete the word "because" (see paragraphs 10 and 11 of the guidance)	3. I consider that this treatment may have been unlawful because

(Continued)

(Continued)

This is the first of your questions to the respondent. You are advised not to alter it

4. Do you agree that the statement in paragraph 2 is an accurate description of what happened? If not in what respect do you disagree or what is your version of what happened?

This is the second of your questions to the respondent. You are advised not to alter it

5. Do you accept that your treatment of me was unlawful discrimination by you against me? If not
   - a why not?
   - b for what reason did I receive the treatment accorded to me, and
   - c how far did considerations of colour, race, nationality (including citizenship) or ethnic or national origins affect your treatment of me?

Enter here any other questions you wish to ask (see paragraphs 12–14 of the guidance)

6.

*Delete as appropriate If you delete the first alternative, insert the address to which you want the reply to be sent

7. My address for any reply you may wish to give to the questions raised above is * that set out in paragraph I above/the following address

See paragraph 15 of the guidance

Signature of complainant ....

Date ....

NB *By virtue of section 65 of the Act, this questionnaire and any reply are (subject to the provisions of the section) admissible in proceedings under the Act and a court or tribunal may draw any such inference as is just and equitable from a failure without reasonable excuse to reply within a reasonable period, or from an evasive or equivocal reply, including an inference that the person questioned has discriminated unlawfully.*

THE RACE RELATIONS ACT 1976 SECTION 65(I)(b)

REPLY BY RESPONDENT

Name of complainant	To ....
Address	of ....
	....
Name of respondent	1. I ....
Address	of ....
	....
Complete as appropriate	hereby acknowledge receipt of the questionnaire signed by you and dated ....
	which was served on me on (date) ....
*Delete as appropriate	2. I ***agree/disagree** that the statement in paragraph 2 of the questionnaire is an accurate description of what happened.
If you agree that the statement in paragraph 2 of the questionnaire is accurate, delete this sentence. If you disagree complete this sentence (see paragraphs 21 and 22 of the guidance)	I disagree with the statement in paragraph 2 of the questionnaire in that
*Delete as appropriate	3. I ***accept/dispute** that my treatment of you was unlawful discrimination by me against you.
If you accept the complainant's assertion of unlawful discrimination in paragraph 3 of the questionnaire delete the sentences at a, b and c. Unless completed a sentence should be deleted (see paragraphs 23 and 24 of the guidance)	a My reasons for so disputing are

(Continued)

(Continued)

b The reason why you received the treatment accorded to you is

c Considerations of colour, race, nationality (including citizenship) or ethnic or national origins affected my treatment of you to the following extent:—

Replies to questions in paragraph 6 of the questionnaire should be entered here

4.

Delete the whole of this sentence if you have answered all the questions in the questionnaire. If you have not answered all the questions, delete "unable" or "unwilling" as appropriate and give your reasons for not answering.

5. I have deleted (in whole or in part) the paragraph(s) numbered .... above, since I am **unable/unwilling** to reply to the relevant questions of the questionnaire for the following reasons:—

See paragraph 25 of the guidance

Signature of respondent ....

Date ....

THE RACE RELATIONS ACT 1976 SECTION 65(I)(b)

REPLY BY RESPONDENT

Name of complainant	To ....
Address	of ....
	....
Name of respondent	1. I ....
Address	of ....
	....
Complete as appropriate	hereby acknowledge receipt of the questionnaire signed by you and dated ....
	which was served on me on (date) ....
*Delete as appropriate	2. I ***agree/disagree*** that the statement in paragraph 2 of the questionnaire is an accurate description of what happened.
If you agree that the statement in paragraph 2 of the questionnaire is accurate, delete this sentence. If you disagree complete this sentence (see paragraphs 21 and 22 of the guidance)	I disagree with the statement in paragraph 2 of the questionnaire in that
*Delete as appropriate	3. I ***accept/dispute*** that my treatment of you was unlawful discrimination by me against you.
If you accept the complainant's assertion of unlawful discrimination in paragraph 3 of the questionnaire delete the sentences at a, b and c. Unless completed a sentence should be deleted (see paragraphs 23 and 24 of the guidance)	a My reasons for so disputing are

(Continued)

(Continued)

b The reason why you received the treatment accorded to you is

c Consideration of colour, race, nationality (including citizenship) or ethnic or national origins affected my treatment of you to the following extent:—

Replies to questions in paragraph 6 of the questionnaire should be entered here

4.

Delete the whole of this sentence if you have answered all the questions in the questionnaire. If you have not answered all the questions, delete "unable" or "unwilling" as appropriate and give your reasons for not answering.

5. I have deleted (in whole or in part) the paragraph(s) numbered .... above, since I am **unable/unwilling** to reply to the relevant questions of the questionnaire for the following reasons:—

See paragraph 25 of the guidance

Signature of respondent ....

Date ....

APPENDIX

NOTES ON THE SCOPE OF THE RACE RELATIONS ACT 1976

Definitions of discrimination

1 The different kinds of discrimination covered by the Act are summarised below (the references in the margin are to the relevant paragraphs in the **Guide to the Race Relations Act 1976**).

2.3 to 2.7 Direct discrimination arises where a person is treated less favourably than another is (or would be) treated because of his (or someone else's) colour, race, nationality (including citizenship) or ethnic or national origins.

Indirect discrimination arises where a person is treated unfavourably because he cannot comply with a condition or requirement which

(a) is (or would be) applied regardless of colour, race, nationality (including citizenship) or ethnic or national origins, and

(b) is such that the proportion of persons of a particular racial group (ie one defined by reference to colour, race, nationality (including citizenship) or ethnic or national origins) who can comply with it is considerably smaller than the proportion of persons not of that group who can comply with it, and

(c) is to the detriment of the person in question because he cannot comply with it, and

(d) is such that the person applying it cannot show that it is justifiable regardless of the colour, race, nationality (including citizenship) or ethnic or national origins of the person to whom it is applied.

2.8 and 2.9 **Victimisation** arises where a person is treated less favourably than other persons are (or would be) treated because that person has done (or intends to do or is suspected of having done or intending to do) any of the following:—

(a) brought proceedings under the Act; or

(b) given evidence or information in connection with proceedings brought under the Act; or

(c) done anything else by reference to the Act (eg given information to the Commission for Racial Equality); or

(d) made an allegation that someone acted unlawfully under the Act.

Victimisation does **not**, however, occur where the reason for the less favourable treatment is an allegation which was false and not made in good faith.

Unlawful discrimination

2 The provisions of the Act which make discrimination unlawful are indicated in the table on the next page. Complaints about discrimination which is unlawful under the provisions in Group A (the employment provisions) must be made to an industrial tribunal. For detailed information about these provisions see chapter 3 of the Guide. Complaints about discrimination which is unlawful under the provisions in Group B must be made to a county court or, in Scotland, a sheriff court. For detailed information about these provisions see chapters 4 and 5 of the Guide.

Exceptions

3 Details of exceptions to the requirements of the Act not to discriminate may be found in the **Guide**. The exceptions applying only to the employment field are described in chapter 3; those applying only to the educational field, in chapter 4; and those applying only to the provision of goods, facilities and services and premises, in chapter 5. General exceptions are described in chapter 7.

(Continued)

(Continued)

PROVISIONS OF THE RACE RELATIONS ACT 1976 WHICH MAKE DISCRIMINATION UNLAWFUL

	Section of Act	Paragraphs of Guide
GROUP A		
Discrimination by employers in recruitment and treatment of employees	4	3.4–3.16
Discrimination against contract workers	7	3.17
Discrimination against partners	10	3.20
Discrimination by trade unions, employers' associations etc	11	3.21
Discrimination by bodies which confer qualifications or authorisations needed for particular kinds of jobs	12	3.22
Discrimination in the provision of training by industrial training boards, the Manpower Services Commission, the Employment Service Agency, the Training Services Agency and certain other vocational training bodies	13	3.24, 3.25
Discrimination by employment agencies	14	3.26
Discrimination by the Manpower Services Commission, the Employment Service Agency and the Training Services Agency other than in vocational training or employment agency services	15	3.29
GROUP B		
Discrimination by bodies in charge of educational establishments	17	4.2–4.5
Discrimination (other than that covered by section 17) by local education authorities	18	4.6–4.7
Discrimination in the provision of goods, facilities or services to the public or a section of the public	20	5.2–5.3, 5.8–5.10
Discrimination in the disposal of premises	21	5.4–5.6
Discrimination by landlords against prospective assignees or sublessees	24	5.7
Discrimination by clubs or associations with 25 or more members (other than clubs or associations covered by sections 11 or 20).	25	5.11–5.13

HEALTH AND SAFETY EXECUTIVE
Health and Safety at Work etc. Act 1974, Sections 21, 23, and 24

IMPROVEMENT NOTICE

Serial No. **I**

Name and address (See Section 46)	To ....
	....
(a) Delete as necessary	*(a)* Trading as ....
(b) Inspector's full name	**I** *(b)* ....
	one of *(c)* ....
(c) Inspector's official designation	of *(d)* ....
	.... Tel no. ....
(d) Official address	hereby give you notice that I am of the opinion that at
	(e) ....
(e) Location of premises or place and activity	you, as *(a)* an employer/a self employed person/a person wholly or partly in control of the premises
	(f) ....
(f) Other specified capacity	*(a)* are contravening/have contravened in circumstances that make it likely that the contravention will continue or be repeated
	....
	....
(g) Provisions contravened	*(g)* ....
	....
	The reasons for my said opinion are:— ....
	....
	....
	....
	and I hereby require you to remedy the said contraventions or, as the case may be, the matters occasioning them by
(h) Date	*(h)* ....
	(a) in the manner stated in the attached schedule which forms part of the notice.
	Signature .... Date ....
	Being an inspector appointed by an instrument in writing made pursuant to Section 19 of the said Act and entitled to issue this notice.
	(a) An improvement notice is also being served on
	....
	of ....
	related to the matters contained in this notice.

NOTES

1 Failure to comply with an Improvement Notice is an offence as provided by Section 33 of this Act and renders the offender liable to a fine not exceeding £400 on summary conviction or to an unlimited fine on conviction on indictment and a further fine of not exceeding £50 per day if the offence is continued.

2 An Inspector has power to withdraw a notice or to extend the period specified in the notice, before the end of the period specified in it. You should apply to the Inspector who has issued the notice if you wish him to consider this, but you must do so before the end of the period given in it. *(Such an application is not an appeal against this notice.)*

3 The issue of this notice does not relieve you of any legal liability resting upon you for failure to comply with any provision of this or any other enactment, before or after the issue of this notice.

4 **Your attention is drawn to the provision for appeal against this notice to an Industrial Tribunal.** Details of the method of making an appeal are given below *(see also Section 24 of the Health and Safety at Work etc. Act 1974)*.

(a) Appeal can be entered against this notice to an Industrial Tribunal. The appeal should be sent to:—

(for England and Wales) The Secretary of the Tribunals
Central Office of the Industrial Tribunals
93 Ebury Bridge Road LONDON SW1W 8RE

(for Scotland) The Secretary of the Tribunals
Central Office of the Industrial Tribunals
Saint Andrew House
141 West Nile Street GLASGOW G1 2RU

(b) The appeal must be commenced by sending in writing to the Secretary of the Tribunals a notice containing the following particulars:—

(1) The name of the appellant and his address for the service of documents;

(2) The date of the notice or notices appealed against and the address of the premises or place concerned;

(3) The name and address *(as shown on the notice)* of the respondent;

(4) Particulars of the requirements or directions appealed against;

and (5) The grounds of the appeal.

A form which may be used for appeal is attached.

(c) **Time limit for appeal**

A notice of appeal must be sent to the Secretary of the Tribunals within 21 days from the date of service on the appellant of the notice or notices appealed against, or within such further period as the tribunal considers reasonable in a case where it is satisfied that it was not reasonably practicable for the notice of appeal to be presented within the period of 21 days. If posted, the appeal should be sent by recorded delivery.

(d) The entering of an appeal suspends the Improvement Notice until the appeal has been determined, but does not automatically alter the date given in this notice by which the matters contained in it must be remedied.

(e) The rules for the hearing of an appeal are given in:

The Industrial Tribunals (Improvement and Prohibition Notices Appeals) (S1 1974 No. 1925) for England and Wales.

and The Industrial Tribunals (Improvement and Prohibition Notices Appeals) (S1 1974 No. 1926) for Scotland.

HEALTH AND SAFETY EXECUTIVE
Health and Safety at Work etc. Act 1974, Sections 22—24

PROHIBITION NOTICE

Serial No. **P**

Name and address (See Section 46) — To ....

....

(a) Delete as necessary — *(a)* Trading as ....

I *(b)* .... — *(b) Inspector's full name*

one of *(c)* .... — *(c) Inspector's official designation*

of *(d)* .... — *(d) Official address*

.... tel no. ....

hereby give you notice that I am of the opinion that the following activities,

namely:— ....

....

....

which are *(a)* being carried on by you/about to be carried on by you/under your control

(e) Location of activity — at *(e)* ....

involve, or will involve *(a)* a risk/an imminent risk, of serious personal injury.
I am further of the opinion that the said matters involve contraventions of the following statutory provisions:—

....

....

....

because ....

....

....

and I hereby direct that the said activities shall not be carried on by you or under your control *(a)* immediately/after

(f) Date — *(f)* ....

unless the said contraventions and matters included in the schedule, which forms part of this notice, have been remedied.

Signature .... Date ....

being an inspector appointed by an instrument in writing made pursuant to Section 19 of the said Act and entitled to issue this notice.

SPECIMEN

NOTES

1 Failure to comply with a Prohibition Notice is an offence as provided by Section 33 of this Act and renders the offender liable to a fine not exceeding £400 on summary conviction or to an unlimited fine or to imprisonment for a term not exceeding two years or both on conviction on indictment and a further fine of not exceeding £50 per day if the offence is continued.

2 An Inspector has power to withdraw a notice or to extend the period specified in the notice, before the end of the period specified in it. You should apply to the Inspector who has issued the notice if you wish him to consider this, but you must do so before the end of the period given in it. *(Such an application is not an appeal against this notice.)*

3 The issue of this Notice does not relieve you of any legal liability resting upon you for failure to comply with any provision of this or any other enactment, before or after the issue of this notice.

4 **Your attention is drawn to the provision for appeal against the notice to an Industrial Tribunal.** Details of the method of making an appeal are given below *(see also Section 24 of the Health and Safety at Work etc. Act 1974)*.

(a) Appeal can be entered against this notice to an Industrial Tribunal. The appeal should be sent to:—

(for England and Wales) The Secretary of the Tribunals
Central Office of the Industrial Tribunals
93 Ebury Bridge Road LONDON SW1W 8RE

(for Scotland) The Secretary of the Tribunals
Central Office of the Industrial Tribunals
Saint Andrew House,
141 West Nile Street GLASGOW G1 2RU

(b) The appeal must be commenced by sending in writing to the Secretary of the Tribunals a notice containing the following particulars:—
(1) The name of the appellant and his address for the service of documents;
(2) The date of the notice or notices appealed against and the address of the premises or place concerned;
(3) The name and address *(as shown on the notice)* of the respondent;
(4) Particulars of the requirements or directions appealed against;
and (5) The grounds of the appeal.
A form which may be used for appeal is attached.

(c) **Time limit for appeal**

A notice of appeal must be sent to the Secretary of the Tribunals within 21 days from the date of service on the appellant of the notice or notices appealed against, or within such further period as the tribunal considers reasonable in a case where it is satisfied that it was not reasonably practicable for the notice of appeal to be presented within the period of 21 days. If posted the appeal should be sent by recorded delivery.

(d) The entering of an appeal does not have the effect of suspending this notice. Application can be made for the suspension of the notice to the Secretary of the Tribunals, but the notice continues in force until a Tribunal otherwise directs. An application for suspension of the notice must be in writing and must set out:—

(a) The case number of the appeal, if known, or particulars sufficient to identify it and

(b) The grounds on which the application is made. It may accompany the appeal.

(e) The rules for the hearing of an appeal are given in:—

The Industrial Tribunals (Improvement and Prohibition Notices Appeals) Regulations 1974 (S1 1974 No. 1925) for England and Wales.

and

The Industrial Tribunals (Improvement and Prohibition Notices Appeals) (Scotland) Regulations 1974 (S1 1974 No. 1926) for Scotland.

Form 21 *The Health and Safety at Work etc. Act, 1974* — Schedule (LP3)

HEALTH AND SAFETY EXECUTIVE
Health and Safety at Work etc. Act 1974, Sections 21, 22, 23, and 24

Schedule

Serial No. **I/P**

Form 22 *The Health and Safety at Work etc. Act, 1974* — Notice of Extension (LP4)

HEALTH AND SAFETY EXECUTIVE
Health and Safety at Work etc. Act 1974, Section 23

NOTICE OF EXTENSION

To ....

....

(a) Inspector's name in full I *(a)*..

(b) Inspector's status one of *(b)* ....

Hereby extend the period specified in Improvement/Prohibition Notice No.:— ....

dated .... until ....

Signature ....

Official Address:— Date ....

....

....

.... Tel ....

Form 23 *The Health and Safety at Work etc. Act, 1974* — Notice of Withdrawal (LP5)

HEALTH AND SAFETY EXECUTIVE
Health and Safety at Work etc. Act 1974, Section 23

NOTICE OF WITHDRAWAL

To ....

....

(a) Inspector's name in full I *(a)*..

(b) Inspector's status one of *(b)* ....

hereby withdraw Improvement/Prohibition Notice No. ....

dated ....

Signature ....

Official Address:—

Date ....

....

....

.... Tel ....

Form 24 Appeal to an Industrial Tribunal under the Health and Safety at Work Act (IT19)

For official use			
Date received	Case number	ROIT	Inits

APPEAL TO AN INDUSTRIAL TRIBUNAL UNDER THE HEALTH AND SAFETY AT WORK ETC ACT 1974

To: *≠The Secretary of the Tribunals
Central Office of the Industrial
Tribunals (England and Wales)
93 Ebury Bridge Road, London SW1W 8RE
Tel: 01-730 9161

*The Secretary of the Tribunals
Cental Office of the Industrial
Tribunals (Scotland)
St. Andrew House, 141 West Nile Street,
Glasgow, G1 2RU
Tel: 041-331 1601

1 Full name of Appellant (or title if company or organisation):

2 Address of Appellant (registered office if applicable):

Tel. No.

3 Address of Appellant or his representative for service of documents if different from 2 above Ø

Tel. No.

4 Details of Notice appealed against:

Prohibition*/Improvement* Date of Notice __________ Serial No __________

5 Address of the premises or place to which the Notice refers:

6 Name and full address of Inspector as shown on Notice:

Tel. No.

7 Particulars of the requirements or directions appealed against:

* Delete as appropriate

≠ In cases of extreme urgency in England and Wales appeals may be taken by hand to an Assistant Secretary of the Tribunals at the appropriate Regional Office of the Industrial Tribunals, the address of which may be obtained from the Inspector.

Ø Please note that if an address is entered here all communications will be sent to this address only.

Form 25 Safety representative: inspection form

Sample of suggested form to be used for recording that an inspection by a safety representative(s) has taken place.

Number

Safety Representative: Inspection form

Record that an inspection by a safety representative or representatives has taken place.

Date and time of inspection

Area or workplace inspected

Name(s) and signature(s) of safety representatives taking part in the inspection.	Name(s) and signature(s) of employer (or his representative) taking part in the inspection (if appropriate)

[This record does not imply that the conditions are safe and healthy or that the arrangements for welfare at work are satisfactory]

Record of receipt of Inspection form by the employer (or his representative)

Signature Date:

Form 26 Safety representative: report form

Sample of suggested form to be used for notifying to the employer, or his representative, unsafe and unhealthy conditions and working practices and unsatisfactory arrangements for welfare at work.

Number

Safety Representative: Report form

Notification to the employer (or his representative) of conditions and working practices considered to be unsafe or unhealthy and of arrangements for welfare at work considered to be unsatisfactory.

This column to be completed by the employer

Date and time of inspection or matter observed	Particulars of matter(s) notified to employer or his representative (include location where appropriate)	Name(s) of safety representative(s) notifying matter(s) to employer or his representative	Remedial action taken (with date) or explanation if not taken. This information to be relayed to the safety representative(s)

[This report does not imply that the conditions are safe and healthy or that the arrangements for welfare at work are satisfactory in all other respects]

Signature of employer (or representative)

Signature(s) of safety representative(s): Date: Date:

Record of receipt of form by the employer, or his representative(s):

Signature Date:

OCCUPATIONAL PENSIONS BOARD
APEX TOWER
HIGH STREET
NEW MALDEN
SURREY KT3 4DN

ELECTION BY EMPLOYER

1 I/We

of

(name and address of employer),

hereby elect that the employment(s) described below, service in which qualifies the earners employed in it/them for benefits under the

(name and address of occupational pension scheme),

shall be contracted-out employment(s) by reference to that scheme for the purposes of Part III of the Social Security Pensions Act 1975/Part IV of the Social Security Pensions (Northern Ireland) Order 1975 from 6 April 1978:—

Employment(s) to be covered by contracting-out certificate A	Description of employees to be covered by the contracting-out certificate (if not everybody in employment(s) at A) B
. . . .	. . . .
. . . .	. . . .
. . . .	. . . .

2 *Members who are unable to complete 5 years' pensionable service before the scheme's normal pension age have been excluded.

*Members who are unable to complete . . . years' pensionable service before the scheme's normal pension age have been excluded.

*No members are excluded on the grounds that they are unable to complete a specified period of pensionable service (not exceeding 5 years) before the scheme's normal pension age.

3 The approximate numbers of employees expected to be covered by the contracting-out certificate will be: Men Women

4 The following are the names and addresses of —

the trustees of the trust(s), if any, under which benefits will be paid

. . . .

. . . .

the insurance company or friendly society (if any)

. . . .

. . . .

the scheme administrator

. . . .

. . . .

**Delete or complete as appropriate*

(Continued)

(Continued)

5 A copy of the notice of the intention to make this election is enclosed. The notice has been given to all employees in (the) employment(s) to which the election relates –

Please tick the appropriate box

by sending or delivering it in writing to each of them: ☐

by exhibiting it conspicuously at the place of work or employment and drawing each employee's attention to it in writing: ☐

in some other manner already approved by the Board. ☐

6 Copies of the notice have also been sent (or delivered) to –

the trustees ☐

the scheme administrator ☐

the insurance company ☐

the friendly society. ☐

7 *I/We confirm that all independent trade unions recognised to any extent for the purpose of collective bargaining in relation to the earners concerned have been given a copy of the election notice and that consultations with them have been undertaken.

*There is no independent trade union recognised to any extent for the purpose of collective bargaining in relation to the earners concerned.

8 I/We apply for the Occupational Pensions Board to determine the question whether the employment(s) described in A of paragraph 1 is/are to be treated as contracted-out employment(s) and if so whether generally or in relation to any description of employees mentioned in B of paragraph 1 and from what date. I/We ask the Occupational Pensions Board to issue a contracting-out certificate accordingly.

Signed ....
(by or on behalf of employer)

Address ....
....
....

Date ....

***Delete as appropriate**

Form 28 Employer's notification of proposed redundancies (HR1)

EMPLOYMENT PROTECTION ACT 1975

EMPLOYER'S NOTIFICATION OF PROPOSED REDUNDANCIES UNDER SECTION 100

Please complete this form and return it to the nearest Regional Office of the Department of Employment.

READ THESE NOTES CAREFULLY BEFORE COMPLETING THE FORM AND SIGNING THE DECLARATION

GENERAL

1 The Employment Protection Act requires employers to notify the Secretary of State for Employment of proposed redundancies involving ten or more dismissals a specified number of days before the first dismissal is to take effect. (See the leaflet Procedure for Handling Redundancies, PL581). Compliance with this requirement does not preclude the employer from postponing or abandoning implementation of the proposals to dismiss if, for example, there is a relevant change of circumstances.

2 Please complete a separate form HR1 in respect of each establishment at which 10 or more employees are likely to be dismissed as redundant.

3 This form is designed to cover the information required by the Secretary of State under Part IV of the Employment Protection Act; alternatively you may write a letter which contains the same particulars as in the form, and send or deliver it to the Regional Office of the Department of Employment.

4 A copy of this notification must be sent to representatives of independent trade unions recognised for any of the categories of workers whom it is proposed to dismiss as redundant.

NOTES ON QUESTIONS

Please write the answers in the spaces provided. If appropriate write NIL. If space is insufficient, continue on separate sheet of paper marking the question number and making a note to that effect on this form.

NOTES ON DECLARATION

The declaration should be signed and dated by the employer, or on his behalf by a person of appropriate status. The position held by the signatory should be indicated.

NB

If rebate against redundancy payments is being claimed you should apply to the Department of Employment separately on form RP 1 which can be obtained from any Redundancy Payments Office, the address of which is available at any Unemployment Benefit Office or Employment Office

DEPARTMENT OF EMPLOYMENT

(Continued)

(Continued)

QUESTIONS

1 Name, address and telephone number of employer.

....

....

....

2 Name of person to be contacted in connection with this form (include address and telephone number, if different from Q1).

....

....

....

3 Address of establishment at which employees are employed, (if different from Q1).

....

....

4 Please state the nature of the main business at the establishment named above.

....

5 (a) What are the main reasons for the proposed redundancies at the above named establishment?

(Please tick the appropriate box(es))

Reduced demand for products or services	A	
Completion of contract or part of contract	B	
Transfer of activities to another establishment following a merger	C	
Transfer of activities to another establishment for other reasons	D	
Introduction of new plant or machinery	E	
Changes in methods or organisation of work	F	
Other reasons	G	

(b) If you have ticked boxes D, F or G please give brief details

....

....

6 (a) What is the total number currently employed at the establishment? ....

(b) What is the total number you anticipate at present MAY be dismissed as redundant at the establishment? ....

(c) If available please give a breakdown of (a) and (b) by occupational groups.

	Employed	Redundant
Manual Skilled		
Semi-skilled		
Unskilled		
Clerical		
Managerial/Technical		

(d) Please state the number of apprentices and long term trainees who may become redundant, if known ....

(e) Please state the number of employees under 20 years old (including apprentices etc) who may become redundant, (if known) ....

(f) Do you propose to close the establishment at which these redundancies may occur? ....

7 On what dates will:

(a) the first proposed redundancy take effect?

Day	Month	Year

(b) the last proposed redundancy take effect?

Day	Month	Year

8 How do you propose to select employees who may be dismissed as redundant? Please give brief details.

....

....

9 Give name(s) and address(es) of trade union(s) recognised for categories of employees it is proposed to dismiss as redundant.

....

....

....

....

....

10 (a) Give date when consultations began with union(s)

Day	Month	Year

(b) Has full agreement been reached? ....

(c) Is the redundancy being handled in accordance with a collective agreement on redundancies? ....

If you answer YES please give brief details or send a copy of the agreement.

....

DECLARATION

I certify that the information given on this form is correct to the best of my knowledge.

Signature ....

Position held ....

Date ....

FOR DEPARTMENTAL USE

1	2	3
4	5	6
	7	

Redundancy Payments Acts 1965 and 1969
(as amended by the Employment Protection Act 1975)

Notice of intention to claim rebate from THE REDUNDANCY FUND

Please read the notes overleaf before completing this notice

(Continued)

(Continued)

NOTES

See also booklet "The Redundancy Payment Scheme", particularly sections headed:

The Redundancy Fund

Rebate from the Fund

How an employer claims rebate

1 Please detach and complete the attached tear-off form and send to the address shown above item 1 not less than 14 days before the expected date of the first dismissals (not less than 21 days if 10 or more employees qualifying for payment are expected to terminate within 6 days of each other). Please explain at item 7 of the form the reason for any delay; failure to give the required notice without good reason may result in the imposition of a penalty up to 10% of the rebate claimed.

"NB: This notification does not satisfy the requirements regarding prior consultation and notification of redundancies laid down under sections 99 and 100 of the Employment Protection Act 1975, details of which may be found in leaflet PL581 — "Procedure for handling redundancies", obtainable free from any jobcentre, employment office or unemployment benefit office."

2 Item 1 of the form — for the purposes of the Redundancy Payments Act an employee is taken to be dismissed from his/her employment if his/her contract of employment is terminated by the employer, with or without notice, or a fixed term of employment expires without renewal of the contract, or the employee terminates the contract with or without notice (being entitled to do so without notice by reason of the employer's conduct). There is no dismissal when an employee accepts an offer of alternative employment (to start within four weeks of the end of the contract) with the same employer, or with an associated employer, or with a new owner of the business (or separate and identifiable part thereof) and remains in the new job beyond the end of the trial period. The trial period is a period beginning at the end of the previous employment and ending 4 weeks after the employee starts work under the new contract. A longer period may be agreed for the purpose of retraining the employee for employment under the new contract.

Conditions relating to redundancy payments

What is meant by "dismissal"?

Is there any entitlement if further employment is offered?

3 Item 1 of the form — Weeks count for payment under the Act in which

(1) (a) an employee is employed for 16 hours or more or in which any part is covered by a contract with the employer which normally involves employment for 16 hours or more weekly, or

(b) the contractual hours of an employee, whose contract of employment normally involves 16 or more hours weekly, are reduced below 16 hours to 8 hours or more weekly; not more than 26 weeks of such reduced hours count between any 2 periods under a contract involving 16 or more hours weekly and weeks exceeding 26 will break continuity, or

(c) an employee who has been continuously employed long enough to qualify for a redundancy payment continues to be employed, although on terms which would not otherwise enable the week to count, provided that he/she does not work under a contract normally involving less than 8 hours weekly and does not, in fact, work less than 16 hours; or

(2) an employee is employed under a contract for 8 hours or more who has been so employed for 5 years or more.

Please tick the appropriate box.
If a week does not count, normally it breaks the record of continuous employment and no period of employment before a break can be counted.

Appendix A Rules for calculating continuous employment (see amending supplement to the Tenth Revision, or later revision of the booklet)

4 Item 2 of the form — An employee who unreasonably refuses an offer of suitable employment with the same employer, an associated employer, or a new owner of the business, made before the end of the job in which he/she is redundant or who unreasonably terminates (or gives notice to terminate) such employment during the trial period (see Note 2 above), is not entitled to a redundancy payment in respect of his/her dismissal. Please tick the box at item 2 if it is likely that any of the employees listed will be offered further employment as described.

Conditions relating to redundancy payments

Is there any entitlement if further employment is offered?

5 Item 3 of the form (and if necessary item 4) — please indicate the reason for the anticipated dismissal of the employees. An employee is dismissed by reasons of redundancy if the whole or main reason is that the employer is closing down altogether or at a particular place, or for some other reason the employer's needs for employees to do work of a particular kind at the place in question have diminished or ceased or are expected to diminish or cease.

Conditions relating to redundancy payments

What is redundancy?
What dismissals are due to redundancy?

6 Item 4 of the form — please use this space for any additional information. If you wish correspondence or enquiries about these redundancy dismissals to be addressed to a particular individual, please give his name, telephone number and extension.

7 Item 5 of the form — please enter the place of work if different from your main address.

8 Item 6 of the form — please enter your tax office and reference number.

9 If you are in doubt on any point, please seek advice from the office to which the completed form is to be returned.

PENALTIES — Any person who makes a statement which he/she knows to be false or recklessly makes a statement which is false in a material particular, or produces a document which to his/her knowledge has been wilfully falsified, is liable on summary conviction to a fine not exceeding £100 or to imprisonment for a term not exceeding 3 months or both, or on conviction on indictment to a fine or to imprisonment for a term not exceeding 2 years or both.

Department of Employment

Redundancy Payments Acts 1965 and 1969

NOTICE OF INTENTION TO CLAIM REBATE FROM THE REDUNDANCY FUND

Full title of firm
(in block capitals) ....

Address ....

.... Telephone No. ....

To: ....

....

1 I declare that the employees whose names are listed overleaf (and on the continuation sheets numbered ....

to ....) are expected to be dismissed, as defined in Note 2 on the tear-off page retained by me, on the dates shown in column 6 of each sheet. Each has been employed throughout the stated period for either –

Please tick the appropriate box

(1) a continuous period of two years as in Note 3(1) on the tear-off page, or ☐

(2) a continuous period of five years as in Note 3(2) on the tear-off page ☐

Please tick if offers of further work are likely

2 I expect that some of the listed employees will be offered further work by this firm, an associated employer, or a successor owner of the business (see *Note 4 on tear-off page*) ☐

3 The reason for the anticipated dismissal (see *Note 5 on tear-off page*) has been ticked in the appropriate box below:–

(1) Closure of the establishment ☐

(2) Removal of the establishment to another area ☐

(3) Reduction in labour force at the establishment due to

(a) general reduction in level of activities ☐

(b) reduction in activities on which the employees engaged ☐

(c) changes in methods of work eg mechanisation, automation ☐

(d) elimination of slack in workloads ☐

(4) Other reasons (specified at item 4 below) ☐

4 Additional information (see *Notes 5–6 on tear-off page*).

5 Address at which the employees work if different from above ....

....

6 I understand that to establish my right to any rebate it may be necessary for you to refer to information given by me to the Inland Revenue and other Government departments and I hereby give my consent to the disclosure of such information for this purpose.

Tax district office/computer centre .... Tax ref No. ....

*7 The reason for the delay in submitting this notification is (see *Note 1 on tear-off portion*)

Signature of employer .... Date ....

Position in firm (eg director, company secretary) ....

* *Delete if inapplicable*

(Continued)

(Continued)

List of employees who are expected to become redundant and be entitled to statutory redundancy payments

IMPORTANT — MEN and **WOMEN** should be listed separately

Name and Initials of employee (state whether Mr Mrs or Miss) (See Note (a)) 1	Occupation 2	National insurance number 3	Date of birth 4	Date employment began (See Note (b)) 5	Date of termination 6	Amount of week's pay (See Note (c)) 7	FOR OFFICIAL USE 8
1						£	
2							
3							
4							
5							
6							
7							
8							
9							
10							
11							
12							
13							
14							
15							

NOTES

(a) Entries in columns 1 to 7 may be carbon copied to form RP2.

(b) The date sought is the start of the period of continuous employment, to which the payment relates, with the dismissing employer or an associated employer or a previous owner of the business.

(c) The amount of a week's pay should be calculated according to the rules explained in Appendix C of the booklet "The Redundancy Payments Scheme". If it is not possible at this stage to calculate the amount in any case, please leave the relevant col 7 space blank and forward the information as soon as possible. Please seek early advice through the office shown above item 1 overleaf, about calculations involving piece workers or shift or rota workers.

FOR OFFICIAL USE

	INITIALS	DATE
RP 1 received		
RP 5 sent		
RP 2/3 received		
RP 2/3 received		
RP 2/3 received		
RP 2/3 received		
RP 2/3 received		
RP 2/3 received		

	INITIALS	DATE
RP 2/3 to RFO		
RP 2/3 to RFO		
RP 2/3 to RFO		
RP 2/3 to RFO		
RP 2/3 to RFO		
RP 2/3 to RFO		

Form 30 Claim for rebate from Redundancy Fund (RP2)

Redundancy Payments Acts 1965 and 1969
(As amended by the Employment Protection Act 1975)

Claim for rebate from THE REDUNDANCY FUND

NOTES

1 Claim for rebate must be sent on the attached tear-off form, to the address shown on the front of the claim form, within six months from the date on which the redundancy payments were made.

2 If any of the redundancy payments for which rebate is claimed were paid following a decision of an industrial tribunal, please quote the tribunal's decision reference(s).

3 If note 2 does not apply and you have not already given advance notice of your intention to make this claim, please complete items 1 to 5 of form RP1 and attach. Failure to give such notice without reasonable excuse may result in the imposition of a penalty not exceeding 10% of rebate claimed.

4 The certificate must not be completed earlier than
   a the latest date shown in column 6 (date of termination), nor
   b the latest date shown on receipt portion of form RP3/RP3(Pen).

5 You are reminded that for the purpose of the Redundancy Payments Act 1965, as amended by the Employment Protection Act 1975, there is no dismissal when an employee is, within four weeks of the date of termination of his contract of employment, re-engaged by the same employer, an associated employer, or by a new owner of the business (or a separate and identifiable part of it) and remains in the new job beyond the end of any trial period. The trial period, applicable where the old and new jobs differ as to capacity, place or other terms and conditions, is a period beginning at the end of the old job and ending four weeks (longer if agreed for retraining) after the employee starts the new job. See the booklet "The Redundancy Payments Scheme": paras headed "Is there entitlement if further employment is offered?" Please note carefully the wording of the certificate at item 1 of the form.

6 The date of the termination to be entered in column 6 of the reverse of form RP2, in the case of an employee who terminated, or gave notice to terminate, alternative employment during the trial period, will be the date his former redundant job ended.

7 An employee who unreasonably refused an offer of suitable employment made before the end of the job in which he was redundant, or who unreasonably terminated (or gave notice to terminate) such employment during the trial period (see note 5), is not entitled to a redundancy payment in respect of his dismissal. Please complete the box at item 2 of the form if any employee has refused an offer, or terminated (or given notice to terminate) further employment during the trial period; also note the reverse of the form as indicated in item 2. Please supply separately details of the offers made, compared with the job in which the employee was redundant, and the reasons for his refusal or termination of the job offered.

8 If you are in doubt on any point, please consult the office shown below the space for entry of your firm's name and address.

PENALTIES

Any person who makes a statement which he knows to be false, or recklessly makes a statement which is false in a material particular, or produces a document which to his knowledge has been wilfully falsified, is liable on summary conviction to a fine not exceeding £100 or to imprisonment for a term not exceeding 3 months or both, or on conviction on indictment to a fine or to imprisonment for a term not exceeding 2 years or both.

(Continued)

(Continued)

DEPARTMENT OF EMPLOYMENT

CLAIM FOR REBATE FROM REDUNDANCY FUND
Redundancy Payments Acts 1965 and 1969

MLH No.
SIC Order No.

When paying rebate please quote reference number

Full title of firm *(in block capitals please)* ....

....

Address ....

Nature of business .... Telephone number ....

To:—

1 I certify that the employees whose names are listed overleaf (and on continuation sheets numbered .... to ....)

(1) (a) have not been re-employed either with this firm, or with an associated employer, or with a new owner of this firm's business (or any separate identifiable part of its business), or

(b) if they have been so re-employed, that they have not remained beyond the end of the trial period. (see Note 5); and

(2) terminated on the dates shown in Column 6 in each case; and

(3) were entitled to redundancy payments in accordance with the Redundancy Payments Act 1965; and

(4) received those payments on the dates shown in the receipt portion of the enclosed statements (forms RP3/RP3(Pen)) which show how entitlement was calculated.

2 I have marked with an *, at the beginning of the relevant line on the reverse, the entry in respect of any employee who refused an offer of further employment, or ended (or gave notice to end) such employment during the trial period (see Notes 5 and 7 of the tear-off notes).

Please tick box if this applied ☐

3 I understand that to establish my rights to any rebate it may be necessary for you to refer to information given by me to the Inland Revenue and other Government departments and I hereby give my consent to the disclosure of such information for this purpose only.

4 Tax district office/computer centre .... Tax ref no. ....

5 I also certify that none of the redundancy payments to which this claim refers is awaiting a decision of an industrial tribunal.

6 I claim rebate amounting to £.................. (~~50%~~ now 41% of the total of col 8 overleaf) and declare that no other claim has been made in respect of the service of these employees between the dates shown in columns 5 and 6.

Signature of employer ....

Position in firm (eg Director, Company Secretary etc) .... Date ....

FOR OFFICIAL USE

To the RFO .... RP2 and RP3/RP3(Pen) checked .... initials Date ....

I certify that forms RP1, RP2 and RP3/RP3(Pen) have been checked and that any necessary amendments which have been made to the claim have been agreed with the employer. No previous claim has been received in respect of any of the employees listed overleaf (and on continuation sheets numbered .... to ....)

Claim is approved for payment £.. Approving Officer ....

Office .... Date ....

FOR USE IN REGIONAL FINANCE OFFICE

Cashier please pay £.. Dr ....

Authorising Officer .... Date ....

Paid by payable order number .... Dated ....

Claim for rebate from Redundancy Fund

IMPORTANT – MEN and WOMEN should be listed separately

	Name and initials of employee (state whether Mr Mrs or Miss) 1	Occupation 2	National insurance number 3	Date of birth 4	Date employment began (See Note(a)) 5	Date of termination (See Note (b)) 6	Amount of week's pay (See Note(c)) 7	Redundancy payment 8	FOR OFFICIAL USE 9
1							£	£	
2									
3									
4									
5									
6									
7									
8									
9									
10									
11									
12									
13									
14									
15									
							TOTAL		

NOTES

(a) The date sought is the start of the period of continuous employment, to which the payment relates, with the dismissing employer, an associated employer or a previous owner of the business, except that no account should be taken of any service in respect of which a redundancy payment has already been made (see declaration at item 6 overleaf).

(b) If these entries are carbon copies of those in the form RP1 but the actual date of termination is different please write in the necessary amendment — See also note 6 on the tear-off.

(c) The amount of a week's pay should be calculated according to the rules set out in Appendix C of the booklet "The Redundancy Payments Scheme".

Form 31 Acknowledgement of liability for redundancy payments (RP2(GP))

Department of Employment **Redundancy Payments Acts 1965 and 1969**

ACKNOWLEDGEMENT OF LIABILITY FOR REDUNDANCY PAYMENTS

Full title of firm ....
(in block capitals please)

Address ....

Nature of business .... Telephone no. ....

To ....

....

On the facts available to me, I certify that the employee(s) whose name(s) is/are listed overleaf (and on continuation sheets numbered .... to ....)

1 terminated on the date(s) shown in column 6

2 is/are to the best of my knowledge entitled to redundancy payments calculated in accordance with the Redundancy Payment Act 1965 as shown on the enclosed statement(s) * RP3/RP22

No other claim has been made by me in respect of the service of the employee(s) between the dates shown in columns 5 and 6

I also believe that the amount of £ .... is the amount of rebate due from the Fund if redundancy payments were made as required by the Act.

I understand that to establish the entitlement of the employee(s) listed overleaf (and on continuation sheets numbered .... to ....) to any guarantee payment it may be necessary for you to refer to information given by me to the Inland Revenue and other government departments and I hereby give my consent to the disclosure of such information for this purpose only.

SPECIMEN

Tax district office/computer centre .... Tax ref no. ....

Signature of * liquidator or other appointed officer / legal representative ....

* Capacity .... Date ....

Address *(if different to that of the firm)* ....

.... Telephone no. ....

FOR OFFICIAL USE

To the RFO RP2 (GP) & * RP3/RP22 checked .... initials .... (date)

I certify that the entries on this form and relevant form * RP3/RP22 are correct and all details and amounts agreed with the * employer/liquidator/trustee/receiver

Guarantee payment of £ .... is approved.

.... **Approving Officer** Date ....

.... Office

FOR USE IN REGIONAL FINANCE OFFICE

Cashier please pay £ .... Dr ....

.... Authorising Officer Date ....

Paid .... date * (By payable order no. .... / By payable orders as shown on attached list)

* Delete inappropriate item

(Continued)

(Continued)

Statement of employee's redundancy payment entitlement

MLH number
SIC order no.

IMPORTANT **MEN** and **WOMEN** should be listed separately

Name and initials of employee (state whether Mr Mrs or Miss) 1	Occupation 2	National insurance number 3	Date of birth 4	Date employment began (See Note (a)) 5	Date of termination (See Note (b)) 6	Amount of week's pay (See Note (c)) 7	Redundancy payment 8	FOR OFFICIAL USE 9
1						£	£	
2								
3								
4								
5								
6								
7								
8								
9								
10								
11								
12								
13								
14								
15								
						TOTAL		

NOTES

(a) The date sought is that of the employee's first engagement by that employer or a previous owner of the business or, if either was a company by a company associated therewith at the time of the employee's transfer to the relevant company.

(b) If these entries are carbon copies of those in the form RP1 but the actual date of termination is different please write in the necessary amendment.

(c) The amount of a week's pay should be calculated according to the rules set out in Appendix D of the booklet "The Redundancy Payments Scheme"

Form 32 Employer's calculation of redundancy payment and employee's receipt (RP3)

Department of Employment
REDUNDANCY PAYMENTS ACT 1965

EMPLOYER'S CALCULATION OF REDUNDANCY PAYMENT AND EMPLOYEE'S RECEIPT

NOTES 1 *If redundancy payment is being reduced because of pension DO NOT USE THIS FORM. Please ask the office which issued this form for the pensions form RP 3(Pen).*

2 *The calculation of payments not arising under the Redundancy Payments Act should be excluded from this form.*

Name of employer ....

....

....

Employee's surname .... initials ....

Employee's address ....

Employee's date of birth ....

Employee's employment began on .... and terminated during the week ending Saturday .... 19......

Non-reckonable periods (employment abroad, on strike, service with the Armed Forces—*see guidance in the booklet "The Redundancy Payments Scheme"*)

from.............................. to .... reason ....

PART I — CALCULATION OF REDUNDANCY PAYMENT

(*See guidance in the booklet "The Redundancy Payments Scheme"*)

1 Total reckonable employment (*exclude employment before age 18. If more than 20 years' employment, enter "20"*)...................... years

2 Number of weeks' pay due .... weeks

3 Amount of a week's pay (*see booklet*)

(1) before applying £100 limit £..

(2) after applying £100 limit £..

4 Amount of redundancy payment (item 2 x item 3(2)) £..

NOTE:- If the employee was aged at least 64 years and one month (man)/59 years and one month (woman) on the Saturday in the week in which the employment terminated, items 5, 6 and 7 below should be completed.

5 Number of complete months by which employee's age exceeds 64 (man)/59 (woman) on the Saturday in the week in which the employment terminated ....months

6 Amount by which redundancy payment is to be reduced $\frac{\text{(item 4 x item 5)}}{12}$ £..

7 Adjusted amount of redundancy payment (item 4 minus item 6) £..

PART II — EMPLOYEE'S RECEIPT FOR REDUNDANCY PAYMENT

Warning—Do not sign this receipt until you have actually received the full amount stated or you may be penalised.

I acknowledge that the redundancy payment amounting to £..

was made to me on (date).. Signature ....

Date..

NOTE: If more than one copy of this form is prepared for payment, the top copy receipted by the employee should accompany the claim for rebate on form RP2

Form 33 Employer's claim to exclude or reduce a pensioned employee's right to redundancy payment (RP3(PEN))

Department of Employment
REDUNDANCY PAYMENTS ACT 1965

EMPLOYER'S CLAIM TO EXCLUDE OR REDUCE A PENSIONED EMPLOYEE'S RIGHT TO REDUNDANCY PAYMENT WITH – I CALCULATION OF THE PAYMENT BEFORE REDUCTION ON ACCOUNT OF PENSION
II CALCULATION OF THE PAYMENT REDUCED ON ACCOUNT OF PENSION
III THE EMPLOYEE'S RECEIPT

NOTE: *The calculation of payments not arising under the Redundancy Payments Act should be excluded from this form.*

CLAIM

PURSUANT TO REGULATION 5 OF THE REDUNDANCY PAYMENTS PENSION REGULATIONS 1965,

I/WE *(name of employer)* ....
claim to exclude the right of the employee to the redundancy payment calculated in Part I below, or to reduce the amount as in Part II .

Employee's surname .... Initials ....

Employee's address ....

Employee's date of birth ....

Employee's employment began on .... and terminated during the week ending Saturday .... 19 ......

Non-reckonable periods (employment abroad, on strike, service with Armed Forces – see *guidance in the booklet "The Redundancy Payments Scheme"*)

from .... to .... reason ....

SPECIMEN

Signature of employer .... date ....

Position in firm (eg *Director, Company Secretary etc*) ....

PART I – CALCULATION OF REDUNDANCY PAYMENT BEFORE REDUCTION ON ACCOUNT OF PENSION
(See guidance in the booklet "The Redundancy Payments Scheme")

1 Total reckonable employment *(exclude employment before age 18. If more than 20 years' employment, enter "20")* ....years

2 Number of weeks' pay due ....weeks

3 Amount of a week's pay *(before applying £80 limit)* £ .... *£ ....

* Enter £80 if the week's pay is £80 or more – this limit is subject to annual review and if there is doubt it should be checked with the office which issued this form.

4 Amount of redundancy payment (item 2 x item 3) £..

NOTE: If the employee was aged at least 64 years and one month *(at least 59 years and one month for a woman)* **on the Saturday in the week in which the employment terminated, items 5, 6 and 7 below should be completed.**

5 Number of **complete** months by which employee's age exceeded 64 *(59 for a woman)* on the Saturday in the week in which the employment terminated .... months

6 Amount by which redundancy payment is to be reduced $\frac{\text{item 4 x item 5}}{12}$ £..

7 Adjusted amount of redundancy payment (item 4 minus item 6) £ ....

(Continued)

(Continued)

PART II – CALCULATION OF REDUNDANCY PAYMENT REDUCED ON ACCOUNT OF PENSION

8 (a) Annual value of pension *(see leaflet RPL 1 paragraph 10)* £ ....

(b) Annual value of lump sum $\left(\frac{\text{lump sum}}{10}\right)$ £ ....

(c) Total of 8(a) and 8(b) £ ....

(d) Annual value of pension and/or lump sum *(item 8(c) rounded DOWN to whole £)* £ ....

9 Annual pay *(item 3 ×52, rounded DOWN to whole £)* £ ....

NOTES: 1 The following formula is explained in leaflet RPL 1 paragraph 10

2 Where the calculation results in a minus quantity, the redundancy payment is "NIL"

3 The resultant sum represents the redundancy payment where pension begins to accrue or lump sum is paid IMMEDIATELY ON TERMINATION; otherwise items 11 and 12 must be completed.

10 Amount of redundancy payment payable after reduction on account of pension:–
item 4 *(or 7 where applicable)*– $\left(\frac{\text{item 4 (or 7 where applicable)} \times \text{item 8(d)} \times 3}{\text{item 9}}\right)$ £ ....

NOTE Items 11 and 12 should be completed only if the pension or lump sum is not payable (or does not accrue) immediately on termination.

11 (a) Date of cessation of employment ....

(b) Date that pension/lump sum is payable or begins to accrue ....

(c) Number of complete weeks between the dates at 11(a) and 11(b) .... weeks

12 Amount of redundancy payment payable :–
item 10 *(nil where appropriate)*+ $\left(\left(\frac{\text{item 8(d)}}{52}\right)^{*} \times \text{item 11(c)}\right)$ #£ ....

* *The amount to be inserted here must not exceed one third of a week's pay, ie* $\frac{\text{item 3}}{3}$ *(see leaflet RPL 1 paragraph 10(3) (b))*

 # subject to an overriding maximum of item 4 *(or item 7 if appropriate)*

PART III – EMPLOYEE'S RECEIPT FOR REDUNDANCY PAYMENT

Warning – Do not sign this receipt until you have actually received the full amount stated or you may be penalised

I acknowledge that a redundancy payment amounting to £....................................

was made to me on ....

Signature ....

Date ....

NOTE If more than one copy of this form is prepared for payment, the top copy receipted by the employee should accompany the claim for rebate on form RP 2.

Form 34 Notification of intention to reduce a redundancy payment on account of pension or lump sum superannuation payment (RP9)

Department of Employment

REDUNDANCY PAYMENTS ACT 1965

NOTIFICATION OF INTENTION TO REDUCE A REDUNDANCY PAYMENT ON ACCOUNT OF PENSION OR LUMP SUM SUPERANNUATION PAYMENT

Notes 1 *Before rebate can be approved in respect of any redundancy payment reduced on account of pension, the Secretary of State must be satisfied that the pension scheme satisfies the provisions of the Redundancy Payments Pensions Regulations 1965 – see leaflet RPL 1, paragraph 2.*

2 *This form should be completed and forwarded according to the scheme (see Part I) which is relevant:–*

SCHEME 1 – with forms RP 2 and RP 3(Pen) when claiming rebate.

SCHEMES 2 and 3 – with form RP 1 when giving advance notice of the expected redundancies.

SCHEME 4 – (a) with forms RP 2 and RP 3(Pen) if the scheme has not altered since copies of the trust deeds and rules were approved by the Department of Employment, OR

(b) to the Employment Exchange at the address shown on form RP 2, at least 21 days BEFORE the date of the first expected redundancy if the scheme has not been approved by this Department or the rules have been altered since approval was last given.

3 *If Scheme 3 or 4 is applicable, PART IIA and B overleaf should be completed and certified by the employer and responsible paying authority respectively.*

PART I – STATEMENT BY EMPLOYER OF DETAILS OF SCHEME UNDER WHICH THE PENSION AND/OR LUMP SUM IS PAYABLE

***Scheme 1** Superannuation benefits under the scheme consist of lump sums only. Payment has been made in full to the redundant employee(s) and receipt(s) is/are attached.

***Scheme 2** The scheme is contracted out of the National Insurance Graduated Pension Scheme.

The number of the certificate of non-participation is ....

***Scheme 3** The scheme is not contracted out of the National Insurance Graduated Pension Scheme but benefits are secured by a contract of assurance or annuity contract with (*please insert name and address of insurance company, friendly society or provident society whose representative has signed the certificate of assurance at PART IIB*):–

....

....

***Scheme 4** The scheme is not contracted out of the National Insurance Graduated Pension Scheme but benefits are secured under an irrevocable trust.

*(a) The trust deed and rules of the scheme have not been altered since a copy of each was sent to the Department of Employment on ....

*(b) A copy of the trust deed and of the rules of the scheme are enclosed (*copy of the trust deed(s) and rules must be certified as a true copy by a responsible person, eg solicitor, accountant, etc.*)

Signature of employer .... Date ....

Status of signatory ....

* *Please delete inappropriate items*

(Continued)

(Continued)

PART II – CERTIFICATE OF ASSURANCE OF PENSION BENEFITS *(Complete ONLY in respect of Scheme 3 or 4)*

A To be completed by the employer

1 Name of superannuation scheme ....

....

2 Name and address of responsible paying authority (*ie the insurance company, friendly society or provident society or, where there is an irrevocable trust, the trustees*):–

....

....

3 Particulars of employees affected:

Surname and initials (1)	National Insurance No (2)					Annual value of pension £ (3)	Date payable (4)	Lump sum £ (5)	Date payable (6)

4 Declaration by or on behalf of employer

I declare that the particulars in columns (3)–(6) of item 3 above have been notified to the employees concerned

Signature of employer ....

Status of signatory ....

B To be completed by the responsible paying authority

This is to certify that the person(s) named in column (1) of item 3 of Part IIA is/are absolutely and indefeasibly entitled to the benefits shown in columns (3) and/or (5) under or by virtue of the recognised superannuation scheme named at item 1 (or would be so entitled but for their being capable, in accordance with the rules of that scheme, of being terminated or suspended for any cause prescribed under the Redundancy Payments Pensions Regulations 1965) and that the benefits are secured in such a manner and such provision is made for their payment as to make the person(s) named at item 3 assured of them for the purpose of the said Regulations.

Signed for and on behalf of the responsible paying authority ....

Status of signatory .... Date ....

NOTE – *If the responsible paying authority is not an insurance company or a provident or friendly society, but benefits are secured by contract of assurance or annuity contract, the name and address of the insurance company or society with which that contract is made should be entered here.*

....

Form 35 Application by an employee for a payment from the Redundancy Fund (RP 21)

DEPARTMENT OF EMPLOYMENT

APPLICATION BY AN EMPLOYEE FOR A PAYMENT FROM THE REDUNDANCY FUND

Office address stamp

FOR OFFICIAL USE
MLH NO. RP 21 A issued Initials .... Date ....

WARNING – Legal proceedings may be taken against a person who knowingly makes a false statement on this form

GENERAL NOTES

1 You should complete this form only if –
   (1) you have been dismissed because of redundancy, and
   (2) your employer has told you that he is unable to make a payment to you or to make the full payment, or he cannot be traced or is deceased, and
   (3) you are not time-barred *(see leaflet RPL 6)*

2 If your employer disputes your right to a payment or has failed to give you a definite answer to a written claim for payment, you should NOT complete this form but seek advice from the office shown above.

3 You will NOT be entitled to a payment if –
   (1) you are over 65 years of age (60 if you are a woman), OR
   (2) you have less than two years continuous employment with your employer after the week in which you attained the age of 18 *(see leaflet RPL 6 for explanation of "continuous employment")*

PERSONAL PARTICULARS

Full name ....Mr/Mrs/Miss

Address ....

....

National Insurance No. .... Income Tax Reference No. ....

Date of Birth ....

PARTICULARS OF EMPLOYMENT FROM WHICH DISMISSED

Employer's name ....

Employer's address ....

....

Employer's telephone no. (if known) ....

Address at which employed, if different ....

....

Date employment began .... Date employment ended ....

Dates of any breaks in this period ....

No. of hours normally worked each week ....
(If less than 16 please attach a separate sheet of paper showing the weekly hours worked, or contracted to work, during the past five years)

NOTE: If you hold a statement from your employer under the Contracts of Employment Act this should show normal hours.

(Continued)

(Continued)

Weekly pay £ ....

Special Pay Arrangements (if any)

NOTE Show your regular agreed pay before deductions of tax etc, but excluding overtime. If you did not receive regular agreed pay, give details opposite of any special arrangements, eg piece work, bonuses

Circumstances of dismissal

NOTE Indicate opposite how your job came to an end, eg closure of company, transfer of establishment to another area, reduction in number of employees

Reason why full redundancy payment not obtained

NOTE Indicate opposite why you have not obtained a full redundancy payment eg insolvency of company, disappearance or death of employer

---

Date on which written application for a payment made to employer ....

PARTICULARS OF NEW EMPLOYMENT, IF ANY, FOLLOWING REDUNDANCY

New employer's name ....

Address ....

....

APPLICATION

I hereby apply to the Secretary of State for Employment for a payment under Section 32 of the Redundancy Payments Act 1965 and declare that the information I have given in this application is correct and may be used in any communication with the employer named (or his representatives). I understand that in order to establish my right to any redundancy payment it may be necessary for you to refer to information given to the Inland Revenue and other government departments as to my remuneration and period of service and I hereby give my consent to the disclosure of such information for this purpose only. If payment is agreed, I request that it be made *to my account at

.... Bank

Code No. [| |] Account No. [ ]

(address) ....

....

* by payable order to my private address

Signature .... Date ....

* *delete inappropriate item*

Form 36 Application for payment of debts owed by insolvent employers (IP1)

EMPLOYMENT PROTECTION (CONSOLIDATION) ACT 1978 DEPARTMENT OF EMPLOYMENT

APPLICATION FOR PAYMENT OF DEBTS OWED BY INSOLVENT EMPLOYER

IMPORTANT: Please read these notes before completing this form.

1 After completion, this form should be sent or returned to the insolvent employer's representative

2 The insolvent employer's representative will be one of the following persons:—
a A liquidator b A receiver or a receiver and manager c The Official Receiver d A trustee

3 Applications should NOT be made directly to the Department of Employment unless you are asked to do so by an official of that Department

4 Deductions for income tax, earnings related national insurance contributions and occupational pension scheme contributions will be deducted from payments due to you where appropriate

PART 1

Full name *(state whether Mr/Ms)* ....

Full postal address ....

....

Post Code .... Tel No. ....

Date of Birth / / National Insurance No. ....

Name of insolvent employer ....

Address at which you worked ....

....

Occupation .... Works/Pay No. *(if any)* ....

Date your employment began / / Gross rate of pay .... * hourly / weekly / monthly *(details of any bonuses, piecework etc included above)*

Date your employment ended / / ....

Name of insolvent employer's representative *(see Note 2 above)* ....

Address ....

.... Tel No. ....

PART 2

Details of debts owed to you by the insolvent employer. Please tick ✓ the appropriate box and indicate where possible the amount you are claiming and the period to which it relates

Wages .... ☐ From / / To / / £ ....

Holiday Pay .... ☐ ....* days / weeks / stamps £ ....

Payment in lieu of notice .... ☐ **IMPORTANT**: If you have ticked this BOX you MUST complete a separate form IP2 available from the person who sent you this form

Other debts *(specify)*

.... From / / To / / £ ....

.... From / / To / / £ ....

PART 3

I apply for payment due to me under section 122 of the Employment Protection (Consolidation) Act 1978 and declare that I have made no other applications in respect of the amounts shown above.

Signature .... Date ....

WARNING: Legal proceedings may be taken against anyone making a false statement on this form.

* *Delete as appropriate*

Form 37 Application for payment in lieu of notice owed by an insolvent employer (IP2)

EMPLOYMENT PROTECTION (CONSOLIDATION) ACT 1978 — DEPARTMENT OF EMPLOYMENT

APPLICATION FOR PAYMENT IN LIEU OF NOTICE OWED BY AN INSOLVENT EMPLOYER

IMPORTANT: **Before completing this form please read all the notes overleaf. It MUST NOT be completed until the end of the statutory minimum period of notice.**

PART 1

Full name *(state whether Mr/Ms)* ....

Full Postal Address ....

....

Post Code .... Telephone Number ....

Date of Birth / / National Insurance Number ....

Name of insolvent employer ....

Address at which you worked ....

....

Occupation .... Works/Pay number *(if any)* ....

Name of insolvent employer's representative *(see Note 5 overleaf)* ....

Address ....

.... Telephone Number ....

SPECIMEN

PART 2

In order to establish your claim against the employer for his failure to give you notice, please answer the following questions:—

1 (a) When did your employment begin? Date / / (b) When did it end? Date / /

2 What was your basic rate of pay? £ .... * hourly/weekly/monthly

3 How many hours per week did you normally work? .... hours. How many days per week did you normally work? ....days.

4 Did your employer give you notice? * **YES / NO**

5 If you have answered **YES**, on what date did you receive the notice? Date / /

6 Have you done any work during the statutory period of notice? *(see Note 1 overleaf)* * **YES / NO**

7 If you have answered **YES**, please state:—

(a) Name and address of your new employer ....

....

(b) Your new occupation .... (c) Date you started work / /

(d) Your gross rate of pay £ .... * hourly/weekly/monthly

(e) Total gross earnings in the period of notice *(including overtime, bonus etc)* £ ....

8 Have you claimed any social security benefits *(eg unemployment benefit, supplementary allowance, sickness benefit)* during the period? * **YES / NO**

9 If you have answered **YES**, please state:— (a) Type of benefit(s) claimed ....

(b) Address of office(s) at which claimed ....

10 Have you received any other incomes during the period? * **YES / NO**

11 If you have answered **YES**, please give full details ....

....

PART 3

I declare that the above information is correct and that I have made no other application in respect of the claim. I hereby apply for any payment due to me under Section 122(3)(b) of the Employment Protection (Consolidation) Act 1978. I give my consent to the disclosure of any information relating to any social security benefit claimed to the employer's representative for the purpose of this application.

Signature .... Date ....

* *Delete inappropriate items*

WARNING: ***Legal proceedings may be taken against anyone making a false statement on this form***

(Continued)

(Continued)

NOTES

1 The amount of payment in lieu of notice payable to you will be based on the statutory minimum periods of notice provided for in the Employment Protection (Consolidation) Act 1978. These periods are:—

a 1 week's notice if your employment lasted for 4 weeks or more but less than 2 years.

b 1 week's notice for each year of your employment if it lasted for 2 years or more but less than 12 years.

c 12 week's notice if your employment lasted 12 years or more.

2 This form **MUST NOT** be completed until your statutory minimum period of notice has expired.

3 Any social security benefits or earnings from a new job payable to you in respect of the period of notice will be deducted from your claim. This is because a payment in lieu of notice is a payment of damages for the employer's failure to give you notice. Damages must be assessed taking account of all incomes payable in the period so that they compensate only for what has actually been lost financially because of the employer's failure.

4 After completion, this form should be sent or returned to the insolvent employer's representative.

5 The insolvent employer's representative will be one of the following persons:—

a a liquidator

b a receiver or a receiver and manager

c the official receiver

d a trustee

6 Applications should **NOT** be made directly to the Department of Employment unless you are asked to do so by an official of that Department.

FOR OFFICIAL USE

*A	unemployment benefit	from	to	£	....
	supplementary allowance	from	to	£	....
	sickness benefit	from	to	£	....
	supplementary benefit	from	to	£	....
	.... (specify)	from	to	£	....
	.... (specify)	from	to	£	....
			TOTAL	£	....

*B No social security benefits payable in period

*C Other information

Signature ....

Date ....

* *Delete inappropriate items*

Form 38 Application for the reference of a recognition issue to ACAS under Section 11 (ACAS 34)

EMPLOYMENT PROTECTION ACT 1975

APPLICATION FOR THE REFERENCE OF A RECOGNITION ISSUE TO THE ADVISORY, CONCILIATION AND ARBITRATION SERVICE UNDER SECTION 11 OF THE ACT

Note: Only an independent trade union may make an application on this form (see definitions overleaf).

1. Name of the independent trade union making the application:

2. Address for correspondence about this application and telephone number:

3. Name and address of the employer from whom recognition is sought:
(If recognition is sought from two or more associated employers please give all their names and addresses).

4. The trade, industry, etc. in which the employer is engaged:

5. The description of the workers covered by the application
(stating where appropriate the part of the undertaking in which they work):

6. Date recognition issue raised with the employer:

7. Does the employer already recognise the trade union to any extent?

SIGNATURE: NAME IN BLOCK CAPITALS:

DATE: POSITION HELD IN TRADE UNION:

(This form may be signed only by an official of the trade union who is duly authorised to make such an application on behalf of the union).

(Continued)

(Continued)

Definitions

For the purposes of the Employment Protection Act 1975:

(1) "Trade union" means except so far as the context otherwise requires, an organisation (whether permanent or temporary) which either -

(a) consists wholly or mainly of workers of one or more descriptions and is an organisation whose principal purposes include the regulation of relations between workers of that description or those descriptions and employers or employers' associations; or

(b) consists wholly or mainly of -

(i) constituent or affiliated organisations which fulfil the conditions specified in paragraph (a) above (or themselves consist wholly or mainly of constituent or affiliated organisations which fulfil those conditions), or

(ii) representatives of such constituent or affiliated organisations;

and in either case is an organisation whose principal purposes include the regulation of relations between workers and employers or between workers and employers' associations, or include the regulation of relations between its constituent or affiliated organisations.

(Trade Union and Labour Relations Act 1974, Section 28(1)).

(2) "Independent trade union" means a trade union which -

(a) is not under the domination or control of an employer or a group of employers or of one or more employers' associations; and

(b) is not liable to interference by an employer or any such group or association (arising out of the provision of financial or material support or by any other means whatsoever) tending towards such control;

(Trade Union and Labour Relations Act 1974, Section 30(1)).

	To: The Advisory, Conciliation and Arbitration Service :-
	EMPLOYMENT PROTECTION ACT 1975: SCHEDULE 11, PART I REPORT OF A CLAIM AS TO RECOGNISED TERMS AND CONDITIONS OF EMPLOYMENT OR AS TO THE GENERAL LEVEL OF TERMS AND CONDITIONS.
Write in name and address of organisation reporting the claim deleting (a) and (b) in a claim citing recognised terms. In a general level claim delete (b) where appropriate.	1. Acting on behalf of ______________________ ______________________ (a) a trade union having as a member a worker to whom this claim relates; (b) an independent trade union recognised by the employer in respect of a worker of the description to which this claim relates. I hereby report a claim to the Advisory, Conciliation and Arbitration Service that as respects
Name or description of worker(s)	
Name and address of employer	______________________, is observing terms and conditions of employment that are less favourable than either A. the <u>recognised</u> terms and conditions or B. the <u>general</u> level of terms and conditions. 2. The following particulars relate to the claim as it concerns <u>recognised</u> terms and conditions of employment: (a) The recognised terms and conditions of employment apply in the following trade or industry or section of a trade or industry in which the employer in question is engaged:- (b) The recognised terms and conditions of employment were settled by the following agreement or award:- (c) The parties to the agreement or the award were:-

(Continued)

(Continued)

3. The following particulars relate to the claim as it concerns the general level of terms and conditions:

(a) The trade, industry or section in which the employer is engaged is:-

(b) The employers in the district in the trade, industry or section, whose circumstances are similar to those of the employer in question and who observe for comparable workers the general level of terms and conditions, are as follows:-

Names and addresses of employers

For official use only

MLH:

REGION:

NAME IN BLOCK CAPITALS:

POSITION HELD:

Address and Telephone Number:

SIGNATURE:

DATE:

Form 40 Report of a claim as to collectively negotiated terms and conditions (ACAS 73)

	To: The Advisory, Conciliation and Arbitration Service:-
	EMPLOYMENT PROTECTION ACT 1975: SCHEDULE 11, PART 11 REPORT OF A CLAIM AS TO COLLECTIVELY NEGOTIATED TERMS AND CONDITIONS.
Write in name of independent trade union	1. Acting on behalf of ____________________ ______________________________ I hereby report a claim to the Advisory, Conciliation and Arbitration Service.
Names, jobs or other descriptions of workers	2. The claim relates to the following worker(s) who are members of the trade union:-
Name of wages council, statutory joint industrial council, Agricultural Wages Board, or Scottish Agricultural Wages Board.	3. These workers fall within the field of operation of:-
* Delete in-appropriate alternatives	4. The claim is as follows: (a) that the union is a party to one or more collective agreements and that those agreements cover a significant number of establishments within the field of operation of the *council/Board referred to in paragraph 3 *generally/in the district in which the worker is employed; and (b) that in those establishments the circumstances of the employer are similar to those of the employer of the worker(s) referred to in paragraph 2 above; and (c) that the employer is paying him/them less than the lowest current rate of remuneration (disregarding any rate agreed to more than 12 months before the date on which the claim is reported) payable to workers of the same description under any of those agreements.

(Continued)

(Continued)

<table>
<tr><td></td><td>5. The following particulars relate to the claim:
(a) The collective agreements referred to in the paragraph 4(a) above are:-</td></tr>
<tr><td>Name of the agreements, dates on which they were made and the parties to them</td><td></td></tr>
<tr><td></td><td>(b) The employer of the worker(s) to whom this claim relates is:-</td></tr>
<tr><td>Name and address of employer to whom the claim relates</td><td></td></tr>
<tr><td>SIGNATURE:</td><td>NAME IN BLOCK CAPITALS:

POSITION HELD IN TRADE UNION:</td></tr>
<tr><td>DATE:</td><td>Address and Telephone No.</td></tr>
</table>

Index

The letter-by-letter system has been adopted. The forms are indexed by the most suitable key-word relative to the subject, i.e. attendance, probation, warning etc. strictly alphabetically. No entries occur starting with 'employee' (or synonyms thereof) or 'employer', but the entry 'employment' refers to, or will lead to, other entries pertaining to connected subjects. Interspersed in the index are entries in italics leading the user to form listed in the table of contents at pp. vii-xii which are co-related. The symbol (O) indicates an obligatory lay-out by virtue of legislation. JM = Johnson Matthey Group; M&S = Marks and Spencer Ltd.